Media, Geopolitics, and Power

THE GEOPOLITICS OF INFORMATION

Edited by Dan Schiller, Pradip Thomas, and Yuezhi Zhao

A list of books in the series appears at the end of this book.

Media, Geopolitics, and Power

A View from the Global South

HERMAN WASSERMAN

UNIVERSITY OF ILLINOIS PRESS
Urbana, Chicago, and Springfield

© 2018 by the Board of Trustees
of the University of Illinois
All rights reserved
1 2 3 4 5 C P 5 4 3 2 1
♾ This book is printed on acid-free paper.

Library of Congress Cataloging-in-Publication Data
Names: Wasserman, Herman, 1969– author.
Title: Media, geopolitics, and power: a view from the
   Global South / Herman Wasserman.
Other titles: Geopolitics of information.
Description: Urbana: University of Illinois Press, 2018. |
   Series: Geopolitics of information
Identifiers: LCCN 2017039630| ISBN 9780252041624
   (cloth: alk. paper) | ISBN 9780252083266 (pbk: alk.
   paper)
Subjects: LCSH: Mass media—Social aspects—South
   Africa. | Mass media—Political aspects—South
   Africa. | Mass media and globalization.
Classification: LCC HN801.Z9 M39 2018 | DDC
   302.230968—dc23 LC record available at https://
   lccn.loc.gov/2017039630

For Helena, Lukas, Daniel and Sophie.

*And in memory of the friend who sat next to me
in the 1994 Stellenbosch University journalism class where
I took my first steps in studying the media:
Gustav Rudolph Thiel (1967–2013)*

Contents

Acknowledgments ix

Introduction 1

PART I: TRANSITIONS

1 From Apartheid to a New Democracy: Areas of Shift 17

2 "This Time for Africa"? Global Media Studies and the View from the South 47

3 A Changing Media Culture: Professional Ideologies between Past and Present 58

PART II: LOCAL CONTESTATIONS

4 Is This Freedom? Media Ethics, "African Culture," and Universal Values 79

5 Global Genres and Local Context: What Controversies around Tabloidization Tell Us about South African Media and Society 97

6 Rethinking Global and Local: South African Perspectives on the "Future of Journalism" 112

PART III: GLOBAL SHIFTS

7 BRICS and Beyond: Mediating New
   Geopolitical Relationships   135

8 New Pressures and Opportunities: Technology,
   Geopolitics, and Social Change   152

   Conclusion   167

   Notes   173

   References   191

   Index   211

Acknowledgments

This book is based on research spanning over a decade, and draws from previously published work, which has been revisited and reworked for the purpose of this publication.

Part of 1, on the media and South African government, appeared in an earlier form as: Wasserman, Herman, and Arnold S. De Beer. "A Fragile Affair: An Overview of the Relationship between the Media and State in Post-Apartheid South Africa." *Journal of Mass Media Ethics* 20, no. 2 and 3 (2005): 192–208.

For the discussion of transitology and social identity in transition in Chapter 1, I drew on parts of earlier published work, i.e., Wasserman, Herman. "Debating the Media, Shaping Identity: Postcolonial Discourse and Public Criticism." *Communicatio* 31, no. 1 (2005): 49–60; Wasserman, Herman. "Identification in Transformation: An Overview of Media Discourses." In *The Political Economy of Transformation of the South African Media*, edited by Anthony Olorunnisola and Keyan G. Tomaselli, 117–132. Cresskill: Hampton Press, 2011; and Wasserman, Herman. "Freedom's Just Another Word? Perspectives on Media Freedom and Responsibility in South Africa and Namibia." *International Communication Gazette* 72, no. 7 (2010): 567–588.

Chapter 2 is based on a keynote address given at the regional conference of the International Communication Association in Nairobi, Kenya, in October 2016.

Acknowledgments

Chapter 3 appeared in an earlier version as Wasserman, Herman. "The Presence of the Past: The Uses of History in the Discourses of Contemporary South African Journalism." *Journalism Practice* 5, no. 5 (2011): 584–598.

Parts of Chapter 4 appeared in a previous version as Wasserman, Herman. "Media Ethics in a New Democracy: South African Perspectives on Freedom, Dignity and Citizenship." In *Global Media Ethics: Problems and Perspectives*, edited by Stephen J. A. Ward, 126–145. Malden: Wiley-Blackwell, 2013. This chapter also draws on previously published articles: Wasserman, Herman. "Towards a Global Journalism Ethics via Local Narratives: Southern African Perspectives." *Journalism Studies* 12, no. 6 (2011): 791–803; and Wasserman, Herman. "Talking of Change: Constructing Social Identities in South African Media Debates." *Social Identities* 11, no. 1 (2005): 75–85.

Chapter 5 draws on extracts from Wasserman, Herman. "Key Trends in South African Society and Media." In *State of the Nation*, edited by Thenjiwe Meyiwa, Muxe Nkondo, Margaret Chitiga-Mabugu, Moses Sithole, and Francis Nyamnjoh, 310–324. Pretoria: HSRC Press, 2014; and Wasserman, Herman. "Attack of the Killer Newspapers! The 'Tabloid Revolution' in South Africa and the Future of Newspapers." *Journalism Studies* 9, no. 5 (2008): 786–797.

Chapter 6 uses extracts from Wasserman, Herman. "Global Journalism 2.0. Beyond Panoramas." *Communicatio* 37, no. 1 (2011): 100–117.

Chapter 7 draws on Wasserman, Herman. "China's 'Soft Power' and Its Influence on Editorial Agendas in South Africa." *Chinese Journal of Communication* 9, no. 1 (2016):8–20.

A part of Chapter 8 appeared previously as a review essay in *Popular Communications* 9, no. 2 (2011): 146–158, titled "Mobile Phones, Popular Media, and Everyday African Democracy: Transmissions and Transgressions." The chapter also draws on an opinion piece written with Sean Jacobs for the *Washington Post*, November 25, 2015: "The Day Mainstream Media Became Old in South Africa." https://www.washingtonpost.com/news/monkey-cage/wp/2015/11/25/the-day-mainstream-media-became-old-in-south-africa/ (accessed June 30, 2017).

These articles are drawn upon in this book with permission from the respective publishers.

I am grateful to several people for their assistance and support during the research contained in this book as well as in the writing process. I have benefited greatly from discussions with colleagues too numerous to mention, but Sean Jacobs, Anthea Garman, Arnold de Beer, Katrin Voltmer and Shakuntala Rao have been constant interlocutors and collaborators at various stages of my research over the past years, in addition to colleagues at the School of Journalism and Media Studies, Rhodes University and the Centre for Film and Media Stud-

Acknowledgments

ies, University of Cape Town. I am very grateful to Yuezhi Zhao for the initial idea of publishing this book as part of the Geopolitics of Information series, and to Danny Nasset for his infinite patience as the deadlines kept whooshing past. Thank you also to Willemien Calitz, Waldo Grové and Nancy Albright for their copyediting of the manuscript at different stages.

As always, my deepest thanks go to my family—Helena, Lukas, Daniel, and Sophie—for contending with my working and traveling, for their support and patience, and most of all for always reminding me that life begins beyond the computer screen.

Media, Geopolitics, and Power

Introduction

When the first democratically elected president of South Africa, Nelson Mandela, was buried at his ancestral home in Qunu on December 15, 2013, this small Eastern Cape village was swamped with international media. On the hills overlooking the valley where a big marquee tent was pitched to host the dignitaries from around the world that came to bid farewell to one of the greatest statesmen of the century, a media village was erected to house the more than 4,000 accredited journalists.[1] Journalists from international networks like CNN, Telesur, Sky, BBC, and Al-Jazeera, along with local camera teams, reporters, and photographers, swamped the hillsides overlooking the valley where the coffin lay of one of the greatest leaders of the twentieth century.[2] These journalists could be seen wandering around the dusty streets trying to explore some new angle on the passing of a global icon.[3] Pictures, sound clips, reports, and commentary flowed from the deep rural village to the furthest corners of the earth. People from around the world could follow in real time the events playing out in Qunu and, in their own way, mediated through television, radio, online news, or social media, share in the moment as if they were there. At the back of the stage from which international dignitaries delivered their tributes hung a picture of the man with the smile familiar in households from Qunu to Quebec.

The highly mediated event that marked the end of Mandela's life concluded twenty-three years of freedom, during which he was constantly in the spotlight of the international media. He had very little privacy since he walked free, with his family relationships, divorce from Winnie-Madikizela Mandela, and marriage to Graça Machel being scrutinized by global media. It was not always thus. Because the apartheid government banned pictures of political prisoners, and the last time Mandela was seen publicly before his release was in 1964, there were three decades during which his face was hidden from the world. So confident were his jailers that he had become the "Man with No Face,"[4] that they allowed him to stroll on a beach during one of his visits to a hospital, knowing that nobody would recognize him.[5] The media was left to speculate on what he would look like after 27 years in captivity. Before his release, *Time* magazine constructed an artist's sketch based on a decades-old photograph.[6] Mandela's release from Victor Verster prison on February 11, 1990, was understandably a huge media event that shaped the collective consciousness,[7] not only of South Africans, but of people around the world. The decades of media blackout that preceded it, and the apartheid government's pressure on local media, left journalists unsure about how to cover it.[8] After all, this is a country where television did not arrive until 1976, after the National Party (NP) government managed to keep it out of the country for many years on the basis of a racist and socially conservative ideology of cultural purity, which included fears of cultural imperialism and the exposure of South African audiences to the portrayal of civil liberties, racial mixing, and cosmopolitanism.[9]

The media ban on showing Mandela's face while he was in prison stands in stark contrast with the iconic global media figure he had become by the time of his death in 2013. By then, in South Africa, the country was firmly located within the globalized media landscape. On election day in 2014, twenty years after the ballots were cast in the first democratic election, the world's biggest search engine[10] devoted a "Google Doodle" to the South African elections.[11] South Africa and the triumphs, trials, and tribulations of the first two decades of its democracy are being mediated globally. International media often project their hopes and fears on the country as an experiment in democracy: here is a country that managed to emerge from colonialism and apartheid and transform itself into a democracy without the bloodshed or type of conflict that usually provides the staple fare for global media when writing about Africa. It soon became clear, however, that the "miracle" of the "rainbow nation" was still far from complete—the country remained marred by huge socioeconomic inequalities, corruption became widespread, violent crime rates were very high, and Mandela's successor, Thabo Mbeki, embarked on a disastrous AIDS policy that denied antiretrovirals to patients in the public health sector and cost the lives of thousands. The story that global media was challenged to tell became much more complex than that of a seamless transition from apartheid to democracy, led by a saintly Madiba.

If the global mediation of South African democracy has often been marked by a somewhat simplistic teleological narrative of liberation from oppression and the emergence of a "rainbow nation," the situation within the country was much more complex.

Under apartheid, the media was strictly controlled with an array of laws—such as the one prohibiting the publication of quotations from or pictures of banned persons that applied to Nelson Mandela—and journalists and editors working for alternative, "underground" antiapartheid media were routinely harassed or imprisoned.

When South Africa became a democracy, the media was granted unprecedented freedom. The new democratic Constitution, adopted in 1996, incorporates a Bill of Rights that guarantees freedom of expression, including freedom of the media. Although the media can therefore operate freely and without fear of government interference or pressure, the relationship between the media and the democratic government has been tense right from the start.[12] Underpinning these clashes are fundamentally different normative conceptions of what the media's role within a postcolonial, "new" democracy, and its relationship to government, should be. Often characterized in terms of a simplistic binary between liberal-democratic notions of "media freedom" and an accompanying adversarial "watchdog" or Fourth Estate role, versus a developmental, collaborative role for the media in aid of a nation-building project, these competing normative perspectives should rather be seen as representing different points on a spectrum that include not only varying views on media-state relations but more deep-seated and historically influenced cultural and social identity positions. Although one can therefore discern ongoing differences of opinion about the media's social positioning, the particular tension between media and state has flared up in recent years. Two key developments have raised renewed concerns that the ANC government might tighten control over the media.

The first of the two recent developments was the passing in 2011 by the South African Parliament of the Protection of State Information Bill (at the time of writing, this Bill still needed to be signed into law). This Bill, dubbed the "Secrecy Bill" by its opponents, is seen as having the potential to reduce the level of access to information by giving officials the power to classify information as confidential, secret, and top secret, thereby preventing not only journalists, but also members of the citizenry and civil society generally, from accessing important information that could keep the security apparatuses of government accountable.[13] The Bill was met with a strong response from civil society, manifesting in a countrywide "Right to Know" campaign by an alliance of media and civil society organizations.

The second development that caused concern about press freedom in South Africa was a proposed statutory Media Appeals Tribunal (MAT), suggested by the ruling African National Congress (ANC) as an alternative to the appeals procedure in the system of press self-regulation, which they see as biased toward the media industry. This move was also met with strong resistance from journalists, media academics, and members of the public. A consequent review of the Press Council's constitution and procedures, resulting in a system of voluntary co-regulation with greater input from citizens, seems to have put the ANC's demands for a MAT on hold.

But in order to understand the South African media's position in postapartheid South Africa, and to assess the distance it has traveled from the apartheid era, it is important to extend the analysis beyond the formal, regulatory dimensions of freedom as reflected in Constitutional guarantees and regulatory processes. In other words, when charting the South African media's change from the apartheid era through the period of transition to the postapartheid era, a separation between political transition and economic and social transition should be avoided. Sparks shows how the academic discourse of *transitology* tends to view the liberal-democratic state in teleological terms as the end point of historical development, and that such democratization comes linked to marketization.[14] This approach also characterized the view of media's relationship to democracy and political transitions more generally. As Sparks shows, several examples in recent years suggest that democratization does not necessarily bring about wide-ranging economic transformation (South Africa is a case in point here); nor does marketization necessarily imply a demand for democratization (the case of China).[15]

The political economy of the South African media in the postapartheid period continued to militate against the democratic gains made on a constitutional level. Socially and economically, democratization remains an unfinished project even after the arrival of political freedom and the extension of citizenship to all South Africans. While the status of citizenship was extended in 1994 to all South Africans regardless of their race, the practice of citizenship in real terms,[16] measured in improved living conditions and access to a mediated public sphere where their voice can be heard and can be seen to make an impact, still eludes the majority of citizens in one of the most unequal countries on earth. This "bifurcated public sphere"[17] can also be seen reflected in the media landscape. The commercial media remain dominated by outlets that cater to an elite who can afford to pay for access or who are attractive to advertisers. Control over the means of production of social reality by the media was, at the time of the democratic transition, in the hands of White capital—something that the first democratically elected president of the country, Nelson Mandela, wasted no time in pointing out.[18]

In terms of the news media, the persistence of historical inequalities means that news agendas continue to reflect a "view from the suburbs."[19] A notable exception here are the commercial, mass-market tabloids that attract a wide readership from among the urban and rural poor and working class, although these papers do not qualify as community or grassroots papers that provide a real counterbalance to the elite perspectives dominating the mainstream printed press, even if they have managed to bring vastly different stories of everyday life into the mediated public sphere.[20] Inasmuch as the continued asymmetries of access to the media, the skewed representation of social reality, and the control over the political economy of the media were inherited from the colonial and apartheid eras, it fell to the new ruling party to set things straight. Already in 1992, two years after its unbanning and as many years before it would assume power, the ANC published its Media Charter, in which it committed itself to redressing the historical imbalances in the media sphere by ensuring greater access to the media by previously marginalized communities. These aims were addressed through a number of legal and regulatory changes that include, as summed up by Fourie,[21] the following:

- The restructuring of the public broadcaster (SABC)
- The establishment of community radio stations
- Facilitating the entry of Black ownership into the media market
- The improvement and extension of telecommunications
- The establishment of regulatory bodies such as the Independent Communications Authority (Icasa), which included the setting of quotas for local content on both public and commercial television and radio stations

The restructuring of the broadcast sector after apartheid was in line with a three-tiered, mixed private-public-community media system built on principles of inclusivity and diversity.[22] A main aim was to transform the South African Broadcasting Corporation (SABC) from a racially divided, state broadcaster into a public service broadcaster serving the needs of a democratic citizenry. Already in these early days of restructuring, the SABC was seen by many in the new leadership as crucial to a "nation-building" or "developmental" project that would assist rather than criticize governmental restructuring efforts.[23] Although structures were put in place to ensure its independence, these structures were gradually eroded through internal reorganizations and the growth of a managerial class at the SABC, including the establishment of measures for more senior editorial control that resulted in political coverage biased toward the ANC.[24] Political interference in content and management of the SABC, as well as an increased reliance on advertising revenue, has brought the broadcaster into a prolonged financial and management crisis that remains unresolved and has led to the emergence of a civil society coalition to campaign to insist its improvement.[25] The chief operating officer of the SABC in 2016, Hlaudi Motsoeneng, was especially controversial and his reign as head of the organization disastrous. A High Court found his appointment as COO unlawful, after the public protector found him to have lied about his qualifications and to have purged some senior staff while giving unjustified salary increases to others, including himself. Nevertheless, the Minister of Communications, Faith Muthambi, made his appointment permanent and appealed the court's judgment.[26] That appeal was lost, but Motsoeneng was subsequently appointed as group executive of corporate affairs, until that appointment was also set aside by a High Court ruling. Motsoeneng was eventually dismissed in June 2017 after he was found guilty in an internal disciplinary hearing. The authoritarian actions and repressive editorial policies put in place by Motsoeneng, such as a ban on coverage of community protests (even in defiance of a finding by the broadcasting regulator that the ban should be reversed), were only the latest manifestations of a broader crisis in which the public broadcaster has been mired since the advent of democracy.

During the transition, a particular attempt was made to strengthen the community media sector through the establishment of the Media Development and Diversity Agency (MDDA). According to the MDDA Act of 2000, community media were defined as media owned and controlled by the community it serves.[27] Banda sees the establishment of the MDDA also in terms of the ANC's "nationalist-reconstructionist ideology that sought to uplift hitherto marginalized groups" and to enable more Black ownership of media.[28] The envisaged increased access that historically disadvantaged communities and individuals would have as owners, managers, producers, and consumers of media would be predicated on the development of media infrastructure made possible through MDDA grants.[29] The MDDA, however, has had to cope with the constraints of lack of funding, continued White dominance of the community broadcasting sector, and the fact that community media continued to model itself on commercial enterprises with little community participation in governance.[30]

In summary, the political economy of the postapartheid media prevented a large-scale, deep transformation of the sector, resulting rather in what Colin Sparks refers to as "elite renewal."[31]

It should be evident from the brief overview earlier that the post-apartheid South African media has been the subject of fierce debates within the country.

As pointed out, these debates largely arose from the political and economic legacies of colonialism and apartheid and attempts to undo them by means of laws, regulation, and ownership changes in the postapartheid era.

The aim of this book is, however, not to provide a picture of South African media in isolation or as a singular point of focus in what has become known as "area studies." Taken as a whole, this book wants to indicate how the local contestations and changes in the South African media landscape after apartheid are intertwined with its changing position in a global media landscape and with the shifts that this global landscape itself continues to undergo. The importance of seeing these local changes and global shifts as intertwined cannot be overemphasized. As will be discussed in Chapter 2, approaching "local" media in the Global South from within its location in the global can contribute to the de-Westernizing of media studies which remains dominated by perspectives informed by social realities in the Global North. The democratization process and internal contestations around the South African media's role and position cannot, and should not, therefore be separated from the country's position within the global economy and geopolitics. On the contrary—the democratization of South Africa was closely linked to the adoption of a particular model of economic development, i.e., neoliberal globalization. But the change from apartheid to democracy, as well as broader geopolitical shifts, brought with it a reorientation toward global media markets that had profound effects on South African media industries and practices.

To understand the extent to which the South African media's relation to the global media landscape has changed since the advent of democracy, it is first useful to contrast the flows and contraflows of media content and capital under apartheid with those that have developed in the democratic era. Second, the extent to which global geopolitical relations—especially the rise of emerging regions in Asia and Latin America—have impacted on the global media sphere is also important to take into account.

Under apartheid, the South African media was isolated and largely inward-focused. Because of an international cultural boycott of the apartheid state,[32] the flow of entertainment media into the country was severely curtailed. Internally, the repressive laws—especially tight during two states of emergency in the 1980s when the apartheid regime forcefully put down mass popular protests—governing the media also had an impact on the ability of local news flowing out of the country. Although South African apartheid, and the increasingly violent response of the White minority regime under the National Party, was a big international story, severe restrictions were placed on domestic and foreign press. These restrictions were aimed at sealing down the resistance and repression in the Black townships and preventing news from entering the international arena. Foreign journalists were denied visas and work permits to enter the country and those that managed to report from within the country were frequently harassed and pressured.[33] During this time, a vibrant alternative, antiapartheid media developed that operated despite these repressive measures (which often resulted in harassment, banning of newspapers, punitive lawsuits, or detention of journalists and editors)[34]. Although flows and contraflows of news and media from and to South Africa were severely curtailed as a result of these measures, it should be pointed out that cooperation between local and international media did occur during these periods in the form of donor funding and general "media assistance."[35] While foreign coverage and international donor funding during the apartheid years were of a different order than direct capital investment and buyouts of media that occurred after apartheid (to which we will return later), it is useful to bear in mind that media flows and contraflows can take different forms under differing circumstances. After the arrival of democracy, media assistance organizations shifted their support from antiapartheid, alternative media to activities such as the training of journalists in the interest of deepening the fledgling democracy. Organizations like Freedom House, the Open Society Foundation, USAid, Hivos, Atlantic Philanthropies and others remain active in the country, inter alia by supporting community media.[36] Ironically, the alternative press of the apartheid era fell victim to the shift from donor funding for nongovernmental entities to new public institutions and capacity building within government[37] to the extent that only one title (the *Mail & Guardian*, and in a different shape and form) of the erstwhile range of alternative publications still exists today. As the South African media's location within the global geopolitical and media landscape is starting to shift again, with its joining of the BRICS (Brazil, Russia, India, China, and South Africa) group of emerging nations and closer ties to China, the historical prominence of Western media assistance organizations is no longer self-evident. It is still too early to tell how these shifts will play out in terms of the norms and practices of South African media in future.

As far as the commercial media is concerned, the demise of apartheid saw the opening up of the media and creative industries in the country to the extent that global media exploded on South African television screens, in film theaters, and on the pages of glossy magazines. For those with access to digital satellite television and the internet, it has increasingly become possible to live in a mediated bubble of European or North American cultural goods, even to avoid local news or cultural production altogether. One way of viewing this process was to see it as South Africa's growing incorporation into a U.S.-led global culture of neoliberalism, a "Pax Americana" that led to the erosion of local cultural specificity. From this perspective, the "neoliberal dismantling" of cultural protectionisms and state interventionism, together with the ruling party's support for detribalization, paved the way for a wave of Northern, mostly U.S., cultural products to sweep across South African media, resulting in increased cultural and linguistic homogeneity.[38] The appeal of English as a lingua franca, even while the postapartheid Constitution recognizes eleven official languages, should be seen against the background of the politicization of cultural and linguistic diversity under apartheid. Apartheid created "antagonistic ethnic consciousnesses."[39]

The opening up after apartheid of South African media to increased global flows has not only had consequences in terms of cultural content but also in terms of the political economy of the local media industry. Boloka points to the licensing of the free-to-air station e.tv as signaling the "entry of global media behemoths."[40] These include Time Warner, which bought a stake in e.tv's holding company. Just about a decade later, the television market again saw the influx of foreign capital, but this time from China, when the StarTimes media group from China purchased a 20 percent stake in the pay-television operator On Digital Media, owner of TopTV, which positions itself as a rival for Naspers's MultiChoice. MultiChoice, the company operating the satellite television platform DStv, has itself already benefited from more globalized markets by spreading its footprint to the rest of the African continent.

The newspaper industry has seen even more tumultuous ownership changes. These change processes were put in motion during the transitional period in response to two pressures—local political imperatives and global economic changes.[41] The political imperative was to restructure print media ownership in the transitional period in response to local political demands for Black representation in what had until then been a largely White-owned industry. Economically, print media capital started globalizing. The result was a series of "unbundlings" of assets in print media in order to sell off constituent parts of companies to Black Empowerment consortia (thus addressing the local political imperative) and subsequent penetration of foreign capital (in the form of Tony O'Reilly's Irish-based Independent Newspapers group that acquired the newly restructured English-language press).[42]

On a much smaller scale, the erstwhile antiapartheid, "alternative" newspaper the *Weekly Mail* was first rescued by the U.K.-based newspaper *The Guardian*—with whom it had collaborated during the apartheid years—from closure in 1998 by buying a share of 62 percent in the publication that was renamed the *Mail and Guardian*. In 2002, the *Guardian* reduced its shareholding to 10 percent, and an 87.5 percent stake was sold to Trevor Ncube, a Zimbabwean publisher.[43]

From these examples of local/global "interpenetration of capitals,"[44] it should already be clear that the globalization of South African media after apartheid cannot be characterized as simply a one-way flow in the mode of cultural imperialism but a hybrid of local political imperatives and global capital flows that resulted in new alliances being formed and new media formations emerging. Moreover, South African audiences are not merely passive recipients of global media, but active participants in meaning-making. The meaning produced in this way can take various forms depending on their position in local cultural contexts and lived realities. Depending on these identity positions, exposure to global media may actually serve to reaffirm localized identities.[45]

Nor has the flow been one-directional. South African cultural industries also benefited from greater access to global markets, creating systems of contraflows into the continent and beyond.[46] So rapid and aggressive has been the expansion of South African media and ICT companies into the rest of the continent that some commentators have considered viewing South Africa as a sub-imperialist or middle power on the continent.[47] Some breakthroughs into the global entertainment industry can also be noted. Witness the Oscar-winning adaptation of Athol Fugard's novel *Tsotsi* or the punk-rock phenomenon *Die Antwoord*, which became a global viral sensation, managing to tap into global markets (even while it is acknowledged that these markets continue to be dominated by Anglo-American media products).[48] The heightened globalization of the South African media industry was led, to a great extent, by the conglomerate Naspers, which successfully managed to reposition itself from a company built on Afrikaner capital (and supportive of the apartheid regime) to one that—especially under the leadership of its CEO, Koos Bekker (who stepped down in 2014)—spread its wings across the African continent and into the Global South with interests, among others, in Brazil and India. It is its holdings in the Chinese company Tencent, however, that has in recent years propelled the company into becoming a global media giant.[49]

This profitability of the South African media behemoth's investment in China points to the recent emergence of China as a player in African markets, which has been the source of much controversy and also signifies most clearly how geopolitical shifts impact on local media industries, practices, and normative frameworks. In 2010, 16 years after South Africa emerged from decades of being a pariah state, it received an invitation from China to join the BRIC group of emerging economies. South Africa's accession to this group, now widely known as the BRICS group, suggests that the country should be taken seriously as a regional power.

Introduction

China's growing presence in African media markets has "challenged liberal orthodoxy" in media as well as government policies on the continent.[50] The often critical response to China's involvement in the African media sphere[51] is based on fears that it represents a media culture that poses a threat to media freedom.[52] In this discourse, it is also interesting to note how global shifts (China's emergence as a player in the global media market) overlap with local political concerns (the internal contestations around the media's role in postapartheid South Africa and government pressure on media freedom). These overlaps are illustrated by the concerns raised when the Independent Newspapers Group—which had been owned by the Ireland-based media conglomerate Independent News and Media plc—was sold to a local consortium, Sekunjalo, headed by Dr. Iqbal Survé, who has close ties with the current ANC government. Sekunjalo was partly funded by a Chinese consortium, and this move was seen as part of a broader trend of the "global see-saw tilting eastward."[53] Taken together with Survé's links to an ANC government that has shown itself as being increasingly intolerant to media criticism, this latest example of Chinese investment in the South African media landscape, following on the establishment of *China Daily* and investment in TopTV, was seen as holding a threat for South African media culture:

> We can assume that this is tied to the Chinese authorities, and their push for a greater media presence in Africa as part of their "soft diplomacy" drive for influence on the continent. The Chinese government, let us say, is not a friend of a free, open and critical media. They are very clear about their national interests, and their firm hand on ensuring their media interests serve them. One has to wonder what will happen when their national interest does not align with ours. This is relevant when Dr Survé has been so vocal about bringing ownership back home. One can safely say now that Independent Newspapers, the country's second biggest newspaper group, is in hands which are closely tied to our ruling party, the ANC. This in itself is neither here nor there, depending on how Dr Survé plays that out and interprets his and his newspapers' roles.[54]

Comments such as these suggest that local contests about the South African media's relationship to political and state power in the postapartheid era coincide with global shifts in the media landscape and geopolitical power relations. These local and global dynamics combine to make the media an arena where proxy struggles about power, identity, and culture are being played out. The confluence of these global and local struggles in and about the South African media in the postapartheid era is the focus of this book. A multidimensional, multiperspectival approach will be followed in which snapshots of these various local contestations and global shifts will be provided. In this way, an overview of various political, economic, social and cultural aspects of the development of the postapartheid media will be given against the backdrop of mediated globalization and a rapidly changing global geopolitics.

The book will be organized into three main sections:

The first will chart the transition from apartheid to democracy, and the impact that the new political order has had on the structure of the media landscape. It will do so by outlining the major shifts in ownership of the media and the changes in the editorial composition of the major media. The major changes in the South African media industry's orientation as it moved outward into the continent and further afield, as well as the fluctuating internal dynamics of the media as a result of the inflow of global capital and changing political-social imperatives, will be discussed. The "glocalization" of content, through the inflow of global media formats like reality TV and tabloids will also be touched upon. Apart from an exploration of the changes in media structures and content, this section will also explore the shifts in media culture, as media practitioners negotiated their own position within a new democracy against the background of memories of their role during apartheid and attempts to reconstruct the memory of past practices in an attempt to meet challenges faced within the democratic era. All of these will be couched in a discussion of the different theoretical frameworks within which the changes in South African media can be analyzed. The debates in the emerging field of transitology, the study of new democracies in the "Third Wave of Democratization" will be compared with political economic critiques of the limits of transformation, "elite renewal," and "elite continuity." The section will conclude with a chapter that draws on interviews with media practitioners remembering their experience under apartheid and comparing that with the current environment, with the aim of understanding how constructions of the past underpin current professional ideologies. In alluding to the professional positioning of media practitioners postapartheid, this chapter will set the scene for the second section of the book, which will focus on the internal contestations around media norms, values and practices in the postapartheid era.

In the second section, the tension between "local" norms and rhetorical claims to indigenous African values on the one hand, and "global" ethical principles and practices on the other, will be elaborated upon. The aim of this section is twofold. First, it will show how the mediated public sphere in South Africa is fragmented by appeals to different cultural and ontological frameworks of meaning, and how the sharp material inequalities, inherited from apartheid and exacerbated by the dominance of neoliberal economic policies, fracture civil society and result in highly asymmetric levels of access to platforms of expression. Historical and contemporary social and political formations influence the various, and competing, normative understandings of what the role of media in a democratic South Africa should be. The focus on the country's emergence as a new regional power within a changing geopolitical landscape can easily obscure these intense internal conflicts and debates as the media paradigm continues to be renegotiated. Second, the focus on the internal contestations will also problematize the notion of "media systems," made famous by Hallin and Mancini's work.[55] Although subsequent revisions and additions of their media system framework[56] have included work on South African media, the extent to which the South African media paradigm borrows from and localizes global media frameworks, as well as the dynamic changes the country's media continues to undergo, raises the question of whether one could talk about a media "system" in contexts undergoing rapid change. To illustrate these shifts and tensions, this section will refer to debates about media ethics and professional values that took place over the two decades following the end of apartheid. These include controversy around the perceived "tabloidization" of South African media as a result of global influences and normative debates about "local" values versus global standards.

The third section of the book will discuss the South African media with a specific focus on the country's position within shifts in global geopolitics in recent years. Most significant among these global shifts is South Africa's accession to the BRICS formation of emerging states. The country's membership of this configuration, especially its relationship to China, has already started to have an impact on media ownership and content in South Africa and has elicited much controversy. The first chapter in this section will outline the regional and global footprint of the South African media to illustrate its position in continued global flows and contraflows. The second chapter will consider how the South African media has framed and represented the country's membership of the BRICS group, with a particular emphasis on the country's developing and often controversial relationship with China amid fears that China's "soft power" initiatives will threaten press freedom locally. The final chapter in this section, before a conclusion that summarizes the main arguments put forward in the book, will explore future challenges and directions for the South African media against the background of continued global geopolitical shifts and the impact of new media technologies on media practices and social change. In ending the book by looking at new global economic and political shifts, the emphasis is reiterated that South African media should not be viewed in isolation or as a particular geographical area of interest but as part of a global mediatized society. Viewed from this perspective, this study of South African media is not only intended as a conversation with global media studies on an applied level, but also as a theoretical and conceptual engagement.

PART I

Transitions

CHAPTER 1

From Apartheid to a New Democracy

Areas of Shift

It might be tempting to cast the development of the South African media post 1994 in a teleological narrative that moves between two binary points—from repression under an authoritarian government to constitutionally guaranteed freedom, from isolation during the apartheid years to the globalization of media capital and content.

However, for several reasons, the picture is not quite as simple. In the first place, the shift from apartheid to democracy does not coincide with a clear move from isolation to globalization. International media already covered South Africa during the apartheid years and there had been international involvement in the form of media assistance to antiapartheid, alternative media. Moreover, despite severe restrictions on the local and international media (such as the prohibition on quoting or depicting "banned persons" like Nelson Mandela), and notwithstanding the fact that television was actively kept out of the country until 1976 and international sanctions severely limited South Africans' exposure to international media, South African publics were not hermetically sealed off from the outside world. Ironically, White South Africans sometimes learned more about race relations from an American television series like *The Cosby Show* than from their own media, as Krabill has pointed out.[1]

Second, while the media did operate under a range of oppressive laws during apartheid, the relationship between media, apartheid, and democracy cannot be cast in a simplistic narrative in which heroic journalists fought an unjust system until they won press freedom. Although this narrative is often expediently used to ward off new pressures in the democratic era (as discussed in Chapter 4), it overstates the mainstream media's resistance to apartheid. Putting aside the independent, alternative press,[2] the mainstream media either supported the apartheid regime, at least toed the official line, or provided a very limited critique of certain aspects of apartheid policy. In other words: "the bulk of the media did little to challenge apartheid."[3]

Third, democratization's gains remain incomplete. In terms of its political economy, it can be argued that the media is now even more concentrated than under apartheid, due to the disappearance of most of the alternative media sector and the growth of big commercial media conglomerates.[4] This situation is exacerbated by the persisting huge disparities in wealth, living standards, and access to resources that continue to present "daunting barriers" to the emergence of a single or homogenous postapartheid public sphere.[5] The contestation about media norms and values, which has already been alluded to in the introduction and which will be discussed in more depth in the following section of this book, has highlighted the differences in opinion about how media should contribute to democratic deepening. What is more, the arrival of democracy has not meant that the media has become completely free from political pressures and renewed threats to its freedom.[6]

There is, however, no question that in many respects the South African media has undergone major changes since apartheid. Whether these changes have been wide and deep enough to refer to a complete "transformation" of the media industry, or whether it would be more accurate to point to the continuation of certain dimensions and tendencies, is a debate that we will return to shortly. It would, however, be useful to attempt to get an overview of the major areas in which shifts did occur during the transition from apartheid to democracy, even as the simplistic dualities outlined above are avoided.

This chapter will first provide a descriptive overview of the changes in four major areas of media structures and practices, so as to indicate how democratization impacted on these areas, rather than providing a critical assessment of the extent to which these changes can be seen as sufficient or transformative enough. The four main areas that will be looked at are the following: ownership and editorial composition, attempts to diversify the public sphere, normative and regulatory frameworks, and conceptions of the relationship between media and political power. Following this overview, some of the debates about how transitions from authoritarian states to democratic ones should be conceptualized will be explored. Like other postauthoritarian countries in central Europe, the Middle East, and Africa, South Africa can be seen as an example of a "new democracy" in which the media has played an important transitional role. Disagreements, however, remain about how this role should be defined, how central the media is to the transitional process, and whether it contributes to democratic deepening or entrenches continuity with the past. The relation between contemporary journalistic identities and roles and a reflection on the media's historical role will be considered in more detail in the following chapter as well.

What this overview of the four main areas of change shows is that a liberal-democratic consensus emerged among the media, in which it positioned itself as independent from the government and as supportive of a free-market environment within which the media can operate as businesses. Despite the clashes between the media and government that occurred when the media's independence was threatened, and the media's professional ideology of an adversarial stance toward government, the media and the ANC government have actually been in agreement over the latter's economic policies adopted after 1994. Some have gone so far as to say that an "academic-institutional-media complex" produced a coherent hegemonic discourse in support of the ANC's neoliberal turn.[7] It may be argued that the media's criticism has been largely directed at instances in which this consensus has not been honored by the ANC, for instance, when corruption undermines the efficiency of "service delivery" (premised on principles of privatization)[8]. This contradictory relationship between a media that vehemently asserts its independence from a government whose policies it has largely been in agreement with, and a government which focuses its attack on media that serves an elite to which it also appeals, can be seen as having played out across different areas. Let us look at each of these areas of shift in turn.

Ownership and Editorial Composition

The changes in media ownership patterns since the advent of democracy have become a productive area of research for scholars of the South African political economy. The private media was subjected to political pressures right from the start of the transition. The ANC had made clear its assumptions that the press was White-controlled and, even when ownership of sections of the press passed into the hands of Black capital, the print media was still being criticized by then president Nelson Mandela for their criticism of the new government. As Tomaselli observes, Black journalists—now entwined with the logic of capital—foregrounded their professional identities as journalists rather than as Black citizens with ideological loyalties to the ANC.[9] The ostensible correlation between economic restructuring and political change in the country was evident, especially in the terrain of the media, partly because of the centrality of this industry to the transition as a whole. As Jacobs points out, debates about the media are often "debates about democracy in disguise."[10]

The ownership shifts were perhaps the most evident in the print media sector while, on a regulatory level, shifts also took place within the broadcasting sector. In the 1990s, in anticipation of the forthcoming democratic elections, the print media embarked on a process of restructuring and "unbundling" parts of its capital to sell off in an attempt to demonstrate its commitment to Black Economic Empowerment (BEE).[11] The company Argus Holdings Ltd sold off a majority share in the *Sowetan*, at the time the daily newspaper with the highest circulation in the country, which under apartheid provided some representation to its Black readership in a society from which they had been disenfranchised—even if its position was not as radically opposed to apartheid as the "alternative" press.[12] The 52 percent share was sold to a Black Empowerment company called Corporate Africa, headed by Nelson Mandela's personal physician, Nthato Motlana, and the remaining stake remained under ownership of Argus. Argus in turn was bought—incrementally but by 1995 in totality—by the Irish-based Independent Newspapers owned by Tony O'Reilly. O'Reilly renamed the company—which publishes major English-language newspapers such as *The Star*, *Cape Argus*, *Daily News*, and *Pretoria News*—Independent Newspapers. In another major restructuring deal, the company that owned the remaining English newspapers, Johannesburg Consolidated Investments (JCI or Johnnic) was unbundled from the mother company JCI. Johnnic had interests in the Central News Agency retail chain, the recording company Gallo, the pay-TV channel M-Net and Times Media Limited (TML, owners of *Sunday Times/Business Times*). The Black empowerment consortium NEC (National Empowerment Consortium, consisting of small businesses and unions supporting the ANC) bought 20 percent of Johnnic in 1996 for R1,5 billion (approximately $380 million at the 1996 exchange rate), at the time the biggest cash deal in South Africa, with the option to increase its stake to 35 percent within 18 months.[13] Through Johnnic's (today called Avusa)[14] companies MultiChoice International and its shareholding in two TML titles, *Financial Mail* and *Business Day*, that were bought by the British-based group Pearsons in 1996, local Black capital entered into the global media market. Black Economic Empowerment capital was later further globalized through the share offerings made to Black investors in M-Net and Naspers, which was built on Afrikaner capital and, under apartheid, supported the National Party and (since the 1990s) became a global media behemoth.[15] The selling off of the "family silver," as Naspers managing director Ton Vosloo described it at the time, to Black-owned companies should be seen as part of a broader attempt by the Afrikaans media to reposition itself in relation to the new political and economic environments and to derive optimal benefit from the political transition. The subsequent global success of Naspers as a multinational media behemoth, with interests in the rest of Africa, China, and elsewhere in the world, is testament to the success of this strategy.[16]

The restructuring of media ownership during the transitional period therefore responded to the domestic demands of aligning the interests of the new political elite and established capital. At the same time, new configurations of the local and the global emerged that had an impact not only on the flows and contraflows of media capital but also on media content and media practices. The acquisition of some of the most important English-language newspaper titles by the Irish Independent group contributed to tensions between the local and the global economies, as the local operation was expected to deliver profits to the Irish mother company. Here was an example of how the global flows and contraflows of media capital also have a direct impact on the cultures and practices of journalism in localities. The Irish conglomerate was accused of "looting" its South African subsidiary to send profits back to Ireland.[17] Local operations were "cut to the bone," replacing experienced journalists with novices and cutting overheads, with the result that the quality of journalism suffered to the extent that the newspapers were seen to have become "sad shadows of themselves."[18] The commercial pressure created by this opening up of the local media industry to global competition may therefore be seen as having "devastating" effects on media practices at the time.[19] Some of these results included a "tabloidization" of the print media, especially; a reduction of staff; a "juniorization" of newsrooms;[20] a preference for commercial imperatives in making editorial judgments; and an erosion of specialized reporting.[21]

In addition to the restructuring of ownership to include Black capital, more Black editorial staff were appointed to newsrooms, some of them occupying senior editorial positions at leading mainstream newspapers. Some of these appointments included: Ferial Haffajee (editor of the quality weekly *Mail & Guardian* before assuming editorship of the Sunday newspaper *City Press* and later becoming editor-at-large of the South African edition of the *Huffington Post*), Justice Malala (editor of the now defunct *ThisDay*), Mathatha Tsedu (editor of *Sunday Times* and *City Press*), Jovial Rantao (editor of *Sunday Tribune*), Makhudu Sefara (*The Star*), Moegsien Williams (*Pretoria News, Argus, Cape Times, The Star*), and Karima Brown (executive editor of Independent titles). But in spite of attempts to change the racial makeup of its owners and editorial staff, critics have pointed out that the print media's class base remains the same[22] and that media continues to operate according to the same functionalistic structural logic of circulation, distribution networks, price structure, and advertising that has as its target the lucrative and arguably still largely White, or at least affluent Black, elite market.[23] In other words, the question posed by these critics is whether the changes to the racial composition of the boardrooms and the newsrooms did enough to transform the media at the level of the public sphere.[24]

Diversity of ownership continues to be an issue in the highly concentrated South African media market. More than twenty years after the arrival of democracy, attempts are still being made to transform the press in terms of the racial composition of its ownership. Parliamentary hearings into print media transformation held in 2011 brought to light that although the number of Black editors of newspapers had increased since democracy, this was not reflected in the political economy of ownership and control. In 2011, Black ownership of the press stood at 14 percent and female representation on media boards at only 4.4 percent.[25] A task team established to hold public hearings into transformation of the print and digital media lasted only six months until two of the four print media companies withdrew from the process in response to a government inquiry into uncompetitive behavior.[26]

The restructuring of ownership and editorial composition of especially the commercial print media can be understood within broader political economy-based analyses of the South African transition. Critics emphasize the extent to which elite interests dominated the negotiated settlement in the years of transition and how neoliberal economic principles continue to determine ANC policy.[27] The shift from the Reconstruction and Development Programme (RDP) toward the Growth, Employment and Redistribution (GEAR) program is often cited as the clearest example of this ideological reorientation on the part of the ruling party. From this perspective, the media forms part of this elite consensus, and the restructuring of media ownership to include new Black owners of capital is no guarantee for a greater diversity of voices and class positions.

Despite the negative assessments that one could arrive at when measuring the limited extent to which the media industry managed to transform itself in the postapartheid era, the ideological lines according to which the media was organized under apartheid have become less clearly defined. Under apartheid, the media had been split along ideological lines that corresponded with language (Afrikaans media was largely supportive of the apartheid government, and mainstream English media was tied to the interests of mining capital, providing a limited, "liberal" point of view).[28] With the demise of the radical, "alternative" media sector, as already described, and despite attempts to strengthen the public and community media sectors, the media landscape remains dominated by commercial media that have proliferated across various platforms—including mobile, satellite, and digital. With the obvious links between different-language media and their ideological orientation having disappeared after apartheid, the commercial media presents itself as ideologically neutral.[29] Therefore, even before any discussion of the media's explicitly stated normative position in relation to the postapartheid government (to which we will return in subsequent chapters), it should be noted that the media's strong commercial orientation, and precisely its ostensibly postideological position, has given it a powerful position from which to become a role player in the political economy in its own right. The free-market principles that it espouses are presented as natural and self-evident, and its construction of social reality therefore is aligned with the overall neoliberal consensus. This is not unusual within the global context. The global media can no longer be seen, at least solely, as a marginal commentator on institutions of power, as has traditionally been the underpinning logic of normative concepts like the "Fourth Estate." It has become a source of power, which "rather than simply mediating between interests, organizes representations in support of their own interests."[30] For this reason, it can even be argued (as Turner does)[31] that we should think about the media as we would of the state, i.e., as "an apparatus with its own interests, and its own use for power."[32]

Indeed, the changes in the political economy of the South African media that occurred around the transition to democracy did serve to entrench the media in a position of economic power and give it a foothold within the new political environment. The ownership shifts that took place in the media industry after apartheid were meant to display the commitment to a newly democratic environment but simultaneously aligned the industry with the market economy in terms of what Sparks called a process of "elite renewal."[33] The process of "unbundling" assets in the print media sector after 1994 and selling them off to Black Empowerment capital (the Johnnic deal) and to international investors (Independent) formed part of what may be seen as "capitalist rationalization," which instead of broadening the public sphere and making it more inclusive, had the effect of narrowing it even further.[34] In South Africa, as in other globalized capitalist economies, "the institutionalized and rationalized nature of the public sphere . . . precludes any significant arrangement that could be said to truly include the pauperized public."[35]

If the Habermasian ideal public sphere is understood to have as one of its characteristics its openness to all citizens, the question that would remain, if viewed from a critical perspective, is whether the South African mainstream media, today, is indeed representing the "public interest" in as wide a sense as it purports to do. It would be unfair and inaccurate, however, to suggest that no attempts were made to redress the imbalances in the public sphere inherited from apartheid. In the following section some of these attempts will be outlined.

Diversifying the Public Sphere

The high levels of inequality in South Africa, among the highest in the world and rooted in a history of systematic underdevelopment of the majority of its citizens, are "vital to understanding everything in the country—including the structure and reach of the different media."[36] During apartheid, the media was largely structured in terms of race and language as these corresponded with struggles for economic and political power.[37] The mainstream commercial print media was broadly divided along ideological lines that corresponded with linguistic differences in the White community, with very limited attempts to cater for Black or "Coloured" (in apartheid nomenclature) audiences (e.g., in separate, "extra" editions). While, as mentioned earlier, English-language publications provided a critique of apartheid rooted in liberal, capitalist interests, Afrikaans-language newspapers served as key institutions for the articulation of nationalist ideology, even while some of them questioned the establishment from time to time.[38] The public broadcaster, SABC, also predominantly served (sometimes competing) White interests.[39] In the structure of its African-language television and radio channels and stations, the SABC was also organized according to the racial and ethnic logic of apartheid. The effect of naturalizing the separateness of different languages and ethnicities was to "imprison African language speakers in their ethnic cultures—the terms and authenticity of which were determined externally, by the dominant white social power."[40]

While the ideological links between language and political positioning faded away in the postapartheid years, as media restructured and repositioned itself according to political and economic demands (as discussed above), market segmentation continued to entrench social differences inherited from apartheid. To a large extent, race, class, and ethnicity (and therefore position in commercial markets) continue to coincide in the democratic era. Newspapers still largely serve an urban elite, with only three newspapers publishing in isiZulu, the most widely spoken of the 11 official languages.[41] The spectacular rise of tabloid newspapers has served as a corrective of sorts by broadening the newspaper market to include a Black working class.[42] However, these newspapers continue to be relegated (see Chapter 5 of this book) to the margins of professional and scholarly journalistic discourses, and their subject matter only rarely spills over into the mainstream press. It may even be possible to argue that the emergence of tabloid newspapers serving the Black working class has provided the mainstream press with an alibi for not paying more attention to the everyday lived reality of the poor majority. What needs to be noted in terms of the introduction of tabloid newspapers to the South African public sphere is that these newspapers have emerged in an era where the death of print journalism at the hands of digital media is accepted as a fact in the Global North. Overall, the internet has not had the same impact on media audiences in South Africa as in many parts of the world where societies are more media-saturated. Access to the internet (and therefore social media use) is not yet as widespread in South Africa, although the penetration of mobile phones is pervasive and has enabled users to access the internet through smartphones.[43] The *Daily Sun* has established a Facebook page where readers engage in lively debates about stories that appeared in the paper. Despite dwindling print circulation figures, advertising in print is still growing, even while advertising on TV has overtaken it in terms of revenue.[44] These statistics underscore the importance of thinking about trends in media use, journalistic production, and the much-debated "future of journalism" in contextually specific ways, as they indicate trends that do not always follow the same patterns as media in the Global North.

Radio and television remain the most popular media across languages and ethnic or racial groups, with 91 percent of South Africans over 16 watching television and 93 percent listening to the radio. Attempts were made to restructure the broadcasting sector so as to widen the postapartheid public sphere. As mentioned in the introduction, the MDDA was established in an attempt to widen access to the public sphere by previously marginalized groups and to enable more Black ownership of the media. Media assistance efforts—support to build and develop community media—have been limited since the demise of apartheid, although international donors continue to support media projects that can be linked to other priority areas like health, social justice, and gender.[45]

The SABC was envisaged as a public broadcaster, accountable to Parliament, and the community broadcasting sector was strengthened substantially. Since democratization, more than 200 community radio stations and five community television stations have received licenses.[46] Both the public and the community broadcasting sectors have, however, been beset by problems. The public broadcaster has been mired in managerial and financial crises, and its credibility has suffered as a result of what is seen as managerial bias toward the ruling party.[47] This bias manifested in, for instance, the authoritarian management style of its former Chief Operating Officer, Hlaudi Motsoeneng, who forbade coverage by the broadcaster of violent protests and suspended journalists who criticized his editorial position. The SABC's dependence on commercial revenue has also hampered its ability to fulfill its public service mandate. Serious allegations of government interference into the operations of the SABC Board were the focus of a parliamentary board of inquiry into the SABC at the time of writing. The board heard of a climate of fear and intimidation created by Motsoeneng, whose appointment by the Minister of Communications, Faith Muthambi, as COO had been deemed unlawful and irrational by the Western Cape High Court.[48]

The community radio sector has also had to face challenges of sustainability due to lack of funding, and many community outlets modeled themselves on commercial media rather than broadening community participation in management and oversight.[49] While community newspapers have shown growth and mainstream print media has been on the decline,[50] many of these papers are owned by big media companies like Media24 and Caxton. In this sector, the concentrated media market has also had an impact. The dominance of big companies in the community newspaper arena has exerted pressure on smaller, independent players. An example of this is the case of a battle between two community papers in the Free State province that, at the time of writing, was being investigated by the Competition Commission. It is alleged that Media24 used its loss-making community newspaper *Goudveld Forum* in such a way as to force the closing of its competitor, a small community paper *Gold-Net News*. Media24 was accused of selling advertising below cost to undercut its competitor, which eventually had to close down.[51] This case is an important one to defend the principle of diversity in the public sphere and to show the importance of independent community media to provide balance to commercial outlets.

The newspaper sector has seen some ownership and managerial changes but not a fundamental transformation.[52] The print media sector continues to be highly concentrated—one of the most concentrated in the world, according to a recent study by Columbia University.[53] The big conglomerates Naspers, Avusa, Caxton, and Independent[54] dominate the sector. The two attempts made to diversify the print sector had to face severe challenges. The Nigerian owned-newspaper *ThisDay*, launched in 2003, lasted a year in the tough print market in which newcomers are treated with hostility. It had to close down as a result of financial problems after it failed to attract enough revenue to sustain its operations. But even if it had survived, it would still have competed in the elite audience niche, and the extent to which it would therefore have managed to bring diversity of perspectives into the print market is arguable. The extent to which editors are able to shift the contours of a debate within the mainstream print market is debatable. Commercial interests are likely to overrule any attempts to frame debates in ways with which the commercially lucrative, upmarket readership is uncomfortable. This, at least, was the contention by the editor of the *Sunday Times* and former chair of the South African National Editors' Forum (SANEF), Mathatha Tsedu, who argued that his 2003 sacking was a result of his attempts to introduce an "Africanization" agenda at this weekly newspaper. Connie Molusi, the CEO of the *Sunday Times*'s holding company, (at the time) Johnnic Communications, acknowledged that the profit motive played a role in the decision to let Tsedu go, but counterclaims were also made that Tsedu was too outspoken against the ANC.[55] Even the mass-market tabloids, which manage to broaden access to the print media to working-class audiences who remain routinely excluded from or marginalized in mainstream print news agendas, still operate within the commercial logic of the big conglomerates (Naspers and Independent) that own them. Their scope of criticism—political, economic, and social—is therefore also limited to those viewpoints that will not alienate their market.

In 2010, another new player came onto the scene in the form of the *New Age* newspaper. It is indicative of the concentration of the print market that this paper is the only mainstream commercial daily that is operated independently of one of the main conglomerates.[56] The company that owned this paper also launched a 24-hour news TV channel, Africa News Network, or ANN7, on MultiChoice's pay-TV digital satellite platform. The paper was owned by the Gupta family, who attracted a fair amount of controversy due to their close ties to President Jacob Zuma. The paper's news is therefore perceived to be less credible because it is seen to be less critical of the government.[57] Such proximity to political power poses obvious problems for editorial independence. A further development in this regard has been the increasing use of social media, especially Twitter, to create fake news and false accounts to discredit critics of the Gupta family and what was seen as their "capture" of the state under Zuma.[58] The extent of this "state capture," and its implications for the media, was still unfolding at the time of completion of this book, with emails to and from the Guptas leaked to the media and a counteroffensive of fake news and intimidation of journalists launched by supporters of the Guptas, including the Black First Land First movement under the leadership of Andile Mngxitama.

Although the *New Age* has been criticized for its perceived friendliness to government, the examples of *ThisDay*'s demise and Tsedu's dismissal show that appraisals of the South African media's role in the postapartheid democracy should extend beyond the dominant analyses that tend to evaluate this role rather one-dimensionally in terms of the degree of its adversity toward government. The economic and social dimensions of the media's positioning in postapartheid society form part of the overall picture and should not be ignored or underestimated. That media markets remain stratified according to race and class (which still largely intersect), that the influential print media still largely provides an elite perspective on social reality, and that community media remains small and underfunded (partly as a result of the limits the commercial media imposed on its contributions to the MDDA)[59] are all reasons for concern. In this regard, the point raised earlier in this chapter about the high level of concentration of media ownership in South Africa should be just as alarming on account of its effects on the vibrancy of debate in the public sphere as the renewed threats to freedom of expression. We will return to some of these other dimensions—the economic and social, in addition to the political—during the course of the book.

Normative and Regulatory Frameworks

As we have already seen in relation to ownership changes, the change from an authoritarian society to a democratic one required the South African media to align itself to a more open, diverse and equal society. It was also noted that despite the entrance of Black capital to the market, and attempts to balance the dominance of the commercial media with public and community media, the South African media industry remains one of the most concentrated in the world. The shifts of media capital changed the racial composition of ownership to a limited extent, but it was argued that the alignment of the interests of media capital and political elites in effect served to entrench elite interests, at least in the print media sector, which saw a process of "elite renewal" rather than a thorough transformation.[60] Adjustment to the new democracy also had implications for the way the media was regulated. Under apartheid, the media was subject to an oppressive set of laws, as mentioned in the introduction to this book. While the advent of democracy brought about the repealing of most of these laws, and allowed self-regulatory regimes for the media, it can be argued that, similar to ownership shifts, the reform of the legal and regulatory frameworks also entrench elite industry interests rather than serve to extend the public sphere. So much attention was (and continues to be) paid to the reform and protection of these self-regulatory procedures in the light of increased political pressures that more substantive questions about the role that the media can and should play in the new democracy and the wider societal context remained unresolved and continue to simmer under the surface of debates about media freedom. In Chapter 4 of this book, I discuss in more depth the distinction between procedural ethical debates and more substantive normative questions to do with the media's role in society, and how these questions underpinned many of the debates that played out in the media sphere during the first two decades of democracy. The purpose of this section is to outline the initial shifts in the regulatory frameworks during the years of transition, and to highlight certain areas of interest that will be explored in more depth in subsequent chapters. This section also links with the previous one in which ownership shifts were described in relation to the change from apartheid to democracy to show how shifts in the regulatory frameworks were underpinned by a renewed commitment by the media to democratic culture.

Under apartheid, the law, rather than ethical principles, formed the yardstick for judging difficult editorial decisions.[61] Apartheid-era laws affecting the media were scrapped as part of the democratization process,[62] but some laws remained. These later provided much cause for concern among the media—for instance, Section 205 of the Criminal Procedure Act, which allows a judge or a magistrate to summon journalists to give testimony about an alleged offense. This section had been invoked on a number of occasions, giving rise to questions about its constitutionality in the light of the protection of freedom of speech.[63] The intervention of SANEF led to negotiations with the Attorney General, Justice Minister Dullah Omar, and Safety and Security Minister Sydney Mufamadi that resulted in a "Record of Understanding" in 1999, which noted the need for case-by-case evaluations and attempts at mediation by the National Director of Prosecutions before subpoenas would be issued.[64] SANEF continued to argue for the repealing of Section 205 as well as other laws like the National Key Points Act that are seen to inhibit media freedom.[65]

The law that perhaps raised the most concern was the new Protection of State Information Bill, dubbed "the Secrecy Bill" by its opponents, which is meant to repeal and replace the apartheid-era 1982 Protection of Information Act. The bill was passed by the National Assembly on November 22, 2011, but still needed to be signed into law at the time of writing. The implications of this Bill, as mentioned in the introduction, raised much concern among the media and civil society and caused a big outcry. These remnants of apartheid laws notwithstanding, the new democratic environment in which the media operated after 1994 is much freer than it had ever been. Freedom of speech, including freedom of the media, is now entrenched in the Constitution, which has been taken to mean that the media should be free to regulate itself and ensure ethical conduct without the threat of legal interference.

The oppressive legal environment of apartheid gave way to a system of self-regulation, with a Press Council and Ombudsman established to hear complaints by the public against the printed media and an independent judicial tribunal, the Broadcasting Complaints Commission (BCCSA), established by the National Association of Broadcasters (NAB) to adjudicate complaints against broadcasters that are members of the NAB. During the fierce debates about press freedom that ensued in the wake of the threats by the ANC to establish a statutory Media Appeals Tribunal and around the passing of the Protection of State Information Bill (see the introduction), the role of the ombudsman came under renewed scrutiny, and following public hearings set up by the Press Council and subsequently by an ad hoc Press Freedom Commission, the Constitution and procedures of the Council were amended to give greater representation to citizens and allow for slightly stronger sanctions.

The new emphasis on self-regulation meant that the media itself negotiated normative frameworks to coincide with the new constitutional notion of a balance of rights (among these, the most pertinent for the media were balancing the right to freedom of speech with the right to privacy and the right to dignity). The normative approach favored by the South African media can be typified as falling within a liberal-democratic, social responsibility paradigm, which originates from the United States[66] but has been adopted in various countries around the world, even if it might not be appropriate for these diverse settings.[67] Retief shows, for instance, how the principles of professionalism and social responsibility espoused by the Hutchins Commission in post–World War II America still influence ethical thinking in the postapartheid South African media.[68] This dominant normative framework, about which there exists consensus among most mainstream media in the country, has, however, not gone uncontested. Several, often heated, normative debates took place in the country during the first twenty years of democracy. These debates will be discussed in more depth in Chapters 5 and 6 of this book. In the current chapter, it is useful to note that one of the major shifts that have taken place during and after the transitional period in the country has been in the area of regulation and normative frameworks, which are also linked to a growing conception of "professionalism" among journalists.

The move away from the legalistic environment of apartheid to an environment where the media was allowed to self-regulate went hand-in-hand with greater claims of "professional" status for media practitioners. Like all other spheres of life in South Africa, the practice of journalism under apartheid was also delineated along racial lines. Most Black journalists belonged to the Media Workers Association of South Africa (MWASA), while the South African Society of Journalists (SASJ), which later became the South African Union of Journalists (SAUJ), had some Black members. Editors belonged to separate bodies—the Black Editors' Forum (BEF) and the Conference of Editors (CoE)—which were amalgamated in 1996 to form SANEF.[69] SANEF had the challenge of contributing to the transformation of an industry that had been ideologically divided under apartheid and continued to be marked by mistrust, while also redefining the role of editors in relation to a democratically elected government.[70] The latter role became especially challenging as the new government started to exert pressure on editors to be less critical and more supportive of its actions. Internal differences of opinion remained around political controversies and issues such as the Truth and Reconciliation Commission (TRC) investigation into journalists' role under apartheid and the Human Rights Commission's investigation into racism in the media.[71] Over the years, however, SANEF has done much to protect the newfound freedom and independence of journalists in the postapartheid era. The organization also mediated between editors and the government when tensions arose. When communication between editors and government threatened to break down during the Thabo Mbeki presidency, SANEF arranged a meeting between Mbeki, cabinet ministers, and editors at the apartheid-era holiday resort of Sun City in Northwest province in June 2001, dubbed the "Sun City Indaba." The topic of the meeting was "The Role of the Media in a Changing Society," and the frank discussions led to the easing of tensions, albeit temporarily.[72]

From a functionalist point of view, the social cohesion brought about by SANEF's attempts to unite Black and White editors and facilitate understanding between media and government can be viewed positively as a way to achieve order and balance in society.[73] The organization of editors into an inclusive, nonracial industry body can be seen as part of the professionalization of journalism in the postapartheid era, as well as part of the rationalization of the industry in response to the demands of the new political environment. Viewed from a more critical perspective, however, the move toward greater professionalization, as seen in the development of a self-regulatory system and the establishment of SANEF, as discussed earlier, is not without its problems. From within the journalism fraternity, objections have been raised that SANEF was not representative of ordinary journalists, especially in the light of increased political and commercial pressures. An informal body of professional journalists, Pro-Journ, intended as the "voice of working journalists," as explained by its founder Michael Schmidt,[74] was established in 2010 to act as a forum for information exchange and support for journalists. But more serious is the concern about the implications of a discourse of "professionalism" on the public. The notion of journalists as "professionals" can entrench narrow and elitist interests, which conceive of media publics in terms of market principles[75]—a concern especially acute in a highly unequal country like South Africa, where access to the media is distributed unevenly.

Christians and Nordenstreng point out that, from a critical perspective:

> One begins to doubt the value basis of professionalism, and sees it increasingly as an ideological smokescreen to protect the proprietors' interests instead of the workers' rights. This is a paradigm shift away from an approach that understands media and journalists as the owners of communication rights and freedoms toward a paradigm whereby the citizens and their civil society are seen as the ultimate owners of freedom of information.[76]

The critical view of professionalization that Christians and Nordenstreng point to also emerged in South African debates, especially regarding what these authors term an "ideological smokescreen to protect the proprietors' interests instead of the workers' rights."[77] The pitfalls of a professional self-definition oriented toward the market rather than the community have been pointed out by two former editors of the erstwhile alternative newspaper, the *Mail & Guardian*, during the debates about the reform of the self-regulatory processes of the Press Council, as well as the deliberations of the Print and Digital Media Transformation Task Team.[78]

SANEF has also come in for criticism. When Jane Duncan indicated weaknesses in the system of voluntary self-regulation[79]—quite a few years before criticism of these weaknesses culminated in reform of the Press Council, in the wake of its own public hearings, and that of the Press Freedom Commission—she argued that SANEF's relationship with the government was a relationship that is too close for comfort. Duncan's call for an approach that sees media independence not as an aim in its own right but as a requirement in order to serve citizens (rather than consumers of their product),[80] resonates with those of Christians and Nordenstreng for media to move away from a "media-centered paradigm" of professionalism toward a "citizen-centered paradigm."[81]

Conceptions of the Relationship between Media and Political Power

The initial years of democracy were marked by a mutual mistrust between the media and government. The government had misgivings about the media's representativeness,[82] and many members of the media industry, in turn, were cautious of possible threats to media freedom posed by the new government. This pessimistic expectation can be interpreted against the background of trends, in Africa, of governmental regulation[83] but has also been linked to "racist and misplaced associations" of the new government with authoritarianism.[84] This mistrust came to a head in two subsequent investigations into the media—the first as part of the TRC's hearings in 1996 and the second as a special investigation into racism in the media by the South African Human Rights Commission in 1999/2000. These investigations had two things in common: they were some of the earliest instances of friction between the media sector and the then newly elected government, and they failed to ask broader, structural questions about the intersection of the South African media, the market and race.[85]

The inquiry into racism in the South African media by the SAHRC led to one of the first clashes between the media and the postapartheid government. The inquiry was established after the SAHRC received complaints from the Black Lawyers Association and the Association of Black Accountants against two newspapers, the *Mail & Guardian* and the *Sunday Times*. The SAHRC decided to widen the remit of the inquiry into the media as a whole and commissioned research into racism in the media. The results of the (methodologically weak) investigation were published in an interim report, which was very negatively received by a hostile media. This report was followed up by hearings in which the input from various stakeholders, including the media, was solicited. In an attempt to ensure participation in these hearings, the SAHRC issued subpoenas to media organizations that carried the threat of fines or jail sentences, should they be disregarded. The media vehemently rejected this approach by the SAHRC, leading to the subpoenas eventually being dropped, but the whole exercise was condemned as McCarthyist and Stalinist.[86]

In this early clash between the media and government, some of the outlines of the many subsequent conflicts and tensions started to emerge. As Johnson and Jacobs point out,[87] the media took a liberal point of view, in which racism is seen as intentional actions rather than structural conditions, with the right to freedom of expression already starting to take precedence over questions of racism in the media or the media's implication in historical, structural conditions of exclusion. As will be discussed in Chapter 5 of this book, the view of media freedom that already started developing in this encounter continues to characterize normative ethical stances in the postapartheid media, namely an emphasis on procedural and regulatory aspects of media freedom and social responsibility but a neglect or avoidance of a discussion of more substantive questions of the media's role in postapartheid democracy. Another dimension of this conflict that continues to characterize media debates a decade and a half later is the narrow focus on rights from an elitist perspective, while socioeconomic rights of the poor majority do not receive the same amount of attention. The danger that Johnson and Jacobs point to as an outcome of the SAHRC conflict, namely "leaving it to elites to contest the content of democracy,"[88] has not yet been averted in the relationship among the media, the government, and the public.

The TRC that was set up to investigate apartheid-era atrocities devoted a special investigation to the role that the media played under apartheid. It concluded that the majority of the media under apartheid had contributed to an atmosphere within which gross human rights violations could take place—either through their support for the apartheid regime, or by the lack of resistance against it.[89] The hearings required the media to occupy several positions—that of actor in the hearings and the site where these hearings played out in the public domain, as well as perpetrators of apartheid, and its victim.[90] The TRC hearings brought to the fore simmering differences in political orientation among members of SANEF as well as in the media fraternity more generally. As Krabill points out,[91] the initial call to hold media hearings, made by the Freedom of Expression Institute, focused on propaganda and state spies in newsrooms under apartheid, with the assumption that the Afrikaans press and the SABC would be the main perpetrators. However, Black journalists and unions demanded that the inquiry also look at the treatment of Black journalists at White, English-language media. This demand undermined claims by such media that they were staunch opponents of apartheid.[92] Some journalists agreed to testify at the TRC hearings in September 1997. The media company Naspers, whose Afrikaans-language newspapers supported the National Party under apartheid, refused to testify. A small group of journalists working for Naspers broke ranks and signed an apology for their complicity to apartheid.[93] The TRC tended, however, to focus on press freedom issues and did not delve more deeply into the wider discourses created by entertainment, advertising, and other programming that could also have sustained the environment that allowed human rights violations to become normalized; nor did it investigate the institutional and organizational machinery that allowed for the production and circulation of these meanings.[94] The role of capital to limit the ability of media to play a more critical role, because of its unwillingness to alienate the apartheid government or because it created and sustained racially determined media markets, also received inadequate attention.[95]

The limited scope and approach of both the SAHRC and TRC investigations meant that opportunities were lost to lay a solid foundation for future debates about the media's role in the new democracy. The methodologically flawed SAHRC investigation highlighted individual cases of alleged racism to make the general point that the South African media was "racist." It focused largely on issues of representation, and, similar to the TRC inquiry, missed the

Chapter 1: From Apartheid to a New Democracy

opportunity to interrogate, in a critical fashion, the bigger questions about the more intricate power relations between race, the market, and the state. A more thorough investigation and addressing of these structural issues could have obviated some of the criticisms that have subsequently come to be leveled against the racial and class-based character of media market segmentation and the lack of community participation in the media sphere. These criticisms continue to reverberate in debates about the lack of transformation in the industry, more than twenty years after democracy.

Clashes intensified after 2010 between the media and the ANC government, when the ANC announced its desire to intervene in the self-regulatory system of the press by establishing a statutory Media Appeals Tribunal. Often conflated with this issue, although not aimed at the media alone, is the much-disputed Protection of State Information Bill. These and other conflicts in the legal-regulatory domain have sometimes led to alarmist responses from the media and the public and direct comparisons drawn between apartheid-era legislation and current pressures, although such comparisons were clearly exaggerated.[96]

In the debates about the media's role in society during the first twenty years after the apartheid era, it became clear that the responsibilities incumbent upon the media operating in this environment were understood differently by different role players. At the core of these debates lie different views of the interests that the media should be serving, as well as diverging definitions of the public sphere and the media's role in this sphere. These views are often (if inexplicitly) informed by different theoretical frameworks, such as notions of development communication that see a collaborative role between media and state, versus liberal-democratic frameworks in which media fulfill a more adversarial role. The range of positions in these normative debates and examples of how they played out in the first two decades of democracy will be discussed in more depth in Chapters 5 and 6 of this book. In the following chapter (Chapter 3), different ways of theorizing the shifts impacting on the media in the areas as described earlier will be offered. In other words, the question will be posed: how should we analyze and understand the various changes that the media underwent during the transition to democracy?

Theorizing the Areas of Shift

Looking at the four areas within which the major shifts took place, we see that despite significant changes—for instance in the editorial composition and the ownership of newspapers, the scrapping of apartheid laws and the relationship between media and the state—certain things clearly did not change. For one, the mainstream media is still dominated by big conglomerates—even more so after the demise of the alternative, antiapartheid press. The level of concentration increased to the extent that, as pointed out earlier,[97] the South African media market is now one of the most concentrated in the world. Soon after the transition, it became clear that commercial interests would dominate not only at the level of ownership, but also in terms of the media's editorial orientation. This refers to the market logic that pervaded all three tiers of the postapartheid media: commercial, public, and community. Commercial media remained focused largely on elite markets, and the most successful attempt to broaden the public sphere as far as the print media is concerned was the introduction of commercial, mass-market tabloids aimed at the Black working class. The community media found support from the MDDA but also found themselves resorting to commercial models when it became difficult to remain sustainable. As for the public broadcaster that continues to be beset by a range of managerial and political problems, its role of providing a counterbalance to the commercial media was limited by its dependence on commercial revenue from advertising. Although media staffing became more representative of the country's demography, the market orientation of most media outlets meant that the extent to which editors could change media discourses was limited by commercial pressures. Another area where the transition to democracy invited some comparisons with the situation under apartheid was the tensions that emerged between the media and the democratic government right from the start. These tensions grew in intensity in the following years as the ANC-led government's intolerance toward the media grew.

It would seem therefore, even from a descriptive overview such as the one provided earlier, that, although significant shifts occurred on the terrain of the media in relation to the new political and social environment during the period of transition and in the years following the formal arrival of democracy, these changes were also limited in important ways. The question then arises of how to understand the shifts and their limitations within broader analytical frameworks. How do we theorize the media's reorientation toward a democratic society, and on what theoretical basis can we evaluate the extent to which that reorientation was truly transformative, or instead circumscribed by a range of factors?

One approach would be to look at the shifts that occurred from the perspective of structural conditions—i.e., to investigate the political economy of the transition, considering issues such as the impact of economic policies on the media and the latter's response to such policies, ownership structures, and the orientation of the media toward its publics, as citizens or as markets, and so forth. Within this approach, different assessments of the media's position in the new South African democracy can be identified in the literature of the transition. These perspectives can be grouped within the broader discourse of *transitology*—the study of the conditions, structures, and effects of the transition to democracy.

A second approach to understanding the media's role in the new South African would be what one could call a more cultural approach, where the role of the media in creating and supporting new civic identities and democratic discourses is evaluated, and the amount of agency that citizens display in appropriating media to reconstruct identities and enact discursive changes is assessed. From this perspective, it is not only the "hard" structures and institutions that give an indication of the robustness and depth of a democracy, but also the "softer" aspects of representation, language, and value systems that display the extent to which democracy influences people's everyday lives and attitudes.

Two different approaches to theorizing the media's position, role, and orientation in relation to the transition to democracy in South Africa will be discussed later. First, the approach of transitology and its contribution to understanding the media in South Africa as a so-called "new democracy" will be considered. Second, the media as a site for the production of new social identities and democratic discourses will be examined, with reference to examples of how the media constructed social and cultural identities and how claims to certain identities obtained political currency in discourses about the media's role in the "new" South Africa.

Both these perspectives are offered with the aim of shedding some light on the terms and conditions under which the South African media made the transition to a democratic environment, how this transition was circumscribed, and why the transformation of the South African media has not been as wide-ranging as might have been expected.

Transitology and "Elite Continuity"

Although the democratization of South Africa followed its own historical trajectory, some comparisons have been made with other erstwhile authoritarian regimes that made transitions to democracy during the same period, such as those in Eastern Europe and the former USSR.[98] South Africa's transition to democracy can be located within the new era of political pluralism, free market economics, and media liberalization that followed the fall of Communism in the 1990s and has become known as the Third Wave of democratization.[99] The theoretical framework of transitology has been developed to draw comparisons between these various regions and the way in which the democratization process went hand-in-hand with marketization.[100] The literature of transitology, as it describes these "new democracies," provides a perspective on the South African media and its role in the democratization process that puts the emphasis on the formal political structures and institutions of democracy. The liberalization of the economy and the establishment of formal democratic institutions and processes like regular elections and constitutionally guaranteed rights (including freedom of the media) would, from this perspective, serve as indications of South Africa's transition to democracy. An assessment of the health of the South African democracy and the media's role in it would therefore also focus on the extent to which these institutions and processes function adequately. The emerging discipline of transitology has become a "growth industry," although the role of the media as a democratic institution has been largely ignored in such studies.[101]

The approach of transitology often relies on the implicit assumption that the introduction of free, independent media will necessarily deepen the practice of democracy. In South Africa, this assumption—although widespread and often invoked in resistance to threats to media freedom—is problematized by the deep inequalities inherited from colonialism and apartheid.[102] As will be discussed in more depth in Chapter 4, these inequalities continue to impact on the South African public sphere and entrench historically determined exclusions from the spaces of democratic deliberation, such as the media. These exclusions prompt us to consider the ways in which the establishment of formal institutions and processes of democracy, such as elections, a Constitution, a free media, and an independent judiciary, have translated into the practice and experience of democracy in everyday life. Chapter 4 explains the distinction (made by Heller in his comparison between India and South Africa)[103] between the status and practice of citizenship as it relates to the media.

Not all critics agree with the usefulness of transitology. Despite the comparisons invited by transitology, the democratization process in new democracies around the world has been "far from uniform."[104] The question has also been asked to what extent the changes in these countries constituted thoroughgoing transformation of society or rather resulted in the repositioning of or partnerships between elites.[105]

Sparks is of the opinion that transitology is experiencing a "crisis" as a result of the wide differences between the "new democracies" of the Third Wave.[106] In China, marketization took place without concomitant democratization, and in Russia the democratic gains after the fall of the U.S.S.R. seem to be in retreat. To its critics, transitology as an approach to understanding the shifts to democracy that gained momentum in the 1990s relies too much on a binary opposition between a fully developed democracy and an authoritarian dictatorship, while the reality in most cases is to be found somewhere in between.[107]

Because of the problems attendant upon transitology's wide sweep of new democracies, Sparks prefers a different concept that encapsulates the ways in which elite classes in transitional societies have managed to entrench their interests across the political and economic changes that have taken place in these countries.[108] The notion of *elite continuity* for Sparks more accurately describes the incomplete nature of the transition from dictatorship to democracy, including the ways in which media structures and personnel often remain intact despite fundamental sociopolitical shifts.[109] The media remains influenced by elites post-transition, and the continued influence of political elites (even if the "race" of that elite may differ, as in the South African case) is especially noticeable in the case of state broadcasters.[110] In many countries that fall under the transitology rubric, major political transitions were not followed by similarly fundamental socioeconomic transitions. Social inequalities remain intact, often widening, and those that benefit economically from the transition are in many cases former elites that have managed to reposition themselves. As Sparks puts it: "Everywhere, a surprising percentage of the new entrepreneurs are simply old bureaucrats in smart new Italian suits."[111] In the South African case, the transition from apartheid to democracy was based on a settlement negotiated between elites, as has already been pointed out earlier in this book. Sparks views this process in terms of continuities between and a renewal of the elite class—the National Party elites relinquished the monopoly over political power, while ANC elites toned down radical claims and instead made concessions that favored business imperatives.[112] The compromise—involving political change and state intervention in the economy via Black Economic Empowerment initiatives that tended to favor a Black middle class but failed to have a big impact on economic inequality and allowed White elites to retain their strong economic position—can also be seen reflected in the media.[113] Political demands resulted in some changes that have already been discussed, such as the strengthening of the community media sector via the establishment of the MDDA, the change of the SABC from a state to a public broadcaster, and some changes in ownership of the print media. However, both the broadcasting media and the printed press remained locked into the dominant market logic that determined the orientation of content toward more affluent audiences, with some notable exceptions such as the new tabloid press (which, however, also served commercial imperatives). From the perspective of elite continuity and elite renewal, therefore, the media was not transformed radically but rather remained "trapped by the unequal social consequences of the apartheid era."[114]

Sparks concludes that the elite continuity model fits the South African transition better than the notion of transitology.[115] While the latter assumes a major shift between the two binary opposites of authoritarianism and democracy, the former accepts that the transformation was not all-pervasive, and that the new democracy—and the media's position in it—still reflects many of the characteristics of society under apartheid. The reasons for his characterization are: South Africa's democratization process did not involve a major change of economic system; the public broadcaster retained much of its former personnel while the press changed ownership but, for the most part, not its orientation toward an elite market; shifts in ownership of the press and commercial broadcasting were linked to political connections among a new elite; political interference in the media remains limited because the new ruling elite is not (yet) as divided as in other new democracies, requiring less control of the media; the revolutionary political changes were not accompanied by a social and economic revolution; and the old political elite were removed but the old economic elite formed partnerships with the new political elite. South Africa has therefore shown that both dictatorship and democratization can be compatible with a market economy.[116] Sparks adds that despite high levels of elite renewal, the transition differed in some respects from the way that this process unfolded in Eastern Europe. South African democracy has been more "sophisticated" in that the masses still have a voice in political processes (unlike in Eastern European countries like Poland where organizations agitating for democracy have been largely demobilized) and that attempts have been made to include underrepresented groups in the media sphere.[117]

The limitations to the transformation of the South African media have already been pointed out, and, as such, these are in line with Sparks's critique of the transitology thesis. The extent to which attempts to include underrepresented voices in the media have been successful in helping those marginalized citizens make themselves heard in policy making can, however, be questioned. These attempts at inclusion—for instance, the strengthening of the community media that has already been discussed in the introduction—have been based on the assumption that all South Africans in the new democracy have certain constitutional rights, including that of freedom of expression. This status as rights-bearing citizens has, however, not been equally visible in terms of its practice in everyday life. This distinction between the status and practice of citizenship,[118] and how this is reflected in media practices, will be discussed in more detail in Chapter 4.

From the point of view of transitology, the political changes in these countries that have made the transition from authoritarianism to democracy have had profound implications for the restructuring of the media and civil society.[119] As has already been outlined, the South African media did become a site where political and economic changes played out (and were contested). Characterizing the media's transition from apartheid to democracy as a negotiation between elites, as argued earlier, does not, however, imply that this process has always been a smooth one devoid of conflict. Disagreements as to the media's role and its relationship to the newly democratic state often arose during the transitional period and continue to arise. These internal contestations, specifically as they apply to the normative frameworks for the media after apartheid, will be discussed again in more depth in Chapters 4 and 5. Within the theoretical framework of transitology, the concept of "media freedom" is often considered an important prerequisite for the establishment and deepening of new democracies. The assumption is that media freedom will allow for rational deliberation in the public sphere, which is conceived of as a "marketplace of ideas." This view has been criticized for its potential to aggravate tensions and conflicts in a transitional context and for privileging the voices of those who have access to mediated communication.[120] In a new democracy such as South Africa, which is emerging from a long history of violent conflict and marked by continued severe economic inequalities, such criticisms become even more pertinent. The increased marketization of media within a globalized, postapartheid context also created tensions between the drive to commercialize media and the need to include previously marginalized groups into the new democratic public sphere.[121] Given these competing imperatives, the importance and meaning of media freedom are all but self-evident.

Usually coupled with the notion of media freedom is that of responsibility, often framed in terms of the "watchdog function" of the media.[122] However, in new democracies, an adversarial or antagonistic media is sometimes seen as undermining the fragile trust put in a new government.[123] Especially in the developing world, it has been argued that the media should support government in its national and developmental goals—being a guide dog rather than a watchdog—even if this means curtailment of press freedom.[124] These demands are often resisted by the media, which safeguards its new independence at all costs. This tension between freedom and responsibility may in new democracies be exacerbated by the deep social divisions inherited from the authoritarian era, which problematize the notion of a "public interest."[125] Although the American-inspired social responsibility model has been seen to enjoy global acceptance,[126] significant differences in meaning or negotiations of the relative importance of central normative concepts have been noted in the Global South. The notion of media responsibility is sometimes also used as a pretext for the protection of powerful interests, as in the case of the "dignity laws" in several African countries that prohibit the media to insult political leaders.[127]

Viewing the transition to democracy in South Africa as part of a global trend linked to the end of the Cold War era suggests certain prima facie commonalities, which could best be studied from a comparative perspective such as transitology or elite continuity. Yet the ways in which democratization, economic marketization and media pluralization have taken place in these transitional contexts display important specificities that require such a comparative approach to be flexible. Structural analyses of political processes and economic structures need to be complemented by attention to the cultural dimensions of these transitions. Analyses of the cultural dimension of the transition, which includes discursive issues of representation, can shed further light on the contestations that marked the transition and how notions such as identity and citizenship can be discursively invoked in a way so as to circumscribe the terms and conditions of the transition.

Social Identities

When theorizing the media's transition from apartheid to democracy, a cultural approach to complement political-economic analyses such as transitology and elite continuity would look at the media not only as *site* and *agent* for change[128] but also as a sponsor of *discourses* of change. This means that the transition to democracy not only impacted the ways in which the media was organized as a social institution or as a form of capital but also impacted the way in which the media was represented in democratic discourses. It has been noted that the media and political fields are increasingly being fused, to the extent that Bourdieu's notion of social capital can be amended to include "media capital"—the media exposure needed by politicians to cement and extend power.[129] But the media does not merely provide a source of power for politicians to draw upon—the media is itself a player in the game of power. The media, as has been noted already, should not be seen as being on the margins of social and political power but as a stakeholder and wielder of power in and of itself.[130] The "mediatization" of public and private life that Couldry talks about[131] can also be noted in postapartheid South Africa, as the media has been central to the democratic discourses within which the transition and the continued contestations in the democratic era have been couched.

Another aspect of the mediation of the politics of transition and democratization that deserves attention is the way in which the media itself became a focus of debate. Such debates can be typified as a meta-discourse on the media, which the media itself helps shape, as Macdonald observes:

> The media can also operate at a meta-discursive level, helping to set the terms in which we think about the media themselves.... [M]any of the issues that we think of as public concerns about the media, ranging from invasions of privacy to anxieties about children's exposure to violence, are themselves orchestrated in terms the media help to shape.[132]

The media therefore occupies a double position—it provides a space for debates about itself, while at the same time setting the parameters of such debates. In many respects, these debates were proxy debates; the media became a bone of contention in what were, in the final instance, negotiations about the reconfiguration of political and social life. To put it simply: when people were talking about the media, they were often actually talking about democracy.[133] These debates, which continue to be intense for more than twenty years after the formal transition to democracy, have wider ramifications than the transformation of the media at the level of ownership or the reconstruction of a regulatory framework for the media to operate in. In the South African case, as a result of the country's history of oppression and resistance based on racial and ethnic categorization, the discourse about the mediatization of politics can also be read as a discourse of *identity*.

In line with the notion of a media meta-discourse, postapartheid identities and their relation to power are not only being constructed by what is said *in* the media, but also by what is said *about* the media. These utterances about the media function as a discourse in the Foucauldian sense in that they produce subjects dependent on the rules determined by those exerting power over the discourse.

For this reason, control of the discourse is important and helps explain why these debates have been so vigorous. In the context of the current discussion about the limits of democratic transformation, it therefore becomes important to analyze not only the structural impediments of ownership, staffing, and the market on democratic transformation and democratic deepening but also the perimeters of mediated discourses and how these attempt to set the terms and conditions for the media's social and political roles. Since various perspectives compete for dominance of these discourses, identity construction is also part of political contests. An illustration of this argument can be found in a series of official statements and presidential speeches made during the tenure of President Thabo Mbeki, who followed the first democratic president, Nelson Mandela, from June 1999 to September 2008. Mbeki's presidency was marked by his controversial denial of the link between HIV and AIDS, and the nonprovision of antiretrovirals in the public health sector. Mbeki's strong emphasis on an African cultural identity and the development of a pan-African consciousness is crucial to note in the current discussion on media and identity discourses. His political style and vision were clearly informed by an assertion of Africanness. This orientation already became clear while he was still Mandela's deputy. At the adoption of the Constitution in 1996, Mbeki made his famous, striking "I Am an African" speech in Parliament,[134] positioning a hybrid South African identity within the broader definition of belonging to the continent. During his tenure as president, Mbeki became known for his pan-African vision, calling for an "African Renaissance" and working as a key architect on the New Partnership for Africa's Development in 2001 and the establishment of the African Union in the same year to replace the Organization of African Unity.[135]

The media was also a prominent feature of official discourse during Thabo Mbeki's presidency, and on several occasions he addressed the media's role directly. These key statements on the media are illuminating for how they positioned subjects and objects in an identity discourse that was—given the centrality of African identity in Mbeki's political ideology—linked to political power. The link between identity, political power, and democratic transition is not limited to South Africa. Ross and Derman point out that orthodox assumptions of identity are challenged in the "new interstices opened up by political transitions."[136] This is applicable to South Africa in two ways. First, the transition to democracy in 1994 brought about a reconfiguration of social relations and power balances that undermined the racial, essentialized identity categories of apartheid. In this transitional space, the South African media had an important part to play in the mythmaking required for this new society.[137] Second, the political transition in 1994 also reintroduced South Africa into the global arena after years of isolation. The renegotiation of identities now not only takes place with the nation-state as its dominant cultural frame[138] but also against the backdrop of global cultural pluralism. Mbeki's discourse of "African Renaissance" can also be seen as a reaction against globalization and cultural imperialism, which may have been experienced as threats to South African culture in the light of the country's greater integration into the global political and cultural order.[139] Questions of identity remain very important when political and economic inclusion and exclusions are addressed. Suttner points out that, "It is necessary to be very conscious of the effect of using some or other 'name' because identity formation carries with it processes that can promote a common society or increase the exclusions that characterized Apartheid."[140]

Around Mbeki's succession of Mandela as president, a shift also occurred in the focus and emphasis of public discourse. Whereas debates in the 1990s were dominated by issues around reconciliation and the "rainbow nation," the focus shifted to issues to do with the reconstruction and consolidation of a specifically African identity.[141] This emphasis on Africa is consistent with what Mangcu called a "more radical Africanist approach" to national politics by Mbeki, as opposed to Mandela's policy of reconciliation between Black and White.[142] Mbeki often remarked on the persistence of racism in the country, appealing to White South Africans' sense of responsibility and seeing the road to reconciliation as going via societal transformation.[143] Mbeki's call for an "African Renaissance" brought to the fore a renewed attention to matters of race and ethnicity, even while it arguably neglected issues of class.[144]

The combination of Mbeki's assertion of a pan-African identity, together with his intolerance of criticism and pressure on the media, ensured that the topic of identity became highly politicized and received much media attention during his tenure. Mbeki's pressure on the media, as well as his controversial HIV/AIDS policies, resulted in a display of antagonism toward him by the local and international media.[145] Identity also featured in Mbeki's statements about (and attacks on) the media. In a speech to SANEF in April 2003, Mbeki put forward the notion of "reporting Africa to the Africans," appealing to the Africanness of journalists: "I am suggesting that the South African media has a responsibility to report Africa to the South Africans, carrying out this responsibility as Africans. . . . I am, of course, proceeding from the assumption that you were African before you became journalists and that despite your profession, you are still Africans."[146] Mbeki urged journalists to be better informed about Africa, saying that some African journalists make themselves guilty of "distorted reporting." What is needed, Mbeki said, was that journalists "know the subject [they] are dealing with."[147]

Questions of identity and race continue to inform debates about the media's criticism of Mbeki's successor, Jacob Zuma, although often in much cruder form. As mentioned above, a Twitter war and the creation of a fake news outlet to delegitimize critics of Zuma and his patrons, the Gupta family, also availed itself of a "white monopoly capital" narrative, although this discourse has now become much more covert and cynical and played itself out behind the scenes, in the more nebulous platforms of the internet.[148]

From this discussion, it becomes clear that the discursive construction of identity in the postapartheid media sphere not only takes place on the level of explicit representation of "race," as the focus of the Human Rights Commission's flawed investigation into racism in the media may have suggested. The debates about the media's role can also serve as processes through which identities are constructed, especially when the media's orientation toward a postapartheid elite (still mostly White, but increasingly including a Black middle class) is considered. Both Sparks's notion of elite continuity, with its emphasis on continued structural inequalities, as well as the cultural dimension of discourses of identity, can be seen to limit the extent to which the postapartheid media could reposition itself as a more inclusive and diverse social institution that retained the possibility of critique.

It should be clear from this overview of the various debates, conflicts, and restructurings since the end of apartheid that the South African media has been involved in an ongoing process of renegotiating its place, role, and function in a democratic society.

Two different approaches to the analysis of these contestations were offered, the *transitology* approach, and its critique in the form of *elite continuity* and the *social identity* approach. These various approaches, although in some ways at odds with each other, can provide us with multidimensional analytical tools to theorize the South African media's internal repositioning in a local context. However, as pointed out at the outset of this book, a localized, "areas studies" approach to the South African media after apartheid is not an adequate way of understanding the intricate flows and contraflows and the complex links between the local and the global that play themselves out in the South African media. Unfortunately, journalism and media studies globally have tended to relegate studies of African media to specialist corners of academia where they are studied either as exceptions to the rules of the media in the Global North or as applications of theories developed elsewhere. A key argument of this book is that the South African media provides us with an opportunity to understand how the local and the global intersect in contemporary global media and how developments in the Global South can also be instructive as to the directions in which global media might be moving. In the following chapter I expand on this argument.

CHAPTER 2

"This Time for Africa"?

Global Media Studies and the View from the South

As we have seen from the overview in the previous chapter, the South African media underwent a number of significant shifts in terms of its ownership, occupational practices, and norms and regulations after the end of apartheid. These changes should not, however, be understood in isolation, as a result only of internal political and social changes and the contestations that accompanied them, but rather considered against the broader background of globalization. Many of the changes that can be seen reflected in the postapartheid South African media can be linked to global shifts in the media industry, changing business models, and the development of new technologies. This is not to say that local changes merely repeated or mimicked changes in the Global North. For instance, the phenomenal rise of tabloid newspapers in the country, at a time when the death of print media was predicted globally, went against the pattern that was widely seen in the media industry in the North. At the same time, elite commercial newspapers in South Africa did suffer huge losses in circulation. While these trends are seemingly contradictory, both are linked to global processes that played out in different ways locally. The rise of tabloid newspapers, while in the first instance a response to the local condition of a continued marginalization of majority poor publics in the country by the mainstream elite press, also fits a pattern of increased commercialization of the media globally. These papers mimic the style and approach of especially the British "red tops" but, in a process referred to as "glocalization," adapted these formats for local audiences.[1] The reception of these tabloids, and their relationship to the communities they serve, in turn took on very local characteristics that illuminate some of the normative expectations of the media in South Africa. These developments will be discussed in more detail in Chapter 5. The decreased circulation of mainstream printed media in the country could in turn be seen as broadly reflecting the same trends as may be found elsewhere in the world. With the increased accessibility of online news sources, at least for those that could afford to connect to these technological platforms, elite audiences increasingly moved online, where news and analysis sites like *News24*, *Daily Maverick*, *GroundUp*, and *The Conversation* burgeoned. In some aspects, these technological developments, however, also differed from similar processes in the North, where fixed-line and wireless internet access is more ubiquitous than in the Global South. Particularly the huge uptake of mobile phones has provided a platform for access to the internet for many South Africans (as is the case elsewhere on the continent) who do not have or cannot afford fixed-line access. These phones also play a significant role in social and political debates and activism, as will be discussed in more detail in Chapter 8 of this book.

Increasingly, major geopolitical shifts such as the rise of China and the emergence of the BRICS group of nations have also had an impact on media in the local context. Chinese media's entry into the continent has been met with vigorous debate and controversy, which again highlighted some of the dominant norms about the South African media's role in society and its relationship with government. Some of the international debates about China's entry into the African media landscape—which extends beyond South Africa but includes the whole region where China's media is actively engaged—also brought to the fore implicit assumptions about African media that exist in Northern journalistic and academic discourses (for instance that African civil society and local journalism are too weak to resist Chinese threats to press freedom). What also became clear from the response to the Chinese media's involvement in the South African media environment is that global developments in the media sphere are often viewed and assessed through the lenses of local political, social, and economic imperatives. These debates will be unpacked more fully in Chapter 7. At this point, it is important to note that local, regional, and global media norms and practices are interwoven and responsive to each other. For this reason, although this book's focus is on South Africa, the developments and contestations that have taken place in the local media cannot be separated from regional and global dynamics.

By approaching the South African media in this way as an interrelated sphere, this book also intends to speak back to media studies as a field where projects such as these are usually relegated to a corner of the field marked by descriptors such as *global media studies, international media studies* or *comparative studies*. This stems from a tradition of looking at the Global South in terms of specific areas of specialization that are assumed not to yield insights or findings that can be integrated into global media studies on a theoretical level.

A key argument of this book is that the South African media provides us with an opportunity to understand how the local and the global intersect in contemporary global media, and how developments in the Global South can also be instructive as to the directions in which global media might be moving. In this chapter, we will expand on this argument in order to locate this book in terms of a broader engagement with media studies as a discipline.

Internationalizing or *Decolonizing* Media Studies

Attempts to internationalize media and communication studies have been a feature of the field for at least 15 years. Curran and Park's book *De-Westernizing Media Studies* was a landmark collection in this regard.[2] In a subsequent collection of essays on international communication,[3] Daya Thussu sees the rapid globalization of the media industries and the internationalization of higher education as key influences on a growing interest in international media studies. The internationalization of the field also included more specific projects that set themselves the task of reflecting on the global state of journalism research,[4] journalism norms and practice,[5] media ethics,[6] and, after criticism of an earlier, highly influential study, of media systems beyond the Western world.[7] Subsequent groundbreaking work in extending the scope of global media studies to focus specifically on new geopolitical formations can also be noted.[8] A significant signal of the importance of "internationalizing" the field was sent by the largest organization in the field, the International Communication Association (ICA) when it held its first (albeit only regional) meeting on the African continent in Nairobi. This came against the background of criticism[9] that the organization had, in the past, presumed internationality but was dominated by participants and members from the Global North, unlike its smaller counterpart, the International Association for Media and Communication Research (IAMCR), which had a greater diversity in membership and meeting locales. In these attempts to internationalize (of which the above is just an illustration rather than an exhaustive list), African examples and case studies have usually been included. Laudable and well-intentioned as these inclusions may have been, they raise larger questions about the terms upon which African media studies are included in the internationalization project. Key among these is the question *for whom* media studies needs to be internationalized and whether these attempts to internationalize have succeeded in unsettling the dominant Western epistemological assumptions underpinning the study of mass media.[10] As Shome points out,[11] the history of media needs to be theorized as a postcolonial issue—that is, one that foregrounds historical linkages, inequalities, and the historical suppression of epistemes of media and communication from outside the West. The call is therefore not for an ahistorical and apolitical "de-Westernization" of media studies, but for a "postcolonial interruption of the history of media as universalized and narrated in the West"[12]—in other words, not merely an inclusion of international diversity but an engagement with "colonial power relations that link media spheres in the West/North with societies in the non-West/South in unequal ways."[13] Shome argues forcefully that a "benign apolitical internationalism" is rooted in a Western, post–cold-war ethos that sees nations as discrete units, and that the decolonization of media studies frameworks rather than a mere internationalization of them should be the goal.[14]

As far as African media studies is concerned, the shared experience of colonial subjection, struggles for independence and continued geopolitical and economic marginalization in the era of globalization suggests that a study of media on the continent should include a focus on the lived experience of Africans in relation to such media, embedded as these are within unequal local and global power relations. The point from which to approach the internationalization or, rather, decolonization of media studies would therefore be rooted in the experiences of those in the South for whom the routes into global media studies have always been negotiated between global frameworks and local experiences.[15]

In the context of this book's focus on the South African media after apartheid, this chapter seeks to locate the current study within broader debates about "internationalization" and "decolonization." The importance of these questions have in recent years been reemphasized by student protests at the country's universities, where students brought the operations of the institutions to a halt to demand "free and decolonized" education. In the light of these demands, it is important that South African media studies scholarship reflects on the epistemological assumptions it is underpinned by and interrogates dominant discourses about global media within which it is located.

Questions we should be asking include:

- What do we mean by "international" or "global" media studies, and what is the place of South Africa within the global media studies field?

- How can a scholarly engagement with South Africa, of which this book is an example, contribute to the de-Westernization or decolonization of media studies?

The central focus is therefore, in the first instance, not only on questions about why and how Africa has been historically marginalized or *excluded* from global media studies scholarship but also on the ways in which it is being *included*. What are the assumptions underpinning a renewed focus on Africa in popular discourses and in communications scholarship? What are the conditions set for this inclusion? What are the modes of engagement?

These questions will be addressed under three headings: media studies *about* Africa, media studies scholarship *from* Africa, and media studies scholarship *with* Africa.

Media Studies about Africa

The Global South, a somewhat slippery category that includes Africa, has become "synonymous with uncertain development, unorthodox economies, failed states, and nations fraught with corruption, poverty, and strife."[16] This is the part of the world that has traditionally served as the raw material from which the Global North weaves its theories. Theory, historically, was the preserve of those schools of thought that could trace their family tree back to Western enlightenment—"the wellspring of universal learning, of Science and Philosophy, upper case" as the Comaroffs would have it.[17] The Global South, including Africa, tends to be the place where you go to find "parochial wisdom," "antiquarian traditions," "exotic ways and means" and, especially, raw data that can be used to support theories developed in, and about, social realities in the Global North.[18] The Indian scholar Vandana Shiva summarized it thus: "the West as theory, the East as evidence."[19]

Knowledge from the South always seems to need qualifiers. Publications in the field routinely assume authority on broad developments in the field, e.g., digital media, political communication, or popular culture, without the need to add the geographical signifier "in Europe" or "in North America." However, for books on film in Nigeria, journalism in South Africa or political activism in Zimbabwe, the label of *comparative, global, transnational,* or *regional* is usually added. Scholarship about media in Africa is therefore likely to be found mostly in the "case study" or "applied" section of books, or in book length studies that signal their regional focus very clearly in their titles.[20] The underlying assumption of the way scholarship from the South is presented and branded in this way is that theories are made in the North and applied, illustrated, or validated in the South. The Ugandan scholar Mahmood Mamdani has put it as follows:[21]

> The assumption that there is a single model derived from the dominant Western experience reduces research to no more than a demonstration that societies around the world either conform to that model or deviate from it.

This epistemological bias against scholarship from the South is compounded by the asymmetrical distribution of knowledge production. Recent figures about scholarly production in scientific journals published by Taylor & Francis show that only 25 percent of authors of journal articles are from developing countries.[22] A large percentage of submissions to journals on African journalism and media studies is produced by scholars located at institutions outside the continent, and these submissions are often couched in methodologies or framed by research questions that speak the language of international scholarship very fluently but may not be the most interesting way to pose questions about local problematics.

Comparative research projects driven by funders from the North sometimes also fall prey to the assumption that research questions developed in established democracies with stable institutions can be exported to questionnaires administered in African contexts. To take one example: an investigation into bribery of journalists (so-called "brown envelopes" or "gombo") in Africa cannot merely be compared in quantitative fashion with similar practices in developed countries. It requires ethnographically embedded research[23] to understand how journalists negotiate tricky terrain in an environment of poverty, corruption, and hardship. These findings, in turn, should inform ethical theories and normative frameworks, instead of being considered curiosities and exceptions to axioms developed elsewhere.

The economics determining knowledge production often also locks African researchers into a consultancy culture, as Mamdani has pointed out.[24] In this culture, research agendas are set by donors and funders in the North, who tend to see the aim of research as finding quick answers with commercial value rather than an exploration of the complexities of problems. The result is research that is demand-driven, rather than problem-driven.

The flipside of scholarship about African communication perceived as being geographically overdetermined and marginalized is the tendency for scholarship to imbue experiences from the Global North with a universal relevance. Critics of hegemonic normative frameworks in media and communication studies have therefore found resonance with postcolonial critiques of the Northern "genealogy of thought" in which scholars in the South find themselves located, and have therefore set out to "provincialize Europe" in the words of Dipesh Chakrabarty.[25]

These critiques have in recent years found further purchase in the changing geopolitical landscape. The emerging economies of the BRICS countries, the "Rise of the Rest,"[26] has intensified the realization that the nation-state is no longer an adequate unit of analysis, but that globally interconnected networks of communication are emerging that require a revision, if not rejection, of theoretical models of "area studies." To do justice to media studies in contemporary Africa would need a contextual embeddedness in rapidly changing societies and an awareness of how shifting geopolitical relations are impacting on the global flows and counterflows of cultural content, capital, and people in and through the continent. An example of these new flows is the increased presence of Chinese media on the continent, which has introduced a different set of media practices, normative frameworks and ownership patterns that have set in motion renewed reflection on, for instance, press freedom in Africa and the idealized role of the media in African societies. We will return to these issues in Chapter 7 of this book.

To argue for a postcolonial critique of media studies is not the same as a rejection, in a simplistic, wholesale, anticolonial rhetorical flourish, of everything that has a whiff of Northern thought about it. Rather, it is a way of reflecting on the Northern history of thought from a vantage point on the margins,[27] making explicit the power relations attendant upon the North-South binary and the ways in which both hemispheres are mutually implicated. We should also realize that these margins are in themselves diverse and heterogeneous. This book focuses on South Africa, which serves as a prime example of how the South also contains a North—i.e., of the vast inequalities and power struggles existing within the margins themselves. Conversely, the African diaspora and the movement of refugees globally also increasingly demonstrate that the North also contains a South. Attempts to achieve greater prominence for African media studies in global contexts should therefore avoid homogenizing, monolithic binaries of North versus South. One way of doing this is to pay greater attention to the diversity of the media content and scholarship that flows *from* Africa.

Media Studies from Africa

To critique the marginality of Africa within the broad field of media studies is not to deny that some progress has been made in recent years to be more inclusive of global perspectives. Popular discourses about Africa have also been changing. News media coverage of Africa has in recent years become more positive, a change from the familiar tropes associated with the "Heart of Darkness"—poverty, war, and disease—which for so long dominated Western media discourses about the continent, as seen in the iconic front page of *The Economist* magazine in 2000 describing Africa as "The Hopeless Continent." Just more than a decade later, the same magazine announced optimistically that Africa was "Rising." The "single story" of despair so critiqued by Nigerian writer Chimamanda Adichie has now been replaced by alternative, more optimistic stories of growth, transformation and success.[28] This changing narrative can at least partly be accounted for by the increase in different voices emerging *from* the continent itself.

As Mel Bunce, Suzanne Franks, and Chris Paterson outline in their recent, updated version of Beverley Hawk's classic text on *Africa's Media Image*, more new voices are emerging from the continent that contribute to a more diverse and more complex picture about the continent starting to take shape in the news media. The establishment and growth of alternative international news organizations, including the Chinese platforms CCTV and Xinhua as well as the Qatar-based channel Al-Jazeera, have contributed to the emergence of alternative media narratives about Africa in recent years, regardless of one's opinion about their journalistic norms and practices.

The increased use of local correspondents, as international news organizations closed foreign bureaus to cut costs, has also contributed to reports that are more contextually informed.

But perhaps the most significant aspect about the new forms of communication coming forth from Africa has been the phenomenal growth of online and mobile media, including various social media platforms. From politics to agriculture, from activism to chatter, from satirical news to Twitter campaigns, digital media have not only provided Africans with new tools to engage each other in their own societies, but also to speak back to the global public sphere. The multitude of online voices speak not only in the hashtag politics of #bringbackourgirls, #Kony2012 or #FeesMustFall, they also speak of the politics of the everyday, fashion, music, religion, and football and an irreverent youth culture that pokes fun at authority.[29]

There are, in other words, now many possibilities for local African voices to be included in popular media as well as in media scholarship. This is not to say that "authenticity" should be fetishized or romanticized—the identity politics through which claims are laid to an authentic "Africanness" can also hide a myriad of sins and agendas. Voices from Africa can often also be homophobic, patriarchal, or ethnically hateful. What is needed is not cultural relativism but a critical dialectic.

Scholarship about the media in Africa still lacks the wide range of lived experience that characterizes studies in this field in the Global North. While good work has been forthcoming on emerging African media cultures,[30] many texts still take the form of providing "panoramas" and "vistas" of African communication landscapes[31] rather than deep, textured engagements with the everyday lived experiences of Africans in communicative and mediated spaces—even if these may not be easily digestible by Northern academic palates. We need more monographs about gaming cultures in Africa, football fandom, cartooning, popular music, and visual storytelling. But we also need to move beyond the case study approach, in which contributors or association members from the South are collected in the way we older people used to do when we collected postage stamps.[32] There can also be a certain imperialistic urge underpinning this desire for collection and exhibition of variety like in a museum, unless we allow these different perspectives to also impact on the central epistemological and methodological assumptions governing our field.

So, if journalists and scholars have in the past decade taken Binyavanga Wainaina's satirical criticism to heart—that there are more ways to write about Africa than in the "broad brush strokes" of AK-47s, naked breasts, and the Starving African awaiting the benevolence of the West[33]—this is largely thanks to the inclusion of more voices that speak *from* Africa rather than just *about* Africa.

But perhaps the best possibility for media studies to move beyond well-intentioned but naive inclusions of Africa is for media studies not to increase scholarship *about* Africa, nor merely to include more voices *from* Africa in order to increase diversity yet limiting them to case studies or examples, but *with* Africa, as part of a critical and ongoing dialectic that will be allowed to impact on theory-building and disrupt dominant frameworks.

Media Studies with Africa

Why then, if not from a misplaced sense of benevolence or scholarly generosity, or an academic savior complex, would international scholars want to engage *with* Africa? The reason why engaging with African scholarship is an epistemological necessity and methodological imperative is not based, in the first place, on a notion of social justice and certainly not on the expediency that a more diverse table of content widens the potential market for "research outputs" in a commercialized global knowledge economy. The simple reason is that an engagement with Africa might do more to enrich scholarship in the North than the other way around.

In the current global era, the challenges faced by media globally are of a nature that requires concerted responses. The increasingly inevitable scenario of irreversible climate change, the global threat of terrorism, food security, and forced migration—these are all challenges where the media has a role to play in providing information, fostering dialogue, and connecting people. These challenges, however, can not be tackled in isolation but require collaborative, interdependent approaches.

When communication in the contemporary, globalized world is considered an inherently relational and interdependent practice, the need to include Africa in these endeavors becomes clear. Across the African continent, contemporary global challenges are playing out in localities, and the creative ways in which African societies are responding to these challenges may be instructive. These challenges include rapid urbanization, economic growth, and rising inequality; conflict and terrorism; humanitarian and health crises; democratic transitions; ethnic and cultural tensions and conflicts; and the phenomenal spread and appropriation of new technologies, especially mobile telephony. (We will return to some of these challenges, and the future outlook, in Chapter 7 of this book.)

The engagement with Africa is therefore born out of the realization that instead of considering the Global South to be lacking, to have fallen behind in a teleological race for modernization, it is in fact in many ways *ahead* of the curve of history—that, in the contemporary, global world, "it is regions in the South that tend first to feel the concrete effects of world-historical processes as they play themselves out, thus to prefigure the future of the former metropole."[34] In other words, if you want to find out what the effects of climate change will be in the North, speak to the farmers in African villages who are already struggling with its impact on their livelihoods. If your notion of European nationhood is confronted by the alterity introduced by refugees and migrants, speak to Africans who have for many years felt the effects brought on by the imposition of colonial borders and displacement of people as a result of civil wars. If you are prompted to find solutions to the implosion of established news media industries in the North, speak to Africans who have been appropriating, adopting, and adapting media technologies in creative ways, from Nollywood to the "please call me" message system on the mobile phone. Learn how African activists combine oral communication in door-to-door campaigns with text messages and the nanomedia of song and dance to protests in ways that have not yet been discovered by those marching against austerity "in the streets of London and Athens."[35] The recent election of Donald Trump as president of the United States of America, his support base and first acts of office (the signing of executive orders that were challenged by the courts and civil society), raise further opportunities for comparative studies of media, populism, and civil resistance against political "big men," of which there are many examples in Africa.

In other words, a scholarly engagement with Africa around these issues at the heart of global communication today should not be motivated by a patronizing desire to "develop" Africa and should certainly not mimic celebrity charity efforts; nor should they rest on a romantic notion that somehow "African culture" holds answers to these problems. Nor would an approach to African communication in a geographically bounded paradigm of "area studies" suffice anymore in an era where Lagos, Nairobi, Johannesburg, and Cape Town are connected to London, New York, Delhi, and Guangzhou in worldwide networks of trade, travel, migration, and digital media. Rather, the engagement should be guided by the realization that challenges to global communication can be addressed only through collaboration and partnership, to mutual benefit.

We have to accept that such engagement will, and should, not always be cozy and smooth. Attempts to de-Westernize communication studies, or, in more contemporary parlance, to decolonize global communication studies, should also be disruptive. This type of disruption is not aimed at closing down opportunities for dialogue but at opening up new avenues of inquiry and understanding. Global media scholarship that includes African media studies as an equal interlocutor should disrupt the dominant ways of thinking about knowledge production, interrogate the history of knowledge production in our field, and address the asymmetrical distribution of power in scholarly organizations and regimes of scientific truth—but always with a commitment to dialogue and engagement. This might imply addressing inequalities in access to scholarly resources, recognizing the limitations of existing knowledge, making explicit the implicit assumptions that govern regimes of scholarly truth, and emphasizing the necessity for Northern scholars to "unlearn their privilege as a loss."[36] A useful term to start describing what decolonization of the field entails might be *critical inclusion*—the notion that widening inclusion at the same time implies an opening up to critique.

CHAPTER 3

A Changing Media Culture

*Professional Ideologies
between Past and Present*

In Chapter 1, we considered the structural changes that the media underwent in the transition from apartheid to democracy, including changes in ownership and editorial staffing. It was pointed out that although significant changes can be noted in terms of both ownership and staffing, the transition included many continuities between the past and the present. The concepts of "elite continuity" and "elite renewal," as coined by Colin Sparks, were used in the chapter to indicate the limits to transformation of the media industry. While it is clear that the transition to democracy did not bring a complete transformation of media ownership and staffing, it was not only the structural dimensions of the media where transformation was limited. As was seen in Chapter 1, the cultural dimension of media discourses imposed its own limitations on transformation. By producing certain dominant notions around identity, journalistic work was circumscribed in important ways, and different normative frameworks were set up in competition with each other. In the previous chapter, the importance of taking African media seriously on a theoretical level was emphasized. To internationalize, de-Westernize or "de-colonize" global media studies, African perspectives on global media should be adopted. However, the discourse of "Africanness" can also be used as a way to exclude certain speakers and construct criticism as antipatriotic, and, in this way, the professional identity of journalists as watchdogs over political power clashes with broader notions of democratic citizenship in the new South Africa.

But how did journalists themselves respond to these discourses in which they often found themselves constructed as being in opposition to a democratically elected government, undermining transformation, and even un-African? How did their own attempts at carving out a new social position legitimate—or at least mitigate—the slow pace and limited nature of media transformation?

In this chapter, journalistic discourses of identity will be examined in order to establish how journalists see their own role in relation to the new democratic order and how they have forged professional identities for themselves to withstand renewed political pressures. In the face of what were perceived as new assaults on journalistic roles and identities in the democratic era, journalists often drew upon the retelling of history to justify their own position in the present. In this chapter, which draws on interviews with journalists from a range of media—from community to mainstream, across the platforms of print, broadcast, and digital—we will see how the reconstruction of a historical narrative supported journalists in legitimating their normative stances and practices in the present, democratic era.

The demise of apartheid in South Africa brought important shifts in the composition of the country's media industry as well as to the professional practices of journalists. South African journalists found themselves having to reorient their professional practices and occupational ideologies—which can be described as the ideas and views through which journalists validate and give meaning to their work[1]—in a social and political environment that was undergoing rapid changes during and after the democratic transition. At the same time as the ground of the local landscape was shifting, radical changes were taking place in the news industry globally that also had an impact on the way journalists viewed their professional identities and the future of journalism as an occupation. Especially in the advanced industrial democracies of the North, wide access to new media platforms created a new class of citizen journalists, and emerging online publications undermined the traditional advertiser-based business model of the print media. The questions being asked about the future of journalism—who qualifies as a journalist, and how will traditional news organizations sustain their businesses—also reverberated in South Africa. Not only did the redefinition of journalism practices prompt reflection by South African journalists on their craft, but the increased competition from global media that became available to local audiences as a result of the opening up of the South African media market to global flows and contraflows[2] also led them to reconsider the specific role they have to play in South African society. The reorientation of South African journalists in relation to global debates about their professional identity and local questions about their roles and responsibilities in a newly democratic society continues to play itself out. Perhaps the most prominent relationship highlighted in these debates has been the one between South African journalists and the government.

South African journalists frequently found themselves at odds with political stakeholders over the appropriate normative framework within which their journalistic practice should be couched. Debates about whether journalists should play an adversarial or supportive role toward the new democratic government often drew on narratives about the media's role during the struggle against apartheid. The constitutionally guaranteed freedom of speech enjoyed by the media in democratic South Africa has also often been compared favorably to the oppressive climate under apartheid. Although journalists have often attempted to show continuity between the role of the media in opposing apartheid and their contemporary role as watchdogs over the new democracy, critics have also contested these views. First, the heroic historical role in which journalists often cast themselves has been shown to be an exaggerated one by critics such as Robert Horwitz, who reminds us that the mainstream commercial English press, tied to big mining companies, only provided a limited critique of apartheid rather than a full-blown, open support for the liberation movements.[3] Second, the media in contemporary South Africa also tends to approach their monitorial role on behalf of a small section of South African society whose interests weigh more than those of the poor majority.[4] These perspectives cast doubt on overblown claims about the media's democratic role under apartheid and thereafter. However, what remains important to note is how these constructions of South African journalistic history operate in contemporary debates—i.e., how journalists use historical constructions to validate and support their normative positions in the current moment.

These appeals to the past may be contrary to the more common association of journalism with the present rather than the past. Journalism is most often seen as concerned more with the "here-and-now than with the there-and-then," with the past seen as falling outside journalists' self-definition of their work.[5] However, journalists' "treatment of the present often includes a treatment of the past" and therefore journalists' role as "memory agents" needs to be taken more seriously.[6] Journalists contribute to the construction of social memory through the subjects they report on, weaving together not only significant news events but also the smaller narratives of everyday life.[7]

In the context of this book's focus on the media's position within the transition from apartheid to democracy, and the shifts and contestations that took place during the first two decades after democratization, this chapter aims to explore how journalistic discourses about the past impact on journalists' self-conception in the present. Following on the previous chapter's focus on how state-sponsored identity discourses attempted to construct normative boundaries for the postapartheid media, this chapter looks at similar debates from the opposing perspective, namely that of journalists. Where state-sponsored identity discourses invoked a past in which the media resisted apartheid and colonialism with the aim of interpellating them (in the Althusserian sense) as Africans (who, by implication, should be less critical of a democratically elected government), journalists may invoke the same past but with the objective of strengthening their own position. Journalism's memory work in this sense extends beyond the construction of the past through news narratives in reportage to the definition of professional ideologies and identities on the basis of a shared past. Conboy reiterates the point that the "sedimentations of its past practice" continue to influence journalism even as it reorients itself toward the future.[8] The relationship of journalists with the past is malleable and dynamic, and the memory work they engage in often takes the form of collective reconstruction of the past to serve their own agendas.[9] In the South African journalism discourses that will be examined in this chapter, the agenda being served by a collective reconstruction of the past relates largely to threats experienced in the present. South African journalists draw on the past to defend themselves against what is perceived as pressures on their professional freedoms. This practice is in line with Deuze's observation that the appeal to ideological journalistic values becomes especially pertinent when journalists are faced with public criticism.[10] The appropriation of historical narratives by South African journalists can therefore be seen as facilitative of a process of reconstructing journalism practice in the postapartheid era. By positioning themselves in relation to a collectively reconstructed past, journalists gain discursive traction in deploying the ideological values of independence, freedom and surveillance of power to ensure journalism's special status in postapartheid South Africa.[11]

To understand how appeals to history have then been used by South African journalists to reconstruct professional norms and identities for themselves after apartheid, we have to ask two central questions:

- What influence do recollections about the past have on how South African journalists construct norms for their current practice, especially in relation to the political sphere?
- How do constructions of South African journalism history feature in discourses of journalistic identity?

These two questions will tell us first about the normative power that history holds over current journalistic practice, and second about how remembrance influences identity. Taken together, a picture of professional identities and norms will emerge that underpins discourses of media freedom and independence in postapartheid society.

These questions will be explored on the basis of in-depth, semistructured interviews that were conducted with journalists to gauge their attitudes toward the past and their views of the role journalism should play in the postapartheid democratic political sphere.[12] These findings will follow after some brief background to the postapartheid South African journalism landscape, in order to contextualize the self-identification of South African journalists in relation to the country's past and the changes occurring in the journalism landscape since democratization.

From Past to Present: Background

During the negotiations and contestations that surrounded the repositioning of South African journalism in a postapartheid sociopolitical context, two recurring issues dominated the debates: the composition of the industry (both in terms of the racial composition of newsrooms as well as the political economy of ownership, access, and control) and the efficacy of the press self-regulatory system. As discussed in Chapter 1 of this book, important shifts have taken place in both these areas since democratization. Questions remain, however, about whether these shifts have been far-reaching enough, and responses to these questions have often been framed in terms of journalists' professional identity and an evaluation of past practices. When White and Black media capital merged as a result of a series of "black empowerment" and "unbundling" deals,[13] the deracialization of the structures of media capital were seen as an attempt toward undoing the history of White domination over the media. However, the underlying commercial logic of the press remained the same, and news media markets continued to be largely racially segmented. The question that emerges is to what extent the reorganization of media capital, as discussed in Chapter 1 of this book, would also succeed in a) broadening access to the public sphere and b) changing journalistic practices to result in a more diverse and inclusive representation of South African social reality.

As was also mentioned in Chapter 2, tensions started to develop between a normative conception of journalism in the postapartheid era as grounded in individual rights and a free-market commercial environment on the one hand, and views that saw a more nationalistic and developmental role for journalism. Shifting from apartheid to democracy meant that the ideological lines that had divided the press landscape before into pro- or antiapartheid camps became blurred. The high degree of political parallelism between the apartheid state and its sympathizers in the Afrikaans press, the liberal parliamentary opposition and its advocates in the mainstream English press, and antiapartheid activists and the alternative press, made way for the politics of the free market, where old political allegiances became redundant and commercially unviable.[14] In other words, the increased professionalization of journalism in the postapartheid era went hand in hand with an increased commercialization of journalism. But as new lines of contestation opened up between the media and the new ANC-led government, journalists started looking for ways to construct a professional identity that would provide them with a solid footing in a politically uncertain new era. Because the new political landscape was, from the start, dominated by one party, journalists—in the liberal mode of the watchdog, adversarial press—often saw themselves as having to perform a de facto political oppositional role.[15] Another contestation—one that we will return to in Chapter 4 of this book—developed between proponents of an "African" approach to normative media frameworks and those that adhered to what was presented as a universal value system (but corresponded largely to a Western, liberal-democratic perspective). These debates can be seen as corollaries to the increased globalization of the South African media industry, where local media had to compete to a greater extent with their international counterparts that entered the local domain, and where South African media also extended their reach beyond national borders. And when the present remained tenuous and the future unclear, journalistic discourses drew on the past to provide beacons for the formulation of norms and values.

The debates about journalism in postapartheid South Africa illustrate how pressing questions about contemporary norms and practices cannot be divorced from history—but in the process, history itself becomes reconstructed in a dialectical relationship with the present. In postapartheid normative squabbles, history has often been used as a weapon in the arsenal of the respective protagonists. In defending their freedom, journalists have frequently pointed to, for instance, historic utterances by struggle icons such as Nelson Mandela.[16]

The past has also often been reconstructed in a way so as to foreground the media's role in bringing down the apartheid regime. Harber refers to the way in which the journalist Nat Nakasa, who died in exile during the apartheid era, has been remembered in contemporary political and journalistic narratives.[17] Nakasa left the country in 1964 to take up a Nieman Fellowship at Harvard. The apartheid government granted him an "exit permit," which made it impossible for him to return to his native country. He committed suicide in New York by throwing himself out of a window in "despair at becoming stateless."[18] In 2014,

Nakasa's remains were returned to South Africa and he was given a hero's reburial. He was widely celebrated by both representatives of the government and members of the journalistic community, as, respectively, a patriot and a critical antiapartheid writer. Harber points out how these different claims to Nakasa's legacy indicate the role of remembrance in contemporary political and journalistic discourses:

> Behind many current South African debates is a battle to control the struggle narrative. It is a tug-of-war between history and heritage, where history is an attempt to uncover and explain the past and heritage is a bid to shape it to serve current political needs. In recent weeks, this has played out in the many tributes to journalism icon Nat Nakasa, who died tragically in exile in 1965 and whose body was brought back from the USA for reburial as part of Heritage Month 2014. It is for journalism researchers and journals such as this to critically interrogate the narratives around such events and rescue the history from heritage.[19]

In the context of postapartheid South Africa, where renewed pressure is being put on journalists to be less critical of government, the celebration of journalist-heroes from the past could bolster their defenses. However, critics of the South African news media have pointed to the less glorious aspects of South African journalism history, such as the skewed racial profile of the journalistic workforce, the complicity of some sections of the news media with the apartheid regime, and the limited, liberal critique offered by others.

The question then becomes one of how history is used by journalists to support normative agendas. In Harber's terms,[20] how is "history" turned into "heritage" and for what reasons? How does the reconstruction of journalism history serve contemporary agendas?

In the rest of this chapter, these questions will be explored by drawing on data gathered in an earlier study through interviews with political journalists in which they were asked to elaborate on their professional self-identity, their role in relation to political authority, and their views of journalism history in the country.[21] The aim of this exploration is to understand how recollections and reconstructions of the past—"memory work"—shape journalists' professional identities and function strategically in their everyday practice, especially with the aim of defending journalism against perceived threats to their freedom and independence.

While the memories of past practices and professional values are reconstructed in the present—therefore flexible and subject to interpretation[22]—these reconstructions are rooted in new ethical frameworks of professional bodies of journalists (such as SANEF) and the legal and political frameworks associated with the state. While the reconstructions therefore enter a contested normative space, they are not merely imaginings without any material context.

Journalists' perception of how the past impacts on their contemporary journalistic values and practices was explored by means of a range of interviews conducted with political journalists working in various media across the country. These interviews formed part of a larger, comparative transnational study on political communication in new democracies.[23]

Between eight and ten political journalists, working for a range of media including commercial and public media, across print, broadcast, and online, were interviewed in each of these countries. Questions were organized into five major categories: orientation toward the democratic system, perception of own role and of counterpart, news production, relationship between media and government/politicians, and personal characteristics. Although these interviews took place in 2008 and 2009, before confrontations between journalists and the ruling party around a proposed Media Tribunal started, respondents were asked to reflect in overarching terms about the relationship between the media and government, about their interpretations of notions of media freedom and responsibility, and about the extent of transformation that had taken place in the news media since democratization. This chapter draws in particular on the interview question "Do you think that the recent past still has an influence on the way in which the media reports on politics in South Africa?" but also situates this question within the responses received from journalists to other, more general questions. Journalists' responses to this question can provide insight into the way in which reconstructions of history operate within an interpretive community and form part of collective "struggle[s] for determining meanings among groups of social actors."[24] The responses from journalists to questions of how the past continues to influence their work can give us insight into how history is interpreted. as well as reinserted into contemporary visions of professional practice, and help us understand the norms governing the relationship between journalists, politicians, and the public in a new democracy.

A particularly strong narrative in recent debates around the role of the media in postapartheid South Africa is one in which the resistance provided by South African journalists under apartheid is celebrated, to the extent that journalism is seen as having contributed to the fall of the regime. This construction of history (which usually omits the support given to the apartheid regime by Afrikaans sections of the press and does not mention the limits to the liberal critique offered by the English-language press under apartheid) is mustered to resist the renewed pressures from the democratic government on the press, which some have compared to the repression of freedom of speech by the Nationalist government.[25] When editors of liberal newspapers in the apartheid era are therefore characterized as having "spent decades opposing press censorship," it is with the purpose of validating their attack on the current proposals by the ANC-led government for a Media Tribunal and a draft Protection of Information Bill as evidence of "ignorance of the lessons of the past."[26]

In defending the current self-regulatory system, the Director of the Press Council (dealing with public complaints) is presented as a "veteran journalist with almost 50 years' experience,"[27] i.e., as someone associated with an idealized journalistic past and who himself has defied previous onslaughts on press freedom. In reporting on a statement by international news agencies decrying the Media Tribunal proposal, their invocation of an idealized journalistic past is also highlighted.[28] These agencies reportedly reminded President Zuma of "how they stood by his party, the ANC, during the struggle era": "The media in South Africa and foreign reporters working in the country told the world about the horrors of apartheid, despite intimidation, attempts at censorship and attacks by the White-led government."

In a more recent incident that also elicited debates about press freedom, the historical closure of antiapartheid newspapers and pressures on critical journalists were also called into remembrance. When Alide Dasnois, editor of the *Cape Times* was fired in 2013, it was widely regarded as a consequence of the intervention by the new owner of the Independent Newspapers group, Iqbal Survé. Dasnois oversaw an issue of the paper that carried a cover story about tender irregularities in the fishing industry, allegedly involving Survé's company, Sekunjalo holdings. Survé is also regarded as being close to the ANC and therefore likely to suppress criticism of the ruling party. In response to Dasnois' dismissal, journalists and civil society organizations like the Right to Know Campaign went into activist mode, protesting her dismissal and demanding guarantees of editorial independence at the Independent group. In an interview about such protest action between the journalist Alec Hogg and the chairperson of the Right to Know Campaign, Mark Weinberg, the historical closure of the *Rand Daily Mail* in 1985 and the subsequent establishment of an alternative, antiapartheid newspaper were recalled:

> ALEC HOGG: What kind of support do you have? I ask this because some years ago in 1985, the Rand Daily Mail was closed down, and the reporters at the Rand Daily Mail together with some well-wishers started a publication called the Weekly Mail, which is now the Mail & Guardian. Do you think that's an option that you might consider?

MARK WEINBERG: Yes, I think you're pointing to a very interesting phenomenon where these big print corporations remain profitable, even under periods of extreme censorship and oppression. With that said and done, I would like to believe that the marketplace would support alternative and independent media. Of course, that's not the experience of many small publishers in the country. Many small companies are alleging anti-competitive behaviour on the parts of the four big monopolies that dominate the industry.[29]

In conversations with journalists, three broad themes emerged from responses to the question of how the recent past continues to shape their contemporary practices. In each of these themes, history was linked to journalism in a particular way that has implications for current normative views and professional attitudes. Several journalists remarked on the fact that history continues to influence their selection of and approach to news reports. What exactly that history is and how its influence plays out in practice was articulated differently by various journalists. Depending on which view of South Africa's media history dominates, various roles for journalism in postapartheid society were envisaged.

The three major themes in journalists' view of the relation between past and present can be described as follows: history as a battlefield: journalism as resistance; history as a wound: journalism as a cure; and history as presence: journalism as continuity.

History as a Battlefield: Journalism as Resistance

The history of apartheid, and the claims made about journalists' resistance to it, continue to be invoked by journalists in the contemporary era to ward off renewed political pressures on journalistic independence. In reflections on journalistic independence, resistance against political interference is sometimes elevated to a component of the very professional identity of journalists, and used to justify claims to a special occupational status for journalists[30] in the postapartheid context:

> Having lived through Apartheid where we had attempts to muzzle us,... at the end of the day the Apartheid regime was not big enough to resource and maintain the kind of oppressive system and regime that it believed it could. [T]here was a very interesting period in the late 1980s where they brought in emergency regulations and it used to take us ten days to two weeks to drive a coach and horses through them, and then we had them bring more. I think

that is another thing worth emphasizing: the history of a very vibrant and vigorous press in this country even during the depths of Apartheid. Visitors always expressed some amazement at the degree of criticism that came out despite a plethora of laws and regulations and all sorts of stumbling blocks that were put in our way. We nevertheless were able to keep going hammer and tongs at the government.

History also becomes a badge of honor and distinction, as when this journalist lamented the fact that young journalists in the postapartheid era are less able to articulate such a clear professional vision, as they have exchanged a strong political identity for one in service of commercial goals.

In these accounts, the history of heavy-handed actions against the media by the apartheid government is called into remembrance, and even if it is clearly acknowledged that the media enjoys constitutionally guaranteed freedom in the postapartheid era, attempts are made to link contemporary political pressures with those under apartheid:

> [I]n the past, even if you would dare, you were very aware of the danger of the state coming down on you or imprisonment or publications being closed down and stuff like that. Now ... the Constitution guarantees you freedom of speech, for instance, but you do get some government officials or ministers who always try to find a way to silence you. Even if they know they are going to lose in court, they will still try ... it comes down to intimidation really.

The ultimate objective of the retelling of history as a terrain of conflict is to construct a professional identity for journalists that is premised on resistance to political authority and editorial independence. That this recasting of history is used as a basis from which to justify an adversarial stance against the current government is not to say that renewed pressures are a figment of journalistic imagination. The point is, however, that journalistic history is remembered selectively and retold purposively.

History as a Wound: Journalism as a Cure

If history was a battlefield, it is understandable that wounds would be inflicted. Another dimension of journalistic narratives about the past was that of trauma—journalists often described history as something that they needed to escape from, or to be cured of. Journalism itself, as it was practiced under apartheid, was sometimes seen as part of the problem. Mistakes committed by journalists at the time, errors of judgment or sins of omission—for instance, not speaking out clearly enough against apartheid, not asking tough enough questions, or even allowing themselves to be drawn into the comfortable sphere of political power—were acknowledged by several journalists as reasons why journalistic history could not be unequivocally retold as a heroic resistance struggle (as some of their colleagues attempted to do, as discussed earlier). In contrast, journalism in the postapartheid era is projected by these journalists in terms of a second chance, a renewed opportunity to rectify some of these mistakes and provide a cure for the wounds of history. Journalism can also play an educational role by reminding the public of this hurtful and unjust past and finding ways of ensuring that history does not repeat itself.

For journalists of this persuasion, it was seen as important to learn certain lessons from the past in order to make sure that the mistakes of the past are not repeated in the present. Journalists therefore reflected critically on their relationship with government as well as their responsibilities toward society as a whole. Illustrative of this orientation is the following response from a journalist to the question about journalism's responsibility toward the citizenry:

> It's a broader question around democracy and the extent to which we open up public debate around crucial issues in South Africa, but do it in a way which is not necessarily divisive and is not necessarily negative, or constantly negative in its approach.... In South Africa what we [are] trying to do, one of the goals, is of course nation-building by trying to heal divisions of the past. The issue is: are our media and our politics aiding that, or is it actually furthering that divide? You know in some critical areas I think that ... it's difficult for the media, because they've got to sell newspapers, and they've got to sensationalize certain things, and at the same time there are a lot of challenges and problems in South Africa and a lot of crises as such that need to be reported on. The issue is how do we strike that balance?

Although journalists were in general fiercely defensive of their editorial independence, the history of racism in South Africa was seen to justify certain limits to press freedom, in the sense that the guarantee to freedom of expression contained in the Constitution had to be balanced with the prevention of hate speech and the protection of human dignity—two countervailing proscriptions also found in the Constitution. This is how one respondent described this balance:

> [T]here must be free flow of information in the public interest for the democratic process to flow. And obviously, there are confines to this: privacy, decency, the fact that you cannot extend your freedom to harm that of another, and no incitement especially given our history of racial hatred, and then no incitement to violence, that sort of basic things.

In this conceptualization, history continues to impact on normative debates in the present as a curtailment of journalistic excesses. A knowledge of journalism history could therefore encourage journalists to take greater responsibility with respect to how they use their freedom and could also provide a source of learning for journalists and publics alike. Journalism can facilitate this learning process first by reminding publics of the country's history—especially the youth who have grown up in a free society and may not be fully aware of the historical context in which the democratic society came into being. But journalists themselves can also form a community of practice to constantly remind themselves of historical mistakes so as to avoid committing those mistakes again.

The imperative of remaining aware of history, and of imparting that historical knowledge to new generations of journalists and publics, was summed up as follows by one journalist:

> [W]e have a certain history. Our history is not the same as many other countries. So when we write we have to sort of keep that at the back of our minds. We don't have to continuously remind ... people. People know. But now and then, based on our history, depending on what the issue is, we have to remind in our reporting, also state the fact that we don't need to have that type of situation again, we need to also educate our readers that the people, especially the young people of today, so that many of them are fully sympathetic to what happened ... we need to educate them ... [to know] that what they have is because of our history ... our struggle ... people who have struggled to [be] where we are today.

Once such historical knowledge would be achieved, the hope was that it would have an influence on how journalists report on politics in the postapartheid context. Knowledge of apartheid history, it was hoped, would enable journalists to take a more critical stance and not take information received from government at face value:

> If you don't understand the history of the country then your reporting is going to be a little bit skewed ... you will just play it straight ahead and you will become a conduit. This is what government says and you will report on it. You have to have a grip on ... the history of this country. Some people don't accept it, unfortunately, but it's a fact that ... a political journalist would not be able to do a proper job unless [you have a solid knowledge of history].

An acknowledgment of the mistakes and omissions committed by journalists in the past would therefore not make journalists more hesitant or reluctant to confront political power in present-day South Africa, but would rather strengthen their resolve to resist renewed attempts at political interference or control:

> I think our papers were the tools in the hands of the previous regime. I think the past experiences would make us more wary of [repeating] that [situation] so to an extent it [works] to our advantage.

From the above responses, it can be seen how the normative roles envisaged for journalism in the current, postapartheid society are validated through an appeal to history, albeit a history that should not be repeated. The litmus test for a socially responsible journalism in the postapartheid era, in this vision, is the extent to which it succeeds in healing the "divisions of the past," cementing over the fractures of the citizenry and enabling journalists and citizens alike to draw on historical lessons in order to avoid repeating them. This means more vigilance over the democratic government, rather than less, but it is a vigilance that does not rely on the narrative of journalists as heroic antiapartheid fighters but as fallible professionals. Notable in this regard is also how this social responsibility role is seen as something to be fulfilled in spite of the political economic pressures in a commercialized postapartheid media landscape. Healing the divisions of the past, while striving to ensure that political power is held to account, is a goal to strive for in spite of the pressures of having to "sell newspapers" and having to "sensationalize certain things."

History as Presence: Journalism as Continuity

In sharp contrast to the views expressed by the journalists quoted so far, who either viewed South African journalism history as one where journalists bravely fought against apartheid or admitted that mistakes were made but that journalists in contemporary South Africa are working in the public interest to ensure that history doesn't repeat itself, is the view that not much has changed. A view of "elite continuity," as found in the literature about media in new democracies holds that economic structures remained relatively intact during the transition to democracy, and that persisting social inequalities are mirrored in the media.[31] This view also underpins, at least partly (insofar as the critiques are not informed by a self-serving deflection of media criticism), some of the ANC-government's critical views of the media. In his defense of the proposed Media Tribunal, President Jacob Zuma, for instance, expressed the view that the postapartheid self-regulatory mechanisms are not accessible to the poor majority and that the proposed Tribunal would act "on behalf of" the poor who cannot afford lawyers.[32]

Some journalists acknowledged a continuity between journalistic practices and attitudes from the apartheid to the postapartheid era, even as they reflected on how journalism practices have changed between different generations of journalists. For these respondents, journalism's history is not purely heroic, and journalism is not easily rid of that history.

On this view, journalistic attitudes have not changed as rapidly as the structure of the media industry did, and the democratization of journalistic mindsets is still an incomplete process, despite progress in terms of racial and gender representation:

> Our newsrooms are a lot more representative of the [country's] demographics than they used to be. But the people who control copy, the transformation is a lot slower there. You have a lot of women journalists who are doing a lot of hard work but not a lot of us [women] are in decision-making positions. There has been a juniorization of newsrooms which has led to a lapse in quality. There has been a massive exodus of trained journalists which has resulted in a weakening of institutional memory. We often make very sloppy mistakes in the media and government accusations that often we are unable to explain complex processes around governance do have some merit. I think we don't take enough responsibility as media for that. On the other hand, we have also seen a rapid advancement of young people, of Black people and of women.

Another journalist pointed out that not all their colleagues "have gotten used to the freedom" of the news media in the new dispensation and continued to approach political news in a similar way as during the 1980s, when sections of the press were either supportive or in collusion with the apartheid regime. The example used by this respondent was the *Citizen* newspaper which, during the 1980s, had been secretly funded by the apartheid government. Other respondents pointed to the public broadcaster, the South African Broadcasting Corporation (SABC), which in their view has been repeating the mistakes of the past by allowing interference by the current, democratic government in ways similar to those of the old regime. Although these observations by journalists clearly served as a means to distance themselves from the way journalism had been practiced in the apartheid era, they acknowledged that some continuity with the past remains, carried forward by journalists from one era to the next. While such generational continuity was viewed in a negative light, the introduction of a new cohort of journalists to newsrooms in an attempt to overhaul the industry was, on the other hand, also seen as having a detrimental influence on the overall "capacity and age and experience of reporters." Several journalists remarked on new, junior journalists' lack of the historical and contextual knowledge required to report on complex political issues or to locate news events within broader historical trends.

These views introduce an ambiguous orientation of journalists toward the past. While their understanding of press freedom and responsibility requires them to reject the failures of journalism practices during the apartheid past, their professional identity (which places a premium on technical skills and values such as truth, accuracy, and surveillance of power) leads them to be critical of the inadequacies of junior reporters—which are seen as resulting partly from the hasty reconstitution of newsrooms in the postapartheid era. This leaves journalists in a double-bind of either having to acknowledge past failures, but then having a weaker position from which to criticize contemporary journalistic weaknesses, or having to defend the "good old days" of technical prowess and underplay the professional blind spots of the past. South African journalism history is therefore used in a contradictory way here—on the one hand, the ignominious parts of that history are rejected in an attempt to validate current practices and ideologies, while a golden era of journalistic skills is called into remembrance.

The continuities between the past and the present, as they play out in journalistic attitudes, routines, and practices, call into question any glib notion of journalism in the democratic era as having made a clean break with the past. One senior journalist gave a sober assessment of the continuities between past and present attitudes and practices, but also saw these continuities as indications of a normative framework that is dynamic for the very reason that it is subject to ongoing contestation. Her response is worth quoting at length:

> Fourteen years in the life of a country is nothing. The contradictions in South Africa are becoming more stark. There was a democratic breakthrough in 1994 but the race and class faultlines are intensifying in many ways and the past is still festering in the present. That is apparent in a whole range of areas: in state institutions, in practices, etc. It is one thing to legislate a set of laws but you can't legislate attitudes—to change attitudes takes time and work. So I think the past is very present in the way political coverage is happening. [L]ook at the media's portrayal of every new ANC leader. When Mandela took over he was a saint, which to me was problematic, but when Mbeki had to take over there was this big exceptionalism around Mandela. There was no other person like him so how could Thabo Mbeki possibly fit his shoes? There was a lot of suspicion around Mbeki; he was an enigma, a silent assassin, etc. until he showed himself as an economic conservative and the checking classes were very happy with him—even though he proved to be quite undemocratic—but he became the person that we could not do without. We had outsourced our responsibilities to him as a leader. That was the basis of the argument that a fallible leader like Jacob Zuma couldn't possibly fill the shoes of the philosopher-king that is Thabo Mbeki.
>
> All of that is in fact prejudices parading as analysis and says more about the cultural preoccupations of the people raising the problem than it does about the subject.

Just because we had a democratic breakthrough does not mean that these institutions are in good shape or that all your contradictions have been resolved—it's an ongoing process. That has become part of the fight over whether the settlement we had in 1994 was an appropriate settlement. That contestation is now in full swing. You have class faultlines, the division between the urban and the rural. . . . It's quite a dynamic process in many ways.

Conclusion

The views of journalists discussed herein displayed the ways in which history continues to impact on current journalism practices and normative positions. However, there remains no clear consensus on exactly how history should inform current normative positions. Three positions emerged from the way history is drawn upon to support journalists' professional identities and norms in the present:

- A celebration of the past: the recasting of journalism's perceived role in resisting apartheid then becomes a justification for a renewed insistence on press freedom in order for journalism to act as watchdog over the postapartheid government.
- A rejection of the past: the acknowledgment of journalism's historic failures and shortcomings is then used as a clarion call for journalists to develop a critical social responsibility in the postapartheid era in order to avoid falling into the same traps as before. This is usually articulated in terms of a critical "watchdog" position in relation to political power.
- No clear break between the past and the present: continuities between past and present journalistic practices are acknowledged. Instead of embracing postapartheid journalism uncritically as an inherently democratic practice, the persistence of inequalities and undemocratic attitudes are conceded, at the same time as the loss of some professional values and technical proficiencies of the past are lamented.

It seems that, in general, journalists in postapartheid South Africa accept that they have to remain vigilant in order to avoid repeating the mistakes of the past. This vigilance is frequently expressed by means of an assertion of journalistic freedom, independence, and social responsibility. While, perhaps for strategic reasons, some journalists choose to emphasize the role that journalism played in resisting apartheid and that it therefore deserves special status and recognition in the postapartheid dispensation (articulated through values such as "freedom" and "independence"), others are more critical of their professional history. For the latter group of journalists, critical scrutiny of the relationship between journalism and democracy should be directed as much toward journalism as toward politicians and institutions of government.

The range of ways in which journalists understand history as having a bearing on current journalism practice and normative orientations suggests that history should be studied with an open mind and a critical attitude in order for contemporary values, norms, and practices to be informed by it. Using history as a mere validation of contemporary practices or a source for sloganeering would be a simplistic and dishonest approach. Instead, normative debates in the present can only be enriched by historical perspectives if history is drawn upon in all its complexity and contradictions.

The extent to which these normative debates about the role of the media in contemporary South Africa have become a key feature of broader discourses about media, citizenship, and democracy in the country will form the focus of the next section of this book. Amid the changes in the South African media's global positioning and the increased external political and economic pressures under which the media operated during the first twenty years of democracy, vibrant and often heated contestations of these norms, values, and practices came to define media debates. This is the topic we will move to next.

PART II

Local Contestations

CHAPTER 4

Is This Freedom?

Media Ethics, "African Culture," and Universal Values

Introduction

The following three chapters of this book will address various aspects that have to do with internal contestations in the South African media and how these relate to broader, global debates about media norms and values and the notion of a global "crisis" in journalism. This chapter provides a broad, largely theoretical, overview of the normative questions about the South African media in a postapartheid era, in particular as these relate to democracy and citizenship. A key distinction to be drawn will be that between substantive and procedural notions of ethics. The overview of these normative contestations will set the scene for a focus (in the following chapter) on one particular example which—in South Africa as it has often been the case in other contexts around the world—has foregrounded different views of the role of media in society, namely tabloid journalism. The question of what the changes in South African journalism contribute to the often alarmist discussions about the future of journalism will then be considered in Chapter 6.

The ethical questions about the media's responsibility toward South African citizens and democratic values, which will be discussed in this chapter, will be developed further to highlight contrasts between local and global ethical frameworks.

In the previous chapter, the normative positioning of journalists in the postapartheid era was considered against the backdrop of history. From the responses of journalists, it became clear that they defined their roles and responsibilities in the democratic era in relation to a reconstructed version of South African history. Looming large in the discourses of journalistic roles in postapartheid South Africa was the notion of freedom and independence, justified on the basis of the remembrance of historical experiences of repression. Time and again, journalists state that they have to remain vigilant, even in the new democracy with its constitutional guarantees of freedom of expression, to avoid new incursions into editorial freedom. They are also wary of repeating the mistake of the past of not offering enough resistance against repression.

These responses, given within the context of historical recollections as in the previous chapter, are resonances from wider, and ongoing, normative debates about the role of the media in contemporary South Africa. The changes that the South African media has undergone as a result of the internal changes and transformations as have been described thus far have meant that these debates have at times been heated, because the media's role has come to be seen as closely tied to highly significant questions of citizenship, democratic debate, and human rights. Changes in the South African media's positioning within global media markets, coupled with changing geopolitics such as the country's membership of BRICS and how these new international relations—for instance, South Africa's relationship with China—will impact on media freedom, have brought an additional layer of complexity to these normative debates. A further feature has to do with the way that the South African media market has developed domestically. The imperative for the media to transform in terms of the respresentativity of its editorial staff, the orientation of its content, and the diversity of its ownership has set in motion wide-ranging contestations of a structural and cultural nature. Structural questions related to the political economy of the media and media pluralism in relation to the public interest in a highly unequal society remain highly relevant in the postapartheid era, where media concentration has increased. At the same time, what can be called cultural-ethical questions to do with professional norms, values, and practice, have become increasingly important as new formats and genres such as social media and tabloid newspapers emerged onto the South African media scene. One of the problems that emerged in the way these debates unfolded was that the structural and cultural aspects of normative frameworks were not always connected. While issues relating to professional journalistic culture were often thrashed out in detail, these were usually contained within procedural understandings of ethical standards, press codes, and regulatory bodies. The structural questions about media ownership and representativity, in turn, were mostly dealt with within a political economy framework. Both these approaches were, however, largely procedural in nature, while the substantive ethical questions about what the role, function, and responsibility of the media should be within a new democracy, a highly unequal country, and a postcolonial society remain largely unanswered.

Let us look at this distinction in more detail first, against the background of different views of the media's role in a new democracy, before considering the specific ways in which this distinction became manifest in South African media discourses.

Media Ethics in a New Democracy

What role should the media play in a new democracy? What are the ethical duties owed by a media to a citizenry that has only recently emerged from centuries of colonialism and apartheid? How should the media orient itself toward a society that is considered the most unequal in the world?

Earlier in this book, the framework of *transitology* and its critiques were discussed with reference to the South African transition from apartheid to democracy. The opening up of a democratic public sphere, the intensified impact of globalization with the end of the country's isolation, and the redefinition of civil society in relation to a now legitimate state[1] had profound implications for the way that the South African media conceived of its role in normative terms. One of the key debates in the literature of transitology is to what extent democratization brought about complete transformation of erstwhile authoritarian states or merely resulted in the repositioning of partnerships between elites.[2] Critics have pointed out that in the South African case, the political system was transformed radically, with citizenship rights now having been extended to all South Africans, but that the "narrowest practical definition of democracy" was used to justify an elite transition from apartheid to neoliberalism.[3] According to this view, the political system was radically reformed, but economic policies adopted after apartheid still favored elites and continued to marginalize the poor majority of South Africans, for whom economic justice is still elusive. As far as the media is concerned, critics point to the fact that the media has largely been supporting this economic arrangement and has offered a middle-class perspective on news events.[4] From this perspective, rights like media freedom were seen as linked to individual rights and therefore supported by the media (arguably also because there is an element of self-interest). Basic economic rights—and the associated human dignity—of those citizens for whom life in the postapartheid democracy is still a struggle for survival would, however, require of the media a more communitarian commitment to social justice and the restoration of human dignity.

The tension between the newly acquired democratic right to freedom of expression and the imperative for the media to contribute to the restoration of the right to dignity remains at the center of debates about media ethics in postapartheid South Africa. The former right—upon which claims to media independence rest—was vigorously defended by the media when self-regulatory procedures came under scrutiny and pressure was put on the media to acquiesce to stronger forms of regulation. Much progress has indeed been made on media ethical *procedures* such as the establishment of a Press Council, Press Ombudsman, and ethical codes that embody constitutional values. At the same time, there seems to be disagreement about the *substantive* issues of how the media could contribute to the improvement of society more generally—toward a "good life for purposes of human flourishing."[5]

The distinction between procedural and substantive ethics can be summed up by looking at the criteria for an action to be judged as ethical. In procedural ethics, an action is considered ethical if the process followed certain "rules" closely. In substantive ethics, "the (substantive) conclusion matters more than how (that is, the procedures) one reaches it."[6] Examples of procedural ethics would be the deontological ethics of Immanuel Kant, in which the rational process of identifying and adhering to a specific *duty* would qualify an action as ethical, or dialogical ethics, where the outcomes of ethical deliberation are assumed to be good as long as that deliberation took the form of dialogue.[7] In contrast, substantive ethics is concerned with the concrete content of the ethical decisions reached more than with the process that was followed. Amartya Sen makes a similar distinction in his discussion of justice.[8] Sen contrasts the procedural form of justice in early Indian jurisprudence, *niti*, with the substantive form, *nyaya*. Whereas the first concept is concerned with the rules and processes that make justice possible, the latter form considers how the rules of justice affect people's everyday lives. As Rao discusses in more detail, the procedural *niti* for Sen is located in the "transcendental institutions" that deliver justice through rules and regulations, whereas *nyaya* refers to the kind of world, the type of society that we want to see emerge from these institutions and their rules.[9] Sen criticizes John Rawls for his "transcendental institutionalism," which Sen sees as an idealistic approach to a perfectly just society, whereas his own comparative approach acknowledges that sometimes a choice needs to be made between various alternative forms of justice that are sometimes in tension.

To apply Sen's distinction between *niti* and *nyaya*, or between procedural and substantive ethics, to the postapartheid South African democracy, one can compare the democratic institutions and processes (e.g., the courts, the free press, the five-year ballot) with the outcomes of these democratic processes and institutions in everyday life—for example, the extent to which all citizens have the opportunity to make their voices heard in democratic debates, or the extent to which the everyday lived experiences of the majority of South Africans have improved. In the first chapter of this book the distinction Heller makes between the "status" of citizenship and the "practice" of citizenship was pointed out.[10] This distinction has relevance for how one thinks about the media's ethical responsibilities pertaining to citizenship and democracy in postapartheid South Africa. For Heller, the "status" of citizenship refers to the legalistic, nominal rights to inclusion into the democratic polity that all South Africans came to enjoy when formal democracy arrived in the country in 1994—this includes freedom of expression and freedom of the media. The "practice" of citizenship, in contrast, refers to the extent to which all South Africans can lay claim to their civic rights in a practical sense. Do all South Africans have a voice in the public sphere? To what extent can South Africans participate in decision-making processes that determine the quality of their daily lives?

The distinction between substantive and procedural justice and between the status and practice of citizenship can also be noted in the different approaches to developing media ethical frameworks for the postapartheid media. On the level of procedural ethics, much emphasis has been placed on refining the procedures and institutions of regulation (through a Broadcasting Complaints Commission) and self-regulation, under a Press Council. The attacks on self-regulation and the ANC's proposed Media Appeals Tribunal have focused on these aspects, but underpinning them was the deeper, unresolved question about what the desired substantive outcomes of ethical institutions and procedures should be. This substantive question is a normative one, i.e., what role should the media play in a transitional, developmental democracy such as South Africa? What exactly is the contribution by the media toward this democracy that these procedures and institutions are meant to facilitate? The separation between procedural and substantive ethics is therefore neither clear nor absolute: procedural ethics implicitly assumes certain substantive goods to exist, whereas substantive ethics needs to be expressed in procedural terms in order to become articulate and intelligible.[11] A problem arises, however, when public debate about media ethics focuses so much on procedures that the underlying, harder questions about the media's role and orientation in society are neglected. It is also instructive to note that questions of media responsibility routinely got narrowed down to issues of self-regulation and professional codes. It may be argued that a notion of ethics that emphasizes professional values and independence is easier to reconcile with the self-interested objectives of commercial media, while more in-depth engagement with substantive ethical questions may necessitate a reorientation toward social justice that would be more difficult to sustain within a market environment.

Debates around the role of the media in a transitional society have frequently resulted in open conflict between the media and the state. Most often, the central roles envisaged for the media have been reduced to the liberal-democratic "watchdog" or "Fourth Estate" monitorial paradigm versus a collaborative developmental one. The normative frameworks in dispute have, however, largely been deductive in nature, derived from media systems theory developed in the Global North. Attempts to critique and "Africanize" these inherited Northern frameworks have in turn frequently lapsed into essentialist identity politics. The result has been a normative impasse, with media ethics being seen largely in formalistic terms, as a strategic ritual to protect an existing corporatist media paradigm on the one hand, and crude political economic critiques and attempts to co-opt the media into political power projects on the other.

The development of new media technologies and the globalization of media, with the resultant fragmentation of audiences and bewildering diversity of perspectives, could lead one to argue that normative frameworks for the media are out of sync with the globalized media culture in which we live. This line of argument forms part of a particularly productive area of research in recent years in the area of global media ethics.

"Universal Values" and "African Culture"

As the South African media made the transition from operating within an authoritarian society to operating within a democratic one, it also extended its presence in the continent and globally. This dual repositioning of the South African media brought with it questions of how local normative frameworks should respond to what sometimes seemed to be conflicting demands for Africanization and globalization.

Despite the pervasive notion that we live in a highly globalized world, and the recurring criticism that media act as agents of media imperialism,[12] global corporate capitalism[13] or the "Pax Americana,"[14] media formats, practices, and underpinning value systems show significant variance around the world. Recent work in the area of journalism studies has shown how media production is premised on local cultural, political, and historical contexts.[15] At the same time, research has also pointed to similarities across media cultures, especially as far as normative orientations and practices like the "ideals of 'objectivity and impartiality'" are concerned.[16] Furthermore, the media texts produced across transnational media may also be read in sometimes radically different ways, as the controversy following the publication of the "Mohammad Cartoons" by the Danish newspaper *Jyllands-Posten* in 2006 and a similar, yet arguably more violent, event when twelve people died in attacks on the offices of the French satirical magazine *Charlie Hebdo* showed. The musical metaphor of "counterpoint," first used by Edward Said to recognize the multiplicity of positions from which texts may be interpreted, has been invoked to indicate the tension between unity and diversity in the production of media discourses and the professional and societal norms and value systems underpinning them.[17] Another way of putting this would be to say that, just as contrasting melody lines mutually constitute a piece of music, cultural identities and normative frameworks are mutually constitutive. During the democratization period, attempts were made to reposition intellectual traditions in relation to a renewed identification of South Africa with the African continent. More widely, institutional transformations were clad in the language of "Africanization," which often did not extend beyond superficial changes of company names or corporate identities, but in some cases did give cause for introspection around issues pertaining to cultural imperialism and South African identity. Examples of these are the restructuring of apartheid-era arts councils and the drawing on African cultural traditions or vocabulary (e.g., *ubuntu* or *lekgotla*) to express management or business concepts.[18] Media institutions and journalism also considered "indigenization,"[19] and debates raged about how media ethics should be more reflective of African values.[20]

When one looks at the meta-discourse about media during the transitional period to which has been referred already in Chapter 1,[21] it emerges that debates about the media were also debates about the kind of democracy envisaged as the ideal for South Africa, and how media came to represent different positions in identity politics. As has already been pointed out, one may perhaps even speak of the media as being a "metaphor" for change, since the media continues to be seen as an index of broader changes in the country—both internally, in terms of who dominates the public sphere, as well as how the South African media reflects the country's position in terms of global power relations. More than being a site or an instrument for transformation, one can venture to say that the media debates form a meta-discourse or a system of knowledge in themselves, through which identities are constructed in relation to power. Simply put, postapartheid identities are not only being constructed by what is said in the media, but also by what is said about the media. For this reason, control of the discourse is important, and this explains why the media as a site and instrument is so vigorously contested.

Debates about the media therefore not only serve the function of transforming the media as an industry or exerting some form of control over its content, but the very debates about the media can also serve as identity-producing discourses. The question of whether the South African media should follow Western norms of "objectivity" and "independence," for instance, or rather opt for a "developmental" model or one underpinned by African philosophy, not only reflect broader concerns about the changing nature of South African society but also have a bearing on how journalists and other media practitioners define their social and professional identities. These identities, in turn, are constitutive of media norms, as the way media practitioners see themselves and their position within South African and global society is likely to influence the construction of norms for their practice. This is what is meant by identity and norms being mutually constitutive.

Identity construction in this context is also part of ongoing commercial and political power struggles. The tensions between local cultural identities and various models of professional norms and values become even clearer when the question of how values and norms for the South African media should relate to global normative frameworks is asked. The question of media ethics—not merely as it pertains to the codified practices of media professionals, but in a broader sense as a framework guiding the moral duties and obligations of the media in relationship to society—is therefore a central one in the analysis of the South African media's position within various transitions.

Global Media Ethics

One of the central questions in media ethics scholarship in recent years has been whether a global media ethics is possible, and what it could look like. One of the most challenging concerns in these debates has been how to account for a diversity of normative perspectives globally while avoiding cultural relativism.[22]

The incorporation of these various "local" perspectives into a global media ethics is further complicated by the fact that "local" or "regional" perspectives may themselves offer competing visions of what a "global" media ethics would look like, or even question whether such a global ethics is possible or desirable.

At first glance, media ethics codes globally agree, at least on a surface level, about certain key normative concepts such as media freedom, truth-telling, independence, and responsibility.[23] Despite its shortcomings and U.S.-centered history, the notion of social responsibility as a central guiding principle for media has found resonance around the world,[24] been adopted in national media systems, and influenced debates about equitable global communication systems, such as those around the New World Information and Communication Order at UNESCO in the late 1970s.[25] However, the wide adoption of the notion of social responsibility may obscure the fact that tensions between freedom and responsibility remain, even in established democracies like the United States[26] and that the framework's genesis in a particular historical and geographic context may make it an inadequate foundation for global media ethics. Although ideas such as media freedom and responsibility are often presented as having universal validity, they are in themselves "local" in that they have originated from particular epistemological traditions rooted in Western thought and experience.[27] This is the point that was also made in Chapter 2 of this book, when the "decolonization" or "internationalization" of media studies was discussed. An attempt to arrive at universal protonorms that may guide a globalized media, such as human dignity, truth-telling, and nonmalfeasance, would only be possible once the realization sets in that northern practices and norms that have become global in their reach cannot claim to be universal knowledge but should be understood as having originated in other specific localities.[28]

Despite the wide resonance of certain "protonorms," local interpretations of these norms are still likely to differ. What exactly human dignity means in a specific context, and how it should be balanced with other values such as truth-telling, is likely to be contested. One only has to look at several conflicts in South Africa around media coverage to see that concepts such as dignity and freedom will be read through the lenses of local histories and power struggles. An example of this was the controversy in 2012 surrounding the South African artist Brett Murray's satirical work, *The Spear of the Nation*, in which President Jacob Zuma was depicted with his genitals exposed in a parody of Lenin. A picture of the artwork was published in the Sunday newspaper *City Press*, which led to a debate about how the constitutional rights to freedom of expression and human dignity should be balanced, and what position the media should take when these values are in tension.[29] A similar tension between the right to freedom of expression and the protection of human dignity erupted some years before in 2007, when the then Minister of Health, Manto Tshabalala-Msimang, was hospitalized for a liver transplant. The *Sunday Times* came into possession of her health records and published allegations of her alcohol abuse and a previous conviction for theft, under the headline "Manto: A Drunk and a Thief."[30] The exposure of the minister's alleged alcoholism and abuse of the state health services through receiving preferential treatment was done in the conventional "watchdog" or "Fourth Estate" mode. According to this approach, truth-telling in the public interest was the primary duty of the media. However, for some, this exposure violated the Minister's right to privacy and dignity, which would have been upheld were an alternative normative approach followed. One such claim was made by the CEO of the public broadcaster, the SABC, Dali Mpofu, who also introduced another perspective on the tension between competing ethical values, namely that of African culture. In protest against SANEF's defense of the *Sunday Times* article, Mpofu broke ties between the SABC and SANEF. He criticized the reporting as "inhumane" and "far removed from the basic value of *ubuntu*."[31] "Shame on all of you," he continued, "especially those who have turned their backs on your own cultural values for 30 pieces of silver, pretending to be converted to foreign, frigid, and feelingless 'freedoms.'"[32] In his response, Thabo Leshilo, then editor of the *Sowetan* newspaper, responded to defend the *Sunday Times* editor, Mondli Makhanya, to say that press freedom should not be seen as a "bourgeois indulgence" or a "white pastime," but that Black editors who support press freedom should not be seen as "black surrogates of the right-wing enemies of the democratic government."[33] In both these cases, the media claimed that publication was in the "public interest," while counterclaims stressed the right to privacy and dignity, even of public figures.

Differences of opinion as to the relative weight of the values of media freedom and social responsibility not only exist between the media, political stakeholders, and the public. Journalists themselves also interpret these values differently, as has been mentioned in the previous chapter.[34] The fact that, in both these cases, "African values" were invoked to counter the media's insistence on its freedom to perform a monitorial role also suggests that a simplistic binary between "local" and "global" ethics will not suffice—the "local" is also contested.

These differences of opinion suggest that grand and totalizing schemes for global media ethics have to make way for more nuanced understandings of the specific cultural and political histories within which ethics is interpreted and operationalized, especially in various settings outside the Northern metropolitan centers. The very notion of universalism, with its historical association with Western traditions of liberalism, also needs to be examined critically.[35]

To reiterate the argument made in a slightly different way in Chapter 2, this introduction of non-Western perspectives into a "global" narrative needs to go beyond superficial and patronizing gestures of inclusion and diversity. A superficial engagement of perspectives on media ethics from the Global South, for instance, as descriptive case studies to illustrate existing theoretical notions, may also render them exotic and static, ignoring the vigorous contestations around central moral concepts that take place in these localized contexts, such as the ones in South Africa mentioned earlier. While it is therefore clear that simplistic notions of the "universal" will not do justice to the global cultural diversity reflected in different ethical norms, the "local" equally is not an unproblematic category through which to approach global media ethics either, as significant contestation may exist between various ethical traditions.

Instead, a contextualized narrative approach to media ethics, which seeks to understand how ethical concepts are interpreted, applied, and given meaning within specific, concrete, geohistorical contexts, would be a more appropriate approach to solve the dilemma of the "local" versus the "global" in media ethics. Such an approach would be rooted in an ethnographic understanding of morality, that is, the realization that "morality is rooted in everyday experience and gains multiple levels of complexity."[36] In following such an approach, the notion of "listening" already alluded to earlier, would be an important one to incorporate. By listening to the voices of those that are usually marginalized from the mainstream mediated public sphere,[37] a richer understanding of how ethical values operate in specific contexts might be arrived at. In this process, the specific conditions under which media in Africa operate would need to be taken into account without resorting to essentialist or romanticized notions of "African culture." In other words, the specificity of the local context, the material conditions under which media operate, and the lived experiences of media producers and consumers in Africa should all be considered and contribute to the development of normative frameworks appropriate to local contexts such as the South African one. An essentialized notion of "African culture," used in binary opposition to media ethical traditions derived from elsewhere, is not helpful. In the past, various attempts have been made to develop African media ethics—some more successful than others. Let us look at some these in conclusion.

Media Ethics in Africa

In an era of accelerated globalization, to a large extent facilitated by global media, African media increasingly has to negotiate the space between ethical norms and practices as these have evolved in a particular sociocultural and political environment, on the one hand, and globalized ethical discourses laying claim to universal validity on the other. An example of the intersection between universal and regional discourses was the landmark Windhoek Declaration on Promoting an Independent and Pluralistic African Press in 1991.[38] In this declaration, African journalists invoked the Universal Declaration of Human Rights as a motivation for the promotion of press freedom in the particular African context. The spread of global media to African audiences (for instance, through satellite television) and the reach of African media to global audiences (for instance, through new media technologies such as the internet often aimed at Africans in the diaspora) have positioned African media ethics in an increasingly transnational context.

These global shifts in terms of global content available on African media platforms, and African media companies expanding their international footprint on the rest of the continent and further afield (the company Naspers, with its operations on the rest of the continent via the digital satellite subsidiary MultiChoice, and its interests in many parts of the world, including the BRICS countries, is a prime example) pose challenges to the conceptualization of media ethics in Africa. Questions such as the following arise: Which norms should be used when evaluating media content in this transnational sphere? Are African ethical norms appropriate to deal with globalized media in a postmodern age? Conversely, can ethical frameworks derived from the Global North provide appropriate guidelines for ethical action in African contexts that differ in many respects from those in which dominant normative media theories have been devised?

As several case studies from Africa have made clear,[39] the circumstances under which African journalists work are often so radically different from those in the North that a wholesale importation of Northern ethical frameworks would be unsuitable for these conditions. More recent scholarly concerns with the question of "global media ethics" run the risk of again (albeit inadvertently) imposing Northern norms under the guise of universalism, as has been argued from the point of view of postcolonial criticism.[40] Perhaps the best-known African response to ethics derived from situations and theories developed in the Global North came from the Zambian ethicist Francis Kasoma.[41] His attempt to construct an Afriethics has, however, invited criticism for its romantic notions of an idyllic African society untouched by the West.[42] Because of the dangers of essentializing African culture when African media practices are contrasted against Western norms,[43] connections have been sought between indigenous ethical frameworks and Western approaches like communitarianism rather than pitting them against each other.[44]

Media ethics in South Africa, especially when related to the broader African context, can therefore be seen as contested terrain. The situation is made more complex by ongoing global shifts in which the South African media is being repositioned in relation to global and regional flows and counterflows of media content and capital. Various normative frameworks continue to coexist and compete for dominance over media ethical discourses. These ethical frameworks also have a political dimension, as they may support conflicting visions of to whom African media owe their primary responsibility, and what their degree of freedom should be. This led to a vigorous and heated debate among journalists and commentators about the appropriate value system for the South African media to follow, the limits of press freedom, and "a Eurocentric and western mindset within journalism."[45]

These local contestations around "universal" or Western norms and African cultural values are further complicated by geopolitical shifts such as the country's membership of the BRICS grouping, especially the closer relationship to China. These global shifts will be discussed in more detail in Section III of this book, but it is relevant to note in the context of debates around normative frameworks that the increased flows and contraflows between Chinese media and South Africa (and other African countries) have given rise to questions about press freedom on the continent.[46]

Development Journalism Framework

One of the defining normative frameworks within which journalists in Africa have understood their role has been that of development journalism. Although originating in Asia in the 1960s, the approach also gained popularity in Africa and Latin America,[47] and, as such, may be seen as a transnational normative framework for developing regions.[48] Development journalism may be seen as an attempt to develop collaboration between media and governments into a normative theory.[49] Responsibility in this framework is articulated in terms of the media's role to promote development, which in practice has mostly meant supporting governments in attaining their economic, political, and cultural development goals. Often seen as antithetical to the Western libertarian approach, development journalism has indeed been vulnerable to abuse by postcolonial governments.

This is not to say that development journalism is incompatible with Western frameworks of social responsibility. When understood as a type of journalism that examines, evaluates, and reports on the relevance and success of development programs (also criticizing governments who fall short of developmental goals), development journalism can be consistent with the social responsibility theory,[50] although arguably such a definition of development journalism might not be based on collaboration anymore.[51] An alternative notion of emancipatory journalism has also been proposed as a way to redirect attention to the way journalism can affect social change and improve people's living conditions instead of focusing primarily on the relationship between media and the state.[52]

Despite the problems inherent in development journalism as a normative framework, it continues to feature strongly in contemporary discourses of African journalism and also informs many of the discursive struggles around journalistic norms in postapartheid South Africa. Because of its association with collaboration with the state, the very notion of development journalism is routinely rejected by journalists.

There are, however, some signs that South African journalists are slowly moving away from thinking about journalistic norms in stark binary terms (e.g., libertarian versus developmental), as a recent study has shown.[53] This study, the South African part of the international Worlds of Journalism project,[54] has found that journalists surveyed do not view criticism of the government as being in contradiction with their responsibility of providing support for the national development project. The survey has shown[55] that although journalists considered the media's role as a watchdog[56] as important, they also demonstrated commitment to their role as supporters of national development.[57]

These types of negotiated positions in relation to various normative frameworks do not necessarily point to contradictions—rather to ways in which African journalists construct their own professional identities in response to changing conditions of practice. As African journalism practices are increasingly infused with global philosophies and ideologies, and African media institutions are integrated into a globalized media landscape, African journalists have to balance globalized assumptions with the expectations and imperatives of the societies in the developing world within which they work.[58] As a result, the role of journalists in developing countries such as South Africa is "complex, sometimes contradictory."[59] In these junctures between global influences and local imperatives, where professional values taken on board from international contexts interflow with local histories, lived experiences, and political pressures, values such as "freedom" and "responsibility"—so often assumed to have universal purchase—may be interpreted and operationalized differently. As Musa and Domatob state:

> At critical junctures, the fault lines in the perceived common ground between development journalists and their Western counterparts have been exposed. From the time of the anticolonial struggles of the 1950s and 1960s to the post 9/11 world, it has become obvious that when First World and Third World journalists say they are committed to truth, freedom, and the common good, they each have different understandings of these concepts or pursue them through different means.[60]

Indigenization of Ethics

The rediscovery of indigenous African values in relation to the media became an emerging normative discourse in the first decade after the end of apartheid in South Africa. As noted above, the South African media—especially when critical of the postapartheid government—was criticized for acting contrary to African values. In these critiques, the concept of *ubuntu*, as mentioned earlier, became a particularly popular one. Such moves to develop indigenous media ethics in the postapartheid environment drew on discourses developed elsewhere in Africa, as a result of increasing political pluralism and concomitant liberalization of the media in the 1990s. The greater freedom journalists started to enjoy brought with it questions about how they would take "responsibility for their unethical actions instead of blaming them on government."[61] Francis Kasoma's "Afriethics" was developed in an attempt to develop an ethical framework based on a strong sense of (religious) morality and communal bonds.[62] For Kasoma, the increased media freedom as a result of media liberalization made it all the more important for African media to remain true to its cultural and societal values:

> The urge to imitate the Americans and Europeans who introduced journalism into Africa—together with colonialism ... and evangelism—seems to have had much more influence on African journalists, than any sense of what would be appropriate, and right, in their own context.[63]

Kasoma stressed that media ethics should take heed of "the African approach to life" even if it does choose to include principles and values from elsewhere.[64] These values are linked to the material conditions within which African journalists work (e.g., poor pay that makes them susceptible to bribes)[65] but is also orientated toward the "family, clan and community" rather than toward the individual. Such a communal orientation, with consensus more important than a majority preference, would distinguish an African ethics from Western utilitarian approaches.[66]

Although Kasoma points out that consensus should not be mistaken for the uncritical support of national unity as imposed by governments, Tomaselli has pointed out the implicit danger in Kasoma's approach, which sees the media more as a "guide dog" than a "watchdog."[67] Attempts to construct or revalidate an African ethics may lapse into cultural essentialism and cultural exceptionalism, which sets African ethics apart from outside critique and serves the interests of an elite class.[68] Attempts to indigenize ethics often treat Africa as a monolith, glossing over complex social and cultural differences and presenting African culture in romantic, idealized terms, with little acknowledgment of how African cultures have been influenced by historical processes such as colonialism, nationalism, and globalization.[69] Fourie takes the critique of African ethics further, by arguing that the idealization of African values is out of step with a globalizing media environment, where diversity and pluralism, rather than static cultural norms, are valued.[70] Perhaps the most pertinent warning against an uncritical reappropriation of "African values" in postapartheid media ethical frameworks has to do with its implications for freedom of speech. As Fourie and Tomaselli have pointed out, using "African values" as a normative basis for media practice can serve as a strategy to dismiss criticism of government as un-African, unpatriotic, or disrespectful toward authority.[71]

These pitfalls do not necessarily mean that the postapartheid ethical frameworks should not have been subjected to rigorous criticism for not being adequately attuned to African social and cultural values. Such a reorientation should, however, avoid romanticized notions of African culture and instead focus on what democratic citizenship and empowerment would mean in a socially and politically specific context.[72] Any reappraisal of African values would therefore have to move away from anthropological notions of African culture as a specific way of life or traditions to instead account for the location of African within global flows and contraflows and the political economy of media in Africa that impose particular demands on journalists and audiences. In these everyday lived experiences, African media practice may differ from Western media practices in important ways that demand different normative frameworks and value sets. Such a recognition would, however, eschew constructions of Africanness as homogenous or African traditions as continuous and stable.

Professionalism and Social Responsibility

As discussed above, calls for the rediscovery of African values have developed into a counterdiscourse in South African normative debates. The imperatives of reasserting media freedom in a democratic environment, albeit one marked by increasing intolerance for criticism and renewed threats to freedom of expression, have led to the bolstering of notions of media professionalism as well as the resurgence of civil society movements aimed at ensuring the free flow of information.

Under the influence of global narratives of media freedom, journalistic professionalism, and democratic participation, South African journalists have laid claim to rights of freedom of speech, editorial independence, and the importance of robust critique. In espousing these rights, South African journalists found support in the interventionist strategies of "media development" or "media assistance" organizations and funding bodies from the North that have as their aim the capacitating of media in the South.[73] Underpinning the capacity-building activities of these organizations in Africa is the assumption that vibrant media will lead to more democratic societies—"media development" therefore becomes "subject to particular cultural and even political preferences."[74] The "political preference" of such nonstate actors involved in the promotion of media ethics in Africa ("through conferences, workshops and symposia"[75]) has more often than not been inclined toward liberalism, seeing the media as linked to individual rights and a free-market environment, and encouraging the professionalization of journalism.

The renewed attempts by the ANC-led government to clamp down on freedom of expression through measures such as the Protection of State Information Bill and the proposed Media Appeals Tribunal have also been met by a strong civil society response. Among civil society organizations, the most prominent grouping has been the Right to Know Campaign (R2K) that has been very active in organizing public protests and information campaigns aimed at strengthening the ability of citizens (including, but not limited to, the media) to engage in robust public debate and the unfettered access to information.

The challenge for both organizations aimed at media development and journalistic professionalism and civil society organizations working to ensure free spaces for democratic debate is to develop strategies that are contextually relevant and responsive to local political and social dynamics. In order to find a place to stand from which to criticize political and economic power, the media and civil society cannot merely adopt liberal values promoted by organizations in the Global North, but neither can they lapse into a romantic essentialism of "African values" that might render them politically impotent. This is an ongoing challenge. Initially, the press self-regulatory system in South Africa was based largely on media ethical codes centered on notions of freedom and social responsibility derived from the Global North. These values have frequently been contested within African media contexts, and government criticisms that the self-regulatory system has a tendency to orientate itself toward a media industry elite have not been without legitimacy. As was pointed out in the previous chapter, the ongoing debates about self-regulation have led to several rounds of revision to the Press Code and regulatory system and to a more robust and citizen-orientated system.

Perhaps the most important observation regarding the ongoing debates about the "Africanization" of media ethics and the attempts to "professionalize" media practices in South Africa comes from White.[76] He argues for an empirical approach to normative ethics in Africa that takes as its starting point not theoretical abstractions but an observation of journalists' reasoning and media practices. In the next chapter of this book, we will focus on one particular example of an emerging media practice in South Africa around which heated normative debates took place. The reasoning about tabloidization brought to the fore the often implicit normative frameworks informing journalists' reasoning and practices. The fact that the tabloid genre—imported from the North and localized in the South African context—was the cause of so much contestation again emphasizes that normative frameworks cannot have "indigeneity" as their only point of reference, but are linked to cultural flows and contraflows between Africa and the rest of the world in a globalized media landscape. Influences from Northern media ethics are adopted, adapted, and resisted in local contexts, and they take on new social and political meanings. These complex processes fragment any simple or monolithic understanding of African ethics. A global media ethics that seeks to incorporate perspectives from Africa would need to be cognizant of the full complexity of media ethics on this continent and take into account how media ethics are operationalized and interpreted in everyday journalistic practice.

CHAPTER 5

Global Genres and Local Context

What Controversies around Tabloidization Tell Us about South African Media and Society

In the previous chapter, the ongoing normative debates on South African media were discussed. The major points of focus were the seemingly opposing discourses of "global/universal" media ethics versus an "African" media ethics. In that chapter, some of the conflicts that arose from different interpretations of what the media's role in postapartheid society should be were also highlighted. It was concluded that global influences are localized in African contexts, and that the local application of global norms are best discerned in the discursive strategies of journalists. In this chapter, the discourses around values and norms are analyzed through the prism of the emergence of a particular style and format, namely tabloid journalism. In the debates around tabloidization, we see the norms around what journalism in a young African democracy should be played out in an environment marked by the twin pressures of commercialization and globalization.

The emergence of tabloid newspapers in the post-apartheid media landscape brought to the surface many of the implicit assumptions about the media's role in the democratic society. Linked to this phenomenon, although much less clearly identified, is the influence of tabloidization on media in general.

In this chapter, the rise of tabloid newspapers will be discussed in relation to the normative debates that we have tracked in the book thus far. The chapter will also refer to recent case studies of mainstream news reporting to indicate how tabloidization as a process has affected journalism beyond tabloid newspapers as such to become a much more generalized phenomenon.

PART II: LOCAL CONTESTATIONS

The Rise of Tabloid Newspapers

When the first South African tabloids burst onto the local media scene roughly a decade after the end of apartheid, they immediately evoked a strong response from media commentators, mainstream journalists, and the broader public. Their bold style, lurid content, and colloquial language were widely decried by those aligned to the mainstream media. The tabloids were seen as undermining the standards of "good journalism" and exploiting their audience by feeding them entertainment and sensation, thereby diverting their attention from serious news and political debate.

The tabloids, however, soon proved to be a runaway commercial success. Such was the impact of these papers on the newspaper market, that the phenomenon received international media coverage and reference was made to a "tabloid revolution" underway in the country.[1] The *Daily Sun* soon took over the prime position as most-read daily newspaper in the country and seemed to buck the trend of declining newspaper circulation at least in the first few years of its existence. The paper's circulation grew by 228 percent in the first year of its existence.[2] In 2008, it sold 500,000 copies a day but was read by 3.8 million readers, due to a high pass-on rate.[3] In recent years, newspaper circulation declined steeply across different titles, and the *Daily Sun* was not spared; however, it still remained on top of the list of daily newspapers, with a total circulation of 273,746 in the fourth quarter of 2014.[4] Other tabloids emerged around the same time, such as the *Kaapse Son* and *Daily Voice*, aimed at a more regional market in the Western Cape.

What made the commercial success of these tabloids socially significant was that they spoke to a readership market that had until that time been neglected by the postapartheid commercial press. The *Daily Sun* in particular targeted a Black working class, the "man in the blue overall," as the late publisher of the *Daily Sun*, Deon du Plessis, famously referred to the average reader.[5] Through a combination of a low cover price and content relevant to the daily lived experience of this readership, the tabloid managed to create a mass readership of a poor and working class, but upwardly mobile and aspirational, section of the Black majority of the country. The *Daily Sun* impacted negatively on the circulation of the *Sowetan*, a mid-market paper aimed at a Black readership and which was the biggest circulation daily in the 1990s.[6]

The introduction of tabloid newspapers to the South African media landscape also signals the extent to which the South African media became more rapidly enmeshed in processes of globalization and "glocalization." The South African tabloids took their cues both in terms of visual presentation and content from their counterparts in the United Kingdom. South African tabloid journalists received consultation from their counterparts at British "red tops" who were flown to the country to give pointers. The rise of this format can, in this regard, be seen as part of the wider interlocking trends of commercialization and tabloidization that have come to be considered one of the key prisms through which we have to view the future of journalism.[7] The media industry in South Africa became an increasingly commercialized one after 1994, manifested by cutbacks in staff, less investment in costly investigative journalism projects and the concentration of ownership into a few hands.[8] The globalization of the tabloid genre and its influence on African journalism can, for instance, also be seen in the rise of tabloid television in Zambia.[9]

However, South African tabloids also adapted the tabloid format to suit the local context. The content of these local tabloids may be presented in an equally sensationalistic and colorful fashion, but the nature of the stories they cover are very different from anything that can be found in U.K. or U.S. tabloids. The debate that ensued in South Africa in response to the rise of the tabloids also pertained to local shifts in the media industry and the media-society nexus that were particular to the time and place of these tabloids' emergence.

The Panic about Tabloids

Despite creating a mass market of newspaper readers almost overnight (although some of these readers migrated from other publications like the *Sowetan*), the new tabloids were not universally welcomed in South Africa. A vigorous internal contestation around journalistic standards and ethics ensued, not unlike similar debates that took place elsewhere in the world.[10] Tabloids were decried for their focus on sensational topics, entertainment news, and the supernatural. They were accused of flouting conventional norms like objectivity, neutrality, and truth-telling through their sensationalist, opinionated, and seemingly far-fetched stories. Feminist critics accused them of objectifying women through their pictures of scantily clad or topless women and fascination with sex. SANEF, media monitoring groups (like the Media Monitoring Project and Genderlinks), and media academics on various occasions lashed out at them for bringing the profession of journalism into disrepute and undermining the human rights culture of the new democracy. At its annual general meeting in 2005, SANEF held a special debate about whether tabloid editors should be allowed to hold membership in the organization.[11] Berger's dismissal of these papers as "not really newspapers," "junk-journalism," and "opportunistically" populist[12] is representative of the dominant view among mainstream academics, journalists, and commentators at the time.

Although these concerns showed similarities with debates elsewhere in the world, the emergence of the South African tabloids within the context of a young democracy meant that these questions also had implications for the negotiations about the role that the South African media should play in a new society and mediated public sphere. In addition to the moral questions raised in these debates, the debate about media standards therefore also had a political dimension. Tabloids were criticized for diverting their audiences away from politics to entertainment, and for depicting the working-class subjects of their stories only in terms of social pathologies of drugs, crime, and violence.

The debates about media standards took on another dimension in South Africa as they occurred at a time when the normative frameworks for journalism were undergoing revision in relation to the evolving relationship of the media and the new democracy. The question was therefore not only *which* standards were the most appropriate for the new democracy—those of the mainstream media that insisted on rational debate, dispassionate reporting, and "serious news"—but also *whose* standards those were and *where* they came from. Were they, in fact, universal, as the proponents of "professionalism" insisted, or were they linked to the specific interests and tastes of the South African elite? Was the strong reaction from the establishment against the tabloids' style and approach rooted in an unwillingness to engage equally with issues and events that reflected the lives of the Black majority working class and poor? In other words, can we read the criticism against tabloids at least partly as a confirmation of Friedman's point that the South African mainstream commercial media still favored the experiences and worldviews of a suburban, largely White, constituency and that this orientation also underpins the dominant norms and standards to which newspapers are held?[13]

A noteworthy element of the criticism against the tabloids was the view that these newspapers were representative of a kind of media globalization that would have detrimental effects on journalism's role in a young, African democracy. In other words, not only were the familiar tropes of media imperialism employed to critique the perceived deleterious influence of tabloids, but the media imperialism thesis was reinvigorated by linking it to the consolidation of the new South African democracy. For instance, Manson decried the local adoption of a "sick British model" that went against the values of "our democracy,"[14] while Berger, lamenting the fact that South African journalism was making "a lot less impact on our transitional society than it could," criticized the adoption of "Fleet Street's tabloid-style fictionalizing

Chapter 5: Global Genres and Local Context

and sensationalism," which "does not make for a valued model of South African journalism."[15]

It is true that the South African tabloids prefer a personalized approach to politics rather than coverage of formal political institutions and processes (the tabloid *Die Son* famously had a slogan "we don't do politics, but we do politicians"). But this is not to say that the content of South African tabloids is devoid of politics. Because these publications present the perspective of the poor and working-class majority of the country that remain marginalized in most print media, they also offer news as it affects those communities. They should not be mistaken for authentic, grassroots publications and remain tied to the commercial imperatives of the conglomerates to which they belong—to some extent they do practice the same "ventriloquism of the masses" that characterizes the popular press throughout history.[16] However, these tabloids have managed to gain the trust of the communities on which they report to the extent that readers report a close identification with these publications as representing their daily lived experience.[17] Because of the trust that communities vest in them, tabloids often obtain exclusive stories ("scoops") ahead of their mainstream rivals. An example that illustrates this is the case of the Mozambican immigrant Mido Macia, who, in February 2013, was dragged behind a police vehicle and later died in custody. This police brutality came to light when a bystander sent cell phone footage to the *Daily Sun*, who then ran the story that was picked up by newspapers locally and internationally.[18] The stories the tabloids report on are often harrowing and certainly not only frivolous or entertaining. The criticism that these papers divert their readers' attention away from politics is therefore not valid. However, they report what can be called a politics of the everyday—highlighting the political significance of the daily lived experience of their readers. Reports about violence, drug abuse, and social problems that beset poor communities are unsparing in their detail but show the precariousness of life for the majority of South African citizens.

Although the new tabloid newspapers were singled out for bringing in foreign, sensationalist, and commercial influences into South African journalism, their emergence was at least partly the result of the opening up of the postapartheid South African media industry to global cultural influences. Tabloidization can be seen as linked to wider processes of globalization and commercialization that have also impacted on other sections of the South African media since the end of apartheid. Already in 2002, a Skills Audit commissioned by the South African National Editors' Forum, brought to light increased commercial pressures and demands, resulting in, among other things, the juniorization of staff and deterioration of skills.[19] A decade later, a State of the Newsroom report found that the media landscape in the country continued to undergo major transitions, largely as a result of the development of new media technologies that had a disruptive influence on media business models and journalism practices.[20] As the industry continued to be impacted by a tight economic climate, wide-ranging retrenchments, early retirements, and attrition were symptoms of a relentless commercial pressure, while new technologies increased the demands on journalists to multitask and upskill.[21] These pressures often resulted in media coverage that was aimed at drawing bigger and more lucrative audiences within a highly competitive local and international market. Processes such as tabloidization should therefore be seen as more widespread than a particular set of newspapers and as resulting from the repositioning of the South African media within a rapidly changing landscape marked by new technological advances, economic pressures, and ongoing sociopolitical change. Although these processes played out in the local media, they cannot be seen as divorced from bigger global shifts. Some examples of local news stories that made global headlines in recent years will illustrate this.

Media, Tabloidization, and Postapartheid Society

Three South African news events in recent years stand out for having received extensive coverage in local and global news media. The Marikana massacre, where workers at the Lonmin mine in North-West province clashed with police, leading to the deaths of 36 mineworkers and two police officers and injuries to 78 others; the arrest and trial of the athlete Oscar Pistorius on a murder charge; and the hospitalization, death, and funeral of former president Nelson Mandela. The Pistorius trial and Mandela's funeral can be classified as "media events" in Dayan and Katz's definition[22] (as respectively "contest" and "coronation"[23]) while footage from the Marikana massacre—while not filmed live in its entirety—became a reference point as a significant disruption in the postapartheid narrative of democratic deepening and the consolidation of human rights. The subsequent Farlam Commission hearings into the massacre would, in addition, constitute a media event of the "contest" kind in that it was intended to reinscribe social cohesion and judicial legitimacy during what became a political crisis.[24]

The related concept of "media spectacles," a feature of consumerist societies and characterized by the commodified representations found in globalized, commercial media, is useful to understand the representation of the abovementioned and other major news events in South Africa that found global resonance.[25] While the notion of "media events" remains a relevant point of

Chapter 5: Global Genres and Local Context

departure, Couldry and Hepp argue for an extension of the concept that "takes account of consumer and celebrity cultures,"[26] which can include: the media's obsession with celebrities (evident from the extent of the coverage of Oscar Pistorius's trial); "disaster marathons," where oppositional discourses compete with hegemonic ones for central attention (to an extent applicable to the relatively long attention span devoted to the Marikana massacre and its aftermath); and the translocal nature of contemporary media cultures (especially evident in the coverage of Mandela's death and funeral), which are all characteristic of media events in a globalized age.[27]

A closer look at each of these three examples will illustrate how the coverage of these major South African news stories, within a globalized media context, took the form of global media events, understood in the broader way outlined earlier—that is, media events that were marked by commercialization, commodification, and tabloidization at the same time as they became spaces for contestation between hegemonic and oppositional news narratives, in translocal spaces.

These three news events can furthermore be taken as illustrations of key trends with regard to the way the South African media is positioned in relation to political life and society, into its third decade of democracy:

- The South African media emerging as a political role player in its own right, with the print media, especially, favoring an elite orientation
- Commercialization and tabloidization
- The globalization of media across new media platforms and channels

In the remainder of this chapter, I discuss each of these trends—which sometimes interlock—that mark the state of the media. These trends also loosely correspond with Zelizer's typology of the "changing faces of journalism."[28] Zelizer contends that the "platforms" of technology, "truthiness" and tabloidization, provide us with entry points into thinking about the future of journalism. If we consider the elite orientation of the print media within the South African context as foregrounding particular truths of the postapartheid South African reality, similarities may be sought with the contestations around truth and reality that mark postmodern media representations in other contexts as well, and which have given rise to the notion of "truthiness."[29] The tabloidization of print media, both in terms of the emergence of new tabloid titles as well as the changes in tone, approach and style of established media, clearly relates to Zelizer's identification of tabloidization as a platform through which to understand the ways in which journalism will continue to evolve. Globalization is a key trend impacting on postapartheid South African media and is in turn closely linked to technological advances such as the spread of internet access in the country, the growth of digital satellite television and the penetration of mobile phones. Let us look at these trends individually.

Media as a Political Role Player

In the postapartheid period, the South African media displayed less overt political parallelism than in the apartheid years, when support for or opposition against the ruling National Party regime largely coincided with the different languages of mainstream media (Afrikaans media being largely supportive, English media adopting a liberal critique), while a vibrant alternative, anti-apartheid media also existed. The arrival of democracy brought a greater professionalization of the media, which included the adoption of press codes that emphasized notions of "objectivity" and "balance," and the assertion of press freedom and independence. From the outset, the democratic government and the media displayed divergent expectations of the media's role in a democratic society, leading to frequent clashes.[30] These tensions continue well into the postapartheid era, with new threats to freedom of expression, such as the proposed Protection of State Information Bill and Media Appeals Tribunal, as discussed in previous chapters.

Although the media in the monitorial role of surveillance of power often claim to be an objective onlooker on political events, especially when their freedom is threatened (for instance by invoking the defense not to "shoot the messenger"), their actual practice often reflects a closer alignment to power.[31]

In the coverage of the Marikana massacre, it became clear that the majority of mainstream news media in South Africa tends to privilege an elite perspective on events of political and economic importance. From the massacre emerged one of the iconic media images of recent years: a row of armed police officers, shooting at approaching miners. The first footage broadcast internationally was shot literally from behind the backs of firing police officers.[32] This vantage point of journalists from the point of view of those in a position of power is further underscored by the emergence later of facts—brought to light first by an investigative journalist for the nonmainstream news website *Daily Maverick*—that the initial reports gleaned mostly from "official" sources were incomplete at best,[33] and perhaps they even obscured much more brutal acts on the part of the police.[34]

Despite frequent claims to neutrality, news media in the postapartheid era have emerged as political role players in their own right. As a rule, the South African media does not openly endorse specific political parties (although there have been exceptions during the first 20 years of democracy, such as the *Financial Mail* under then editor Peter Bruce backing the United Democratic Movement in the 1999 elections). The South African Broadcasting Corporation (SABC) often stands accused of being pro-ANC and allowing political interference at the broadcaster. Support for particular parties, however, most often takes an implicit form, for instance, keeping certain issues on the news agenda or giving more prominent space to the voices of certain constituencies. This is not only the case with the commercial elite media—the *Daily Sun* tabloid also made its support for Jacob Zuma clear ahead of the party's elections at Polokwane in 2007, although it did not openly declare for Zuma.[35] Subsequently, this and other tabloids have taken somewhat of an oppositional stance to the government, for instance by paying extensive attention to community protests. A tabloidized, commercial approach to big media events should therefore not necessarily be seen as apolitical in nature.

Mostly, however, the way that the mainstream commercial print media performs a political role lies in the way it selects and presents—frames—issues, namely from an elite, middle-class perspective. The truths of the South African reality portrayed especially in the print media therefore remain partial. This is due in part to the political economy of most commercial media (with the exclusion of the mass-market tabloids, serving big working-class audiences, on a different economy of scale), which tends to favor lucrative audiences that are attractive to advertisers.

In addition to the economic reasons for the mainstream media's inclination toward middle-class audiences, the liberal-democratic consensus among these media, in accordance with the dominant "watchdog" normative role, also inclines them toward adversarial political coverage of government. While a critical stance toward government would be in keeping with this monitorial role, as described by Christians et al.,[36] in South African political journalism, this usually translates in practice into support for the opposition political parties. Among these, the Democratic Alliance as the official opposition receives the lion's share of airtime and page space. Previous research has indicated that journalists also see their own roles in terms of providing a type of informal opposition toward the hegemony of a dominant ruling party.[37]

The confluence of the political economic imperative, as well as the role-orientation of South African journalists toward opposition parties, results in a mainstream commercial media (again with the exception of the tabloids) where the dominant voices are those of elite sources.

To return to the example of the Marikana massacre: in his research, Peter Alexander found that journalists paid very little attention to accounts of the events of the massacre alternative to those given by mainstream sources. He explains this in an interview with Mandy de Waal:

> What was apparent to me on both Saturday and Monday, when the ministerial group was there, was that journalists just stand around but don't really investigate or speak to any of the workers.... The journalists interacted with the politicians, the police and sometimes with AMCU (the Association for Mineworkers and Construction Union) or NUM (the National Union of Mineworkers). But there are hardly any accounts of events from people who were on the mountain when the massacre occurred.[38]

The voices that the South African media consumers kept hearing in the initial reports about Marikana were those of people in authority. In her analysis of the sources consulted by journalists at mainstream South African newspapers (*Business Day*, the *Star*, the *New Age*, the *Citizen*, the *Times*, *Sowetan*, *Beeld*, *Die Burger*, *Mail and Guardian*) in the run-up to and the immediate aftermath of the Marikana massacre (August 13–22, 2012), Jane Duncan found that workers were used as sources for information in only 3 percent of the stories.[39] The majority of sources were business (27 percent), mine management/owners (14 percent), political parties (10 percent), government (9 percent) and the police (5 percent). A commissioned study by the media analysis company, Media Tenor, over a longer period, from August 24 to September 19, found that only 15 percent of the sources in reports related to Marikana had mineworkers as their sources. Politicians and trade union officials made up the bulk of the sources, with mining management given the same proportion of coverage as sources than the mine workers (15 percent each). The highest volume of coverage came from *Business Day* newspaper. This paper was more critical of the events than others and focused on the economic impact of the unrest. The alignment of mainstream journalists with "authoritative" sources in positions of power led Duncan to dub the South African media's coverage of the Marikana massacre the local version of "embedded journalism."

The mainstream media's adversarial stance toward government can also be noted in the coverage of the hospitalization and later death of former president Nelson Mandela. Mandela's illness and death provided opportunities for the media to lash out against the current president, Jacob Zuma, and negatively compare the current government with the one that Mandela had led:

> The more Mandela is idealized, the more Zuma's (not inconsiderable) faults are progressively magnified. Whereas Mandela is lionized, Zuma by contrast, is reduced to caricature, to the embodiment of everything wrong with

South Africa. It perhaps goes without saying that neither of these portrayals is wholly accurate or completely rational in nature. This dynamic reflects something of the country's speculation on its own identity. It represents also the country's inability to bring together what is best and worst, what is most inspiring and most dismaying, in our recent history. One is reminded of the resentful words Oliver Stone puts into Richard Nixon's mouth in a scene from his (1995) film *Nixon*. Staring with bitterness at a portrait of Kennedy and wondering why the American people loved the younger man so much, he laments: "When they look at him, they see themselves as they want to be; when they look at me, they see themselves as they are."[40]

The tensions between the mainstream media and the government, and the political implications of this tension, therefore show no sign of abating. It could also be argued that the elite print media exaggerate the importance of formal politics in people's everyday lives. A recent study of media use by the youth suggests that the importance of mediated politics in young citizens' lives may be overstated.[41] If there is one section of the South African print media that understands that it is the experience of everyday life, rather than formal politics, that constitutes the "political" in the lives of the majority of South Africans, it is tabloid newspapers.

Commercialization and Tabloidization

As mentioned earlier, the emergence of tabloid newspapers almost a decade after democratization in South Africa has been one of the most interesting developments in the postapartheid media landscape.

The fact that these tabloids were vilified by the professional media establishment despite their commercial success and unprecedented popularity among those audiences who felt marginalized by mainstream media suggests that the dominant normative standards of South African journalism are set and controlled by a societal elite. Journalists in mainstream media tend to consider themselves members of a profession and because of their background and social position may not share the lived experiences of those whom tabloids report on. Their professional ideology of independence, detachment, and "objectivity" also inclines them negatively toward the sensationalism, overt emotionality, and garishness that characterize tabloid journalism. As mentioned above, the sensational approach of the tabloids also regularly led to criticism that they divert their audience's attention away from serious news and politics toward emotional responses to events.

Such objections against the tabloids are, however, based on a narrow view of what constitutes political discussion and underestimated the importance of emotional engagement and passion in political debate in the public sphere. As Dahlgren remarks, "traditionally, passion is conceptualized as distinct from reason, and viewed as functioning in opposition to self-control."[42] This binary opposition between emotion and reason translates in the media context to a binary between "serious" and "tabloid," or even between "news" and "entertainment." The divisions often indicated in newspapers between "news," "features," "politics," "entertainment," "sports" and so on, obscure the overlaps between them and ignore the way in which "entertainment" can also be political, or the way in which moral outrage against the abuse of power, and critiques of authority, can be present in humor and laughter. Literature on tabloid culture has often drawn on Bakhtin to compare the characteristics of tabloid media with the carnival, where laughter, bad taste, the spectacle, and offensiveness were used to subvert hegemony.[43] Similarly, tabloid media's highly personalized, subjective, and emotional approach can be read as resistance not only to societal and political authority, but to the very authority of institutionalized media norms that represent elite views and tastes.[44] Counter-perspectives, however, highlight that these tabloids can also reinforce some patterns of social domination, especially when viewed from a gendered perspective.[45]

The journalism establishment gradually softened its stance toward tabloids, perhaps on account of their huge commercial success. The Standard Bank Sikuvile awards (previously the Mondi Shanduka award) for print journalism, awarded by Print and Digital Media South Africa, now include a category for "popular journalism." Although arguably working to entrench the view of tabloid journalism as distinct from "real" journalism like investigative and feature journalism, this formal recognition of good tabloid journalism is a far cry from the initial denigration tabloid journalists had to endure from their colleagues. This growing recognition of tabloids as a now entrenched part of the South African media landscape might also be a response to what has become a global trend, according to Zelizer.[46] She identifies "tabloidization" as one of the central "platforms of inquiry" through which to understand changes in journalistic orientations and practices globally. In a global context, where traditional forms of journalism are increasingly under threat, tabloidization has been considered by some observers as a way to enhance the traditional print and electronic news media. While tabloidization is frequently associated with "trivialization, celebrity gossip and human interest stories," it is also often used as a scapegoat onto which mainstream journalism can deflect its challenges and shortcomings.[47]

That the binary between "serious" news and tabloids is a false one, and should in the South African context rather be seen as a continuum becomes evident when considering the way in which news events are selected and covered by mainstream media. Tabloidization as a trend, especially as it relates to a greater commercialization of not only the commercial print media but also broadcasting (including the public broadcaster) and the electronic media, is increasingly a key feature of the South African media in the postapartheid era.

Of the above-mentioned recent media events, the coverage of the Oscar Pistorius case most clearly displayed these trends of tabloidization. Media purported to analyze Pistorius's killing of his girlfriend within a broader societal context (for example, by attempting to understand Pistorius's personality, his motivation, or what the event told us about gendered identities and roles in South Africa), but the cumulative effect of the massive amount of coverage generated by the event was that of a media spectacle that drowned out other important political stories, like the launch of Mamphela Ramphele's new political party Agang that occurred at the same time.[48] In this regard, the Pistorius case could be seen as an illustration of how the notion of the "spectacle," as conceived by Guy Debord and developed by Hardt and Negri,[49] operates. The spectacle can be defined as an "integrated and diffuse apparatus of images and ideas that produces and regulates public discourse and opinion":

> In the society of the spectacle, what was once imagined as the public sphere, the open terrain of political exchanges and participation, completely evaporates. The spectacle destroys any collective form of sociality—individualizing social actors in their separate automobiles and in front of separate video screens—and at the same time imposes a new mass sociality, a new uniformity of action and thought.[50]

Although some media reports attempted to locate Pistorius within the broader context of a violent, patriarchal, and macho South African culture, the reason why the story received (and would continue to receive) such immense global interest was Pistorius's individual profile as a sport star of global renown. The effect of the spectacle around Pistorius was that the killing of Reeva Steenkamp came to be seen in terms of an individual's misdeed, dislocated from the broader societal scourge of gender-based violence. The Commission for Gender Equality criticized this style of reporting as presenting Steenkamp's death as "an unfortunate aberration, rather than part of a broader pattern of gender-based violence in South Africa."[51] In other words, reporting the killing of Reeva Steenkamp by her boyfriend as the Oscar Pistorius Spectacle encouraged South Africans to remember that "they are not Oscar and that Oscar isn't them."[52]

PART II: LOCAL CONTESTATIONS

This type of tabloidization of the South African media that reports broader societal problems as individual pathologies is arguably more damaging to democratic debate than the popularization of journalism in the form of tabloid newspapers that can enlarge the public sphere and make previously marginalized sections of the society feel included as citizens in media debates and representations—even while such representations are not without their problems.[53]

The coverage of former president Nelson Mandela's illness also at times demonstrated this type of tabloid sensibility. Although one could argue that the media attention focused on the former president's condition was rooted in the universal love and admiration for Mandela, the coverage sometimes did take the form of a morbid "death watch," with journalists camped on a "stakeout" outside the hospital where Mandela was being treated.[54] This minute-by-minute coverage of Mandela's illness was lambasted by his daughter Makaziwe as "violating all boundaries" of his and the family's privacy and dignity, and she accused the foreign media in particular of being "racist" and "vultures."[55] Parallel to the coverage of the former president's hospitalization, considerable media interest was generated by the feud between the Mandela relatives about the reburial of the former president's relatives, which would have implications for the gravesite of the statesman, and in turn for the potentially lucrative deals that may be struck around the site. The distasteful family wrangling was denounced by Archbishop Tutu as a selfish tarnishing of Mandela's name,[56] but the feud, and the media attention to it, showed no signs of abating as Mandela lay critically ill in the hospital. Indeed, Schechter's statement was true: Nelson Mandela's final battle was to die with dignity.[57] In turning his illness and death into a spectacle, mainstream media coverage often became indistinguishable from tabloid fare.

The Globalization of Media across New Media Platforms and Channels

The media events listed in this chapter all extended beyond the confines of South African media to a translocal space. The Marikana massacre, and, to a lesser extent, its aftermath in the form of the Farlam Commission, the Pistorius case, and Nelson Mandela's illness were all covered by major global news media. While this global attention sometimes exacerbated the jockeying for position by local news actors (for example, members of the Mandela family showing preference for coverage of their father's funeral by CNN rather than by the SABC, because the former would presumably be more lucrative[58]), it also meant that South African audiences with access to global media via satellite television or the internet could now choose from a bigger range of perspectives on stories of interest to them. The downside of this global coverage was that it exerted intense pressure on local news outlets to compete with much bigger global news industries, with increased tabloidization and commercialization of news agendas and approaches being the almost inevitable result.

While local audiences do not uncritically consume global media but interpret global content within the specificity of their local context, the influence of global media styles and genres on local media production is undeniable. At the level of ownership as well as content, the former media giants from the "West" are lately receiving competition from their counterparts in the "Rest."[59] Chinese media are spreading their influence across Africa. In South Africa, this includes a stake by a Chinese consortium in the Sekunjalo group's purchase of the Independent Newspapers group, as well as extending the distribution network of their English-language newspaper, *China Daily*, in South Africa. Despite the sometimes alarmist terms in which these developments have been viewed, these developments should not be seen in terms of crude "media imperialism" theories but rather in the light of South Africa's own repositioning in relation to changing geopolitics, as well as its membership of the BRICS group—a relationship that will increasingly be mediated.

Perhaps the biggest downside of the increased globalized nature of South African media is, however, the further marginalization of minority voices and grassroots news that may not be considered attractive or important enough in a media landscape that is increasingly dominated by big players—South African players included. To some extent, the tabloid newspapers and community radio stations still counter this commercial dominance, but they are also hampered by problems regarding funding and sustainability. Ironically, the global reach, ease of access, and affordable production opportunities afforded by new media have also given rise to web-based publications like the *Daily Maverick* and *GroundUp*, which provide much-needed alternative perspectives on news.

In all these cases of the global interpenetration of media that has reshaped the South African media in the postapartheid era, technology has played a key role in broadening the reach of media and creating new opportunities for interaction and user-generation of content. It should, however, be borne in mind that access and use of media technology is still divided asymmetrically across the South African population.

The next, and final, section of this book will look in more detail at South African media's location in a translocal, globalized media space. In this section, the global shifts that impacted on local media, often resulting in increased and new forms of contestation, will be discussed.

CHAPTER 6

Rethinking Global and Local

South African Perspectives on the "Future of Journalism"

A book focusing specifically on South African media runs the risk of being classified under "area studies," as an isolated case study located outside the more familiar discourses about media in the Global North. The stated focus of this book—on local contestations and global shifts—is meant to be understood as interlinked. South African media is first meant to be understood as heterogeneous, contested, and fractious, and then as being located within a broader global context marked also by heterogeneity, difference, and power struggles. This chapter uses debates about the "future of journalism" and the notions of a global "crisis" in journalism as a point of departure to argue for an approach to South African journalism that is aligned with recent calls for a new way of doing global journalism studies.

In the previous chapter, the introduction of tabloids into the South African media landscape was used as a case study to illustrate two points about the relationship between global shifts or trends and local contestations and debates. It was pointed out that the arrival of tabloids in South Africa resulted from both local and global developments. First, the tabloid format is a globalized one, with a long history in the West. The continued popularity of tabloid genres can also be seen as one of the key prisms through which to view the future of journalism globally.[1] The South African tabloids were clearly modeled on their international counterparts, even though they were strongly localized in terms of content, language, and approach. Their success in the South African marketplace was also related to specific local factors other than content. These local factors included the demise of the erstwhile alternative print media, the rise of a new, socially mobile Black readership, and the continued marginalization of perspectives of these readers in the mainstream print media. The link between global shifts and local contests can also be seen in the debate about media standards in South Africa, which was reignited when tabloids came onto the scene. Claims by dominant stakeholders in the media industry to uphold standards that were perceived as conforming to a global professionalism came up against counterclaims that those norms represent the interests of a specific local elite, which cannot be taken to represent all perspectives in South African society.

Another question that was raised by the emergence, and especially the unprecedented success, of these tabloids was to what extent the South African media market deviated from global trends as a result of particular local exigencies. While newspapers were seen to be in crisis globally, and the future of journalism was called into doubt, tabloid newspapers in South Africa rose to prominence and popularity. Years after their establishment, tabloids remain a strong feature of the South African print media market even if their circulation also shows signs of slowing down. In this chapter, the questions about the relationship between the local and the global in South African tabloids are extended to apply to the South African journalism landscape more broadly. These questions include: To what extent can current global notions of "journalism in crisis" be applied to the South African media landscape? How should we understand South African journalism within a global context? How can the study of South African journalism be included in a study of global journalism trends and shifts without reducing it to a case study to support theories developed elsewhere? How should we conceive of "local" and "global" journalism(s) in a globalized era of interlinkages and interrelationships? How is South African journalism located within debates about "the future of journalism"?

Notions of "Crisis" as an Example of a Universalizing Discourse

The current debates taking place internationally often assume that journalism is in "crisis," that the end of journalism is nigh and that emergency measures have to be taken to rescue journalism from an otherwise inevitable decline.[2] Zelizer cites several pessimistic studies with "predictions of widespread doom" arising either from failing business models, the changing nature of audiences and disillusionment of the youth with traditional models and platforms of journalism.[3]

These predictions about journalism's future are instructive for the questions in the last section, precisely because they tend to assume a universality when thinking about "crisis," even as they include international perspectives. As Zelizer points out: "the notion of crisis that has prevailed among many observers rests on particular temporalities and geographies at the core of its imaginary."[4] Such a conception of the current state and future of journalism globally, she argues, loses from sight both the contingencies and differences between different futures of journalism.[5] Therefore, more nuanced responses than a uniform "repair" of a simplified notion of crisis are required—starting with a different definition of uncertainty and change that does not present a crisis that needs to be solved by returning to normality and routine, but by "confronting the internal noise, incongruities, inconsistencies, and local situated particularities" that make up the contemporary journalism landscape and to understand crises as potentially "transformative turning points."[6] These discourses of "crisis," which the current climate of uncertainty and change has given rise to, are also linked to a particular "Anglo-American mindset" about what journalism should look like and how it should function in a democracy.[7] As such, particularly important when journalistic crises are discussed, is to acknowledge that "crisis has different drivers in different locations."[8] In the South African context, the rapid changes that the media landscape has undergone as a result of the country's opening up to global media markets, the rapid technological advances that have caused middle-class audiences to migrate online, and the shifting and often testy relationships between media, society, and state can all be seen as such transformative drivers that create moments of challenge and "crisis." Yet, as has been discussed in previous chapters, these confrontations, challenges, and crises can all be seen as part of the journalistic paradigm still taking shape in the country, even as old ways of doing are often defended and attempts are made at repairing old paradigms.[9] The South African media has not been immune to the storms raging in the global media landscape, and locally this turmoil has also resulted in cutbacks, contractions and a consolidations landscape.[10] But despite the similarities between the challenges faced by South African media (especially print) and their global counterparts, the local media environment is not merely a carbon copy of the global one. The atmosphere of uncertainty in the South African media landscape is exacerbated by political turmoil and ongoing normative debates, as Harber and Krüger point out in their preface to the 2014 South African *State of the Newsroom* report:

> This turmoil is a global phenomenon as newsrooms take on the challenges of new technologies, but it has distinct local characteristics, particularly because

of the on-going demands of social and political transformation needed to create a media which can best serve democracy and deal with the legacies of apartheid.[11]

Furthermore, the trend in South African media has not only been a downward one. In parallel with the decline in mainstream, commercial print media, there has also been a noted expansion of offerings in especially the broadcast and community print media sector—adding to the diversification of the South African media that has been a problematic aspect since the advent of democracy (see Chapter 1 of this book), as well as a recurring criticism leveled against the media by the ruling party.[12] Some of these shifts—such as the acquisition of Independent Newspapers by the Sekunjalo consortium and the work of the MDDA to support community media—have already been noted in preceding chapters of this book. In this chapter, the focus falls on how these and other developments in the local media landscape prompt us to think about how journalism in the South African context is situated at the nexus between the local and the global. The historical, social, political, and economic specifics of the South African situation militate against an uncritical and universalizing application of notions of a "crisis" and the "future of journalism" to the local context. While these trends do find some application in the South African situation, they do so in ways that follow other, more complex trajectories than merely a replication of global trends. The questions asked by Waisbord have relevance here: "What is the relevance of talking about 'journalism in crisis' in regions where journalism has been in perpetual 'crisis' amid economic unpredictability and political instability?" and "Do trends [such as the perceived decline and "crisis" of journalism—HW] have the same intensity and impact on journalism and news? Are they driven by similar causes? What explains the different changes in journalism across countries and regions?"[13]

"Crisis," "Future," and Global Journalism

While local specificities are important to note when thinking about South African journalism in relation to these global trends, the other extreme of parochialism should also be avoided. Recent scholarship has seen the rise of calls for a global approach to journalism that takes account of the growing global interconnectedness and reflects an awareness that certain problems and issues require a global response. Berglez, for instance, argues for a global journalism that emphasizes interdependencies and interrelationships on a global scale.[14] Other commentators, such as Robertson and Silverstone have pleaded for a morality underpinning global media that would forge connections between "us" and "them" in a way that would foster greater identification with a global Other.[15]

Berglez's argument for journalism that is more global in its outlook stems from his assessment of the global media as having become globalized in their scope and focus, yet still narrow in their perspective and approach. In other words, the media still tends to present news from a domestic perspective—events from "elsewhere" are either newsworthy because they can impact on "us," locally, or they remain distant events that can be consumed by audiences as spectators but remain at some remove from their daily lived realities. Berglez therefore argues for a type of global journalism that emphasizes the links between "here" and "there" and journalists that can explain the relevance of news events and processes on "all of our lives."[16] His is a warning that the media is not doing justice to the complexities and importance of our new, intertwined global reality—marked by global crises such as terrorism, nuclear threats, and climate change—and are therefore missing out on the opportunity of contributing to a more global democratic culture.[17]

The growing international scholarly discourse on mediated cosmopolitanism and global media ethics supports Berglez's view that a global outlook on journalism should entail more than merely more international coverage.[18] Adopting global journalism as an epistemology and a practice would require a fundamental shift in the way journalists think about news events—not as "domestic," "international," or "foreign," but as "global" and interlinked.

How would this be relevant for South African journalism? There are certainly many issues covered in the South African media that could benefit from a more global approach, especially given the increased geopolitical shifts and connections already remarked on earlier in this book. For instance, the increased involvement of China in South Africa could pave the way for more investigation of the interrelationship between these countries in managing poaching, while the effects of climate change on Africa call for reporting that looks at the interdependency of the Global North and the Global South and their respective locations in the global political economy. Approaching journalism in this way would require journalists to not only adopt a new epistemological framework through which to think about the intersection of the local and the global, but also to acquire skills, knowledge, and resources to make these connections. This, in turn, has implications for training and education of journalists.

The global journalism envisaged by Berglez and others would be especially appealing to news consumers in the Global South, who too often remain the objects of reporting rather than the subjects in their own narratives. It should pave the way for a more immersive, ethnographic approach to journalism that strives to understand societies in depth, rather than parachuting in when big news events occur. But most of all, the kind of global journalism that Berglez proposes—if asymmetrical power relations and the political economy of global news production are also addressed—will put the Global South on a more level footing with the North when global news events are framed. This kind of global journalism should no longer treat the South as providing the raw material or "case studies" for the news narratives determined by the North, but engage the South as coproducers of news narratives.

The question regarding a more global outlook on journalism is directly related to the overall focus of this book, namely the ways in which the South African media have changed in the democratic era as a result of both global shifts and local contestations. The challenges facing South African media in the postapartheid era certainly have much to do with the major political and social changes that have prompted the South African media to reconsider its role, values, and norms in relation to the changing society. But as has become clear from the outline of various developments such as the interpenetration of local and global media formats and capital (the Sekunjalo deal, the rise of tabloid media, the global expansion of Naspers, and the rise of online media—to be discussed in a later chapter), a primarily localized or parochial understanding of the changes that the South African media continues to undergo would be insufficient. But this point leads us to an even larger question, namely how the repositioning of South African media in the democratic era can serve to illuminate a broader need for a revision in the field of journalism studies itself. The debates about the "future of journalism" have suggested that journalism scholarship globally usually takes its cues from the Global North. As Berglez's argument has suggested, however, contemporary journalism studies cannot be satisfied with parochial or nation-based approaches.

Intentions to de-Westernize media and journalism studies by including perspectives from outside the European and American context should be recognized—the classic among these is Curran and Park's *De-Westernizing Media Studies*, but subsequent works in journalism such as Wahl-Jorgensen and Hanitzsch's *Handbook of Journalism Studies* have also sought to include case studies from the South. There is, however, a growing realization that these attempts to diversify the scope of journalism and media studies are still premised on the nation-state or geographic regions as units of analysis, and that this configuration may already have become too static to deal with a dynamic global news environment where issues—climate change, terrorism, the global economic downturn—are not in the first instance nation-specific but have to do with the interrelationship between countries, regions, and supranational formations of power. Even the notion of "transnational" news becomes problematic because it uses the nation-state as a basis for comparison, in the face of arguments that supranational organizations or regional regimes have eroded the significance of nation-states,[19] or that nations are not homogenous internally.[20] New paradigms of interconnectedness, which also acknowledge older, subordinated histories, such as the growing field of "Indian Ocean Studies," might suggest the way forward. Moorthy and Jamal have argued that while "area studies provides the close-ups," a paradigm such as Indian Ocean studies allows us to "pan out" and "mediates between the expansive homogeneity of the global and the minutiae of the local in its rooted particularity."[21]

When questions around a global "crisis" of journalism and the future of journalism practice and journalism studies are considered, the challenges facing scholars are twofold. First, the globalization of media and the growing interrelationship between various regions of the world through such media necessitate an approach to journalism that emphasizes connections, interdependencies, and global challenges. The work on global media ethics in recent years is a good example of how a specific area of journalism studies has responded to the globalization of media. Similarly, the journalistic work that followed on massive data leaks like the Wikileaks information dump and the leaking of the so-called Panama papers in 2016 has shown how investigative reporting can "join the dots" between events "there" and political implications "here." A South African example of this would be the inclusion of Khulubuse Zuma, nephew of South African President Jacob Zuma, in the list of names revealed by the leak of the Panama papers. Khulubuse Zuma was implicated in a questionable and lucrative oil deal in the Democratic Republic of the Congo (DRC) that was allegedly made possible by President Zuma's visit to the DRC's President Joseph Kabila. Local political patronage, regional power relations, and global information leaks come together in the journalism following on the Panama Papers leaks.[22]

Yet to merely celebrate the emergence of such global journalism practices—while highlighting interconnections and interdependencies and providing a framework through which to think about global challenges such as terrorism, climate change, financial crises, and corruption—could fall into the "world is flat" trap,[23] in which globalization is celebrated for the connections it creates but less attention is paid to its attendant inequalities and power relations. The second challenge of thinking about the future of journalism practice and journalism studies in the current global moment, especially when such thinking is done from the Global South, is to avoid succumbing to simplistic views of the world as simply having shrunk or of media globalization as having created a level playing field for journalists and audiences around the world. This utopian notion is especially seductive in the study of new media technologies and their supposed "revolutionizing" impact on journalism. For a genuinely global journalism studies to be developed and become established, teaching and research in this field have to escape the "epistemological essentialism" that still continues to mark a field that, despite some laudable efforts to include global perspectives in the field of "international journalism," remains embedded in the European and North American theoretical and methodological traditions.[24]

There have been some laudable and important efforts to include global perspectives.[25] The limitations of these contributions have often been that they collect case studies from outside the Global North without necessarily using the input emerging from these case studies to challenge the dominant theoretical assumptions of journalism studies, such as the relationship between journalism and democracy, the normative foundations for media ethics or the relationship between technology and society. Even when global perspectives on theoretical debates are acknowledged as necessary, the impression may be (albeit sometimes unfairly) created that the "global context" was added as an afterthought[26] or inadvertently awarded a marginal position to the developed world.[27] Of course, the problem is compounded by political economic reasons, i.e., the lack of access by academics in the developing world to international conferences or shortages of funding to conduct extensive surveys in Southern contexts. Whatever the reason for good intentions not coming to full fruition, the danger remains that the North will continue to provide the theoretical narrative for the field of journalism studies, while examples from elsewhere are used to provide local color, as it were, to serve as evidence for the theoretical argument made by the North. This is tantamount to what Shiva referred to as "the West as theory, the East as evidence."[28]

The result is that dominant debates in journalism studies still largely center around challenges and dilemmas faced in the Global North. For instance, around the time that the debates about the "crisis" in journalism started gaining momentum and the death of newspapers was widely heralded, the print media continued to grow or at least sustain itself in developing markets in Asia and Latin America,[29] and South Africa saw a tabloid newspaper explosion.[30] Although South African print media, including tabloids, have since seen a decline in readership as has also been the case internationally, this has not always been equally precipitous, and other local factors (such as lack of affordable access to online media) play an important role in these dynamics. The point is that experiences in the Global North are often too easily extrapolated and universalized to become the hegemonic perspectives in the field.

In turn, contributions from journalism studies in the South have often been bound to national contexts, and even when contributions from the South reach international journals and conferences they often fail to impact on central research agendas or theoretical frameworks. Too often, the result remains a "panorama of the field" rather than a coherent attempt to revisit central epistemological and methodological assumptions on the basis of the diverse range of experiences uncovered.[31]

There have been some important exceptions. Löffelholz and Weaver's collection makes a call for journalism research across national, cultural, and disciplinary boundaries, and engages with fundamental epistemological and methodological questions.[32] Thussu's collection on the internationalization of the broader field of media studies takes perspectives from the developing world and emerging democracies seriously on a range of aspects pertaining to media studies, which include challenging the disciplinary location, research methods, and pedagogy of media studies.[33] The hosting of the 2nd World Journalism Education Congress in Grahamstown, South Africa, in 2010[34] was also a historically significant event in terms of creating a presence for Africa on the global journalism studies calendar.

Weaver and Löffelholz's assertion that "journalism research can no longer operate within national or cultural borders only"[35] is an important one and has to be reflected at the level of journalism teaching and scholarship as well. Too much of global journalism studies remains at the level of well-intentioned but broad panoramas and vistas from afar without allowing such views to permeate back to the foundations upon which journalism studies rest. The teaching and research of journalism studies needs to become genuinely global in a way that is inclusive, self-reflexive, and participatory. Attention to local contexts such as the South African one is important to provide correctives on assumptions derived from the North and then universalized—but these local contexts should also be recognized as themselves being heterogeneous, contested, and diverse. Regional perspectives are useful as a way to escape from nation-based perspectives collected in a panoramic fashion, but such regional perspectives should again allow for contestations, differences, and specificities within them. Moreover, the relationships and interdependencies between countries, regions, and other parts of the world need to come into play in analyses of global journalism, instead of collecting individual case studies with the assumption that together they can provide us with a full picture. As stated elsewhere, the study of South African journalism and media should ultimately be aimed not at providing material to support Northern theories but to contribute to the development of theory and methodologies in its own right, not merely to slot into global research agendas but to help shift the assumptions and question that underpin these global agendas.[36] Such an undertaking requires a contextual embeddedness in order to understand journalism as a set of values and practices that cannot be divorced from sets of power relations, steeped in history and intertwined with very specific economic and political struggles. As Waisbord reminds us, the approach to media in regions such as Africa as distinct "areas" for study is a remnant from the Cold War—"an imperialistic approach that envisions the world in countries and regions as distinct and manageable units of analysis. It embodies a vision that separates academic knowledge into distinct geopolitical units and different from the 'universal' theorizing supposedly conducted in the West."[37] Instead, Waisbord argues—as does this book—for an understanding of the specifics of countries and regions "within existing debates and lines of inquiry," to "position a specific local/national/regional study within a broad debate in the field."[38] Such an approach would square with the idea of a critical global journalism, in which the local and the global are seen as mutually interdependent and provide a perspective from which notions of the "future" and "crisis" of journalism could be considered more holistically. What would such an approach look like?

The Foundations of Critical Global Journalism

Just as "international journalism" is not conceptually rich enough to capture the interconnected practices of journalism in the contemporary global mediascape, the inclusion of "international journalism" as a separate and distinct field of teaching and scholarly inquiry is not an adequate response to the challenge of globalizing the field of journalism studies. What is required is an orientation that takes into account the varied and multiple ideologies, practices, and institutions of journalisms around the world, yet seeks interconnections and comparisons between them. Instead of treating them as marginal cultural curiosities or, conversely, succumbing to cultural relativism in which different sets of practices are uncritically accepted in the name of diversity, journalisms outside the dominant centers of scholarly production should be engaged with robustly. In the domain of research, this means engaging with journalisms other than those practiced in North America and Europe on an equal theoretical footing and not only as examples or illustrations of journalism "elsewhere." In teaching, this means that merely including a module on "global journalism," or even a course in "international reporting" is not enough but that the reorientation toward the global should place across the curriculum.

The new challenges facing journalism in an interconnected world have not rendered all old questions obsolete. The perennial question of inequities in global communication—perhaps most classically represented in the MacBride report,[39] continue to be examined, for instance, in the World Summit on the Information Society meetings held in 2003 in Geneva and 2005 in Tunis, and a WSIS+10 review meeting in December 2015 at the UN headquarters in New York. Global inequalities of access and use therefore need to be at the center of debates about the "the future of journalism." A critical global journalism would emphasize how, despite the current global mediated moment highlighting some radically new questions, long-standing debates have not lost their relevance overnight even though they might have to be rephrased. The complexity of contemporary global journalism demands new approaches to global media inequalities that no longer understand the world in terms of centers and peripheries like in the days of the New World Information and Communication debates, partly as a result of the rise of regional media centers.[40] More critical observers point to the ways in which these globalized media "continue to reproduce the hierarchical relations of race, gender, and nation articulated in Euroamerican colonial ideologies."[41] Critical global journalism studies would therefore resist easy belief in the myths that media globalization, aided by the spread of digital media technologies, necessarily equals communicative equality.

The inequalities caused and/or exacerbated by uneven globalization do not, however, take the form of a neat North/South bifurcation. Severe inequalities also exist between elites and the poor within countries of the "developed" world and within the "developing" world. Because of the hegemony of English within the international field of journalism studies, English-speaking scholars from the South (e.g., South Africa or India) may be privileged over 'Northern' scholars from non-English-speaking countries such as Romania or Portugal. A critical global journalism, based on the principles of interactivity and participation,[42] would therefore continue to explore ways in which the dominant globalization paradigm might offer ways for journalism to facilitate global social change not only in the South but also in situations of inequality that persist in the Global North. This would require the development of a theory of global journalism for social change that goes beyond earlier paradigms such as modernization, imperialism, or empowerment that tended to be based on a core-periphery view of global communications.[43]

The rapid development of digital media technologies offers contradictory and complex perspectives on global journalism.[44] For some observers, these technologies provide the opportunity to overcome the old divisions between mediated centers and peripheries, providing vehicles for contraflow, hybridity, and glocalization. For others, these technologies exacerbate the global divisions between centers and peripheries and widen the divide between them. A critical consideration of new media technologies should therefore be central to the study of global journalism, as well as its pedagogy. The potential of digital media technologies to facilitate greater participation and multidirectional communication has been seen by cyber-optimists as a way toward greater empowerment of and participation by those people who have formerly been constructed as the objects of news reports.[45] In global journalism terms, this has been taken to mean greater empowerment of the developing world. This includes Africa, where access to and appropriation of digital media technologies have been on the increase to the extent that the continent "can no longer be blindly characterized as sitting on the cusp of the digital revolution," despite many obstacles still in the way.[46] The internet and related platforms are fraught with contradictions that have complicated rather than solved global media inequalities,[47] and therefore their application for journalism and appropriation in everyday life and broader citizen engagement have to be understood contextually, as Mabweazara points out: "By exclusively using Western yardsticks to assess developments in Africa, we inadvertently run the risk of glossing over issues of vital concern to local contexts and experiences. This has dire implications for the conclusions reached and for broader efforts to closely understand digital practices and cultures in Africa vis-à-vis elsewhere."[48]

In view of these power relations within which global journalism remains embedded, a critical global journalism will therefore not simply collapse the "local" into the "global," but will have to find new ways of critically relating the local and the global, via the national and the regional. One approach to this conundrum is the notion of "critical regionalism," which is a way to reconceptualize the notion of the "local" as dynamic and changing. A critical perspective on regions such as (southern) Africa, and their location in power relations and struggles, "shifts the emphasis away from the products of regional culture to the processes by which ideas about regions come into being and become influential."[49] Critical regionalism offers a new way of looking at the local—as complex, dynamic rather than static, enmeshed within larger regional geographies, yet not collapsed into or subsumed by them. Such a perspective would avoid thinking about "Western," "African," or "Latin American" journalism in any monolithic fashion. A critical regional perspective would resist thinking about the globalization of media as a one-directional, imperialist force emanating from the Global North and instead paying attention to local appropriation of globalized formats such as tabloid newspapers[50] or 24/7 infotainment outside the Anglo-American world.[51] Such analyses would, for instance, look for signs of hybridity or glocalization in the way that global formats are appropriated and adapted for local contexts.

A critical regional approach to global journalism would also seek to encourage greater comparative work within regions of the Global South. As a result of the often violent and tumultuous national histories of countries in regions such as Africa or Latin America, scholarly attention in these regions has often been directed inward to national media and its relationship to state and society. But global shifts in the communication landscape will demand that comparative studies of journalism in rising regions such as the BRICS formation[52] or "Chindia"[53] become imperative.

Critical studies of journalism in the global context, viewed from the perspective of those on the margins, are important not only for those scholars and researchers located in the Global South. The experiences of the periphery can highlight the limits of the dominant assumptions about journalism in the center[54] and so may contribute to the de-Westernizing or internationalizing of media studies[55]—even while for those on the periphery, media and cultural studies have always been involved in a process of negotiations between local experiences and global epistemologies.[56]

What implications might such an approach have for journalism education and scholarship?

Teaching Global Journalism

The case has been made thus far in this chapter for a critical global journalism studies as a response to radical shifts in global journalism practices, institutions, and professional ideologies. The need to rethink journalism studies, not only in terms of scholarship but also on the level of pedagogy, also arises as a result of changes in the global higher education landscape. Thussu, writing from a position in U.K. tertiary education, remarks on the popularity of media studies with students from across the world, who have become increasingly mobile and seek higher education at universities outside their own national context.[57] These students can enrich classroom discussions with a diverse range of views resulting from their different backgrounds. However, they will also demand that curricula shift to accommodate their experiences and perspectives and validate their understanding of journalism. In some respects, the response to student demand for tertiary education in the United States or United Kingdom may be seen as a commodified response to the neoliberal globalization of higher education. Foreign students routinely pay higher fees than "home" students, and market considerations may often be the driving force behind "international journalism" courses in these metropolitan centers. Universities in the developing world, on the other hand, are drawn into international collaborations and exchange programs with universities in the North, which brings an influx of foreign students into developing world campuses and vice versa and also bringing with them increased revenue. The political economy of these global flows in tertiary education notwithstanding, the coincidence of the current commercializing moment in global higher education with the shifts in global journalism practice may contribute to the evolution of journalism studies to "truly reflect the landscape of a globalized and interconnected planet."[58]

While the march toward further commercialization of the international student market seems to be unstoppable, a wave of student protests against rising fees resulted in the shutdown of South African universities at the end of 2016. The #FeesMustFall movement prompted a serious engagement with questions around the commercialization of higher education in the country and raised questions around the "decolonization" of the curriculum in general. These demands included the broad discipline within which journalism studies are taught in the country, namely communication studies, and questions of curriculum reform also permeated the debates at the annual conference of the South African Communication Association (Sacomm) held in Cape Town in September 2015. The South African student protests were followed by similar protests in the United Kingdom: students at Sheffield University protested the marketization of higher education; students at Jawaharlal Nehru University in Delhi, India, were arrested for "anti-Indian" slogans; and students in Oxford—like their counterparts in Cape Town—demanded the removal of a statue of the colonialist Cecil John Rhodes. The student protest movement, while responding in the first instance to highly localized power struggles, therefore received global resonance. We will return to the #FeesMustFall movement in a subsequent chapter, when the use of social media by student activists will be examined as an illustration of how the media landscape in South Africa is changing and as an indication of what the future of media and politics in the country may hold.

The demand to understand all journalism as global journalism in this sense does not mean that the local becomes unimportant—on the contrary, the local attains even greater importance as its global resonances are explored, and as the local is also embedded in the regional. This reorientation in perspective requires that global journalism becomes a dimension of the journalism studies curriculum as a whole, i.e., that all subjects are taught with some global dimension. Let us look at some suggestions where this can be done.

Political Economy of News. The debates around the "future of journalism" referred to earlier tend to be characterized by alarmist tones. Although there have been participants in these debates from outside the European-American axis, the panic about the imminent death of newspapers especially has been informed largely by the situation in the North.

A study of the political economy of journalism in various regions would be one area where a global approach to journalism might complicate or undermine dominant assumptions about "global" trends regarding convergence, the death of print, and the failing of existing business models for journalism. A closer study of the political economy of news in other parts of the world may expose these assumptions as less universal than they may claim to be. However, a global journalism approach to the political economy of news would not see the news industry in these localities in isolation, but as part of complex interconnections between localities, regions, and transnational movements of capital. For instance, knowledge of the specific local historical and political circumstances surrounding the South African media's reentry into the global media landscape after apartheid (for instance the relationship between Independent's Tony O'Reilly and Nelson Mandela, or Naspers's ideological repositioning after its former association with the apartheid regime[59]) is required to understand the interpenetration of media capital in these multinational companies.[60] Similarly, the rising influence of China in the African mediascape (which will be dealt with in more detail in the following chapter) has introduced new sets of political-economic power relations that could alter the course of journalism on the continent in ways that may not be replicated in the parts of the Global North on which projections about the "future of journalism" are predicated.

While these specifics of the political-economic context in the South should be taken seriously in order to arrive at more diverse projections about the future of journalism, trends in conglomeration and concentration that do have global resonance are equally important to understand in terms of how the transnational flows of capital can impact localities.

Such a structural study of the interdependence as well as the variances between news industries worldwide on a macro-level should, however, be complemented by closer attention to the micro-picture of localities, which requires a more cultural, ethnographic approach to news and its audiences.

Audience Studies. The characteristics of a critical global journalism included an emphasis on the differential power relations between various points of access and consumption of global news around the world. These power relations emerge from a closer look at how journalism practices, institutions, and ideologies are manifested within their specific contexts, and how global structures are negotiated and contested within local settings. To achieve such a critical understanding of global journalism, a structural study of the political economy of news and its future is not enough. While political economy approaches to global journalism can provide a structure for the way transnational flows of capital are interconnected around the world, it requires a more detailed contextual complement in order to establish how these economic conditions—about which alarmist speculation currently abounds in the field of journalism studies—actually influence journalistic practices, attitudes, and patterns of consumption around the world.

Equipping students of global journalism with the methodological skills developed in sister fields like cultural and media studies might help them understand the everyday practices of and relationships between journalists, citizens, and institutions in contexts that differ from theirs or from those usually highlighted in journalism textbooks. Anthropological approaches and ethnographic methods become especially pertinent to address questions in underresearched areas of global journalism in the Global South in order to build theory inductively. Because postcolonial or postauthoritarian regions have historically seen much conflict between journalism and governments, the prism through which journalism in these countries has been viewed has largely been that of freedom of speech and independence from state interference. These concerns remain important in many areas of the world. But too often, this view of journalism in the globe's regions becomes a debate about citizens without citizens, limited to a clique of professional journalists, academics, and advisors. Berger points out that the issue of audience studies was largely ignored by the political economy orientation of the NWICO debates.[61] Critical global journalism in the age of the internet would need to take account of how audiences are now able to relate much more directly to global news content, e.g., via social media platforms or citizen journalism. Furthermore, the way in which audiences outside the Global North interact with journalistic tools and platforms in their everyday lives—for instance, through mobile phones rather than through fixed-line connections, or integrated into oral networks, or as rituals aimed at increasing social capital in a modernizing environment, and so forth—may be very important to problematize dominant assumptions about journalism's role in society and to understand the different ways in which individuals, communities, and national publics are interconnected in the global journalism landscape.

Ethnographic audience studies are also important to understand the much-vaunted potential of the internet to create a global public sphere in which citizens from around the world would be able to participate. The internet has undoubtedly shifted conceptualizations of news audiences. Rusbridger provides a vivid illustration of how the newspaper he edited at the time, the *Guardian*, has grown from a predominantly British one to a trusted global news brand to the point where its online version ranked higher against its global competitors than its print version ranked against other U.K.-based newspapers.⁶² Although the *Guardian*'s increased global audience has turned its journalists into "unintentional foreign correspondents,"⁶³ the link between having a global audience and providing genuinely global news content or taking global angles on stories is not always self-evident. As Berger observes, news websites in the United States often provide only internal links and have a largely national character even if they have a global audience.⁶⁴ The effect is the internationalization of national (e.g., U.S. or U.K.-based) news to a global audience rather than the emergence of a truly supranational public sphere. Users' ability to personalize news preferences on web browsers may further contribute to the filtering out of international news, thus amplifying the existing parochialism in Northern-based news production.⁶⁵ Exactly how audiences outside the global centers of production make meaning—decode locally what has been encoded elsewhere—can properly be established only through ethnographic studies. Such consumption would, however, be considered against the background of the political economy of global news as mentioned earlier, for, indeed, "meaning is made in the context of certain constellations of power."⁶⁶

Journalism, Democracy, and Development. Apart from the prism of "press freedom," other favorite tropes through which global journalism discourse engages news contexts outside the dominant Anglo-American world are those of "development" and "democracy."

Globalization poses new questions for thinking about development journalism. The old models of center-periphery approaches to development are being challenged by the emergence of rising powers like China, India, Brazil, Russia, and South Africa, which at first glance indicate the potential for "developing" countries to successfully navigate global markets to their advantage. Yet internally in these countries, huge inequalities persist (South Africa and Brazil being two of the most unequal countries in the world). Media technologies such as the internet and the mobile phone have vastly increased the opportunities for journalists in the developing world to participate in a global conversation. Yet the neoliberal, unequal globalization of the media industry continues to set terms and conditions that limit the range of options of what can be said in that conversation. For some (e.g., Thussu⁶⁷), the spread of infotainment is an example of how the global media industry has hollowed out journalistic narratives; while others have pointed to the clamor of glamour and lifestyle reporting that drowns out the voices of development journalists trying to make the voices of the poor and the marginalized heard. The Indian journalist Palagummi Sainath provides a vivid example to illustrate how establishment journalism in the developing world buys into the Western narrative of countries like India as "shining examples" of liberalized trade in the global marketplace, while hiding or ignoring globalization's underbelly: in the same year that 512 journalists were accredited to cover a gigantic Fashion Week in India in 2006, a total of 1,520 cotton farmers committed suicide because the price of cotton has been destroyed by global trade policies, which include subsidies for U.S. and E.U. farmers.[68] Yet not a single correspondent of that country's mainstream media has a full-time beat to cover labor or poverty.

The dimension of "development," and its relation to "democracy" and "press freedom," would be important components of a critical global journalism studies characterized by goals of inclusiveness and diversity. But here, as in other focus areas of global journalism studies, it would be important to challenge assumptions of "development" and the role of journalism within democratic debate, as these have been shaped by the normative assertions of journalism studies in the North. Alternative ways of viewing "development journalism" against emerging (and in themselves limited and problematic[69]) paradigms of globalization should be explored. Such exploration would, as in other dimensions of critical global journalism, be premised on finding the interconnections between journalism in the developing and developed regions of the world in ways that defy the easy and utopian visions of globalization as alluded to earlier.

Global Journalism Ethics. A critical, contextually engaged global journalism studies would not only interpret the global media landscape but seek ways of changing it for the better. An academic field that takes its responsibility in this regard seriously would therefore not be content with only descriptive or analytical studies of global journalism, but would construct an ethical response to the changing global media environment.

In an era where media platforms increasingly have a global reach, journalists' ethical obligations can no longer be understood simply in terms of local or national audiences.[70] The by now well-known example of the Danish cartoons in the *Jyllands Posten* that offended Muslims globally illustrates how what is seen as freedom of speech in a Western liberal democracy does not unproblematically translate to contexts of reception everywhere. The global reach of media also raises dilemmas for representation, e.g., how audiences relate ethically to the portrayal of distant suffering.[71] The complex questions raised by the multicultural nature of diasporic media within nation-states, as well as the sometimes conflicting interpretations of central ethical concepts such as "truth," "human dignity," "freedom," and "responsibility" across borders pose challenges for the field of journalism ethics that requires a global outlook, rather than an Anglo-American one masquerading as universal or well-meaning attempts to include examples of ethical thinking from "elsewhere" to fit an existing theoretical framework.

However, the answer does not lie in the type of counterreaction that offers an unhelpful dichotomy between "African ethics"[72] and "Western ethics." A crude "us" and "them" opposition could stifle free expression instead of opening journalism ethics up for debate.[73] Instead, attention should be paid to how journalism ethics is being negotiated or glocalized in local settings.

Even appeals for a moral cosmopolitanism and greater sensitivity for distant suffering brought closer to global audiences via primarily television[74] are often premised on the benevolence of a Western audience, people who are to be convinced that sufferers elsewhere are "like us" and therefore worthy of empathy.[75] A cosmopolitan outlook of this kind, however generous and kind in its orientation, is not necessarily a critical one, which engages the asymmetrical distribution of communicative power in a globalized world head-on; or if it is, the perspective is most often that of the media producer or user based in the Global North.

New Media Technologies. Previously in this chapter it was mentioned that the sense of the world as being interconnected is largely facilitated by pervasive new media technologies. These technologies should indeed be central to the study of global journalism today, but not in a mere pragmatic or deterministic way. Critics like Nordenstreng have warned against the "Nokia syndrome" in media studies, where technology dominates curricula to the extent that other communication phenomena are neglected or the study of technology is undertaken without sufficient disciplinary depth.[76]

As argued earlier, a critical global journalism would explore the interconnections between local and global news events, remain attentive to the asymmetrical power relations in the global news industry, and be based on the ethical understanding of collaboration and openness. As Berger observes, the way new media technologies enable extranational reporting of news requires us to rethink definitions like "local," "foreign," or "international" news.[77] He correctly observes that news stories are often hybrids of these different classifications, more so now that the internet has delinked the location of news producers, distributors, and consumers from the content of news stories.[78] News on the internet, he argues, counts simultaneously as all the variants of global, international, local, and other news.

Of course, it would be imperative for journalism courses aimed at equipping future journalists with the skills they will need in the contemporary converged newsroom to give students as much exposure to the technical aspects of using new media technologies. But it would be very short-sighted to imagine that technical skills are all that journalists need in order to flourish in a new global journalism landscape. Journalism courses that approach students as if they can continue to work as a distanced elite, professional class will have to make way for reflection on how journalism has become a more collaborative (or "mutualised"[79]) field of practice.

When considering the role of new media technologies in refashioning a form of global journalism, it should not be assumed that they are neutral tools in a technologically determinist way; nor should the use of these technologies be seen as universally normative for journalism practice everywhere. Instead, their use within global journalism should be reflected on critically.

A critical global journalism would have to incorporate the study of new media technologies not only on the practical level but on a more reflective intellectual level as well. Critical approaches to media globalization will puncture the often exaggerated and technological determinist views of the potential of new media technologies for the future of journalism by studying the use of these technologies within the overarching structural economic conditions as well as their actual everyday use. This would mean taking into account the enormous disparities worldwide regarding access to the internet, for example, but also the creative ways in which people in the South appropriate and adapt technologies to suit their various sociocultural and economic settings. Students in the South could be encouraged to find examples of such adaptations in their everyday lives and reflect on how such practices invite theorizations about the relation between new media and society that differ from those that dominate scholarly literature produced in the North—for example, how mobile phones are adopted in African societies,[80] how the Web is accessed via intermediaries,[81] or how new technologies are combined with traditional media by social movements.[82] Simplistic notions of how new media technologies can achieve the modernization of societies by "leapfrogging" over stages in a uniform trajectory to development will be discarded in favor of more nuanced, culturally informed approaches to the study of the implications of these technologies for the relationship between journalism and society in the developing world.

Conclusion

The contemporary global media landscape demands a critical study of how journalism practices and institutions relate to processes of globalization in a way that moves beyond older notions of communication between nation-states. A recurring point of focus in debates about the current status of journalism globally has been the facilitative role played by new media technologies. This chapter has argued that to understand the complex and often contradictory status of contemporary journalism, the study of new media technologies in global journalism has to be viewed as part of a multidimensional reorientation of the field toward the global. Such a reorientation should be *critical*—based on the scrutiny of the power relations inherent upon global journalism today—as well as *cultural*, in that it should be informed by an ethnographic approach to the everyday practices of and relationships between journalists, citizens, and institutions. For researchers and students of journalism, the challenge lies in contextualizing their own experiences of journalism against a wider, comparative background of similar contexts, which includes more specific attention to the Global South. If a sustained engagement between journalism studies of the North and the South, and within the regions of the South internally, could be achieved, tangible headway could be made in the internationalization of journalism studies.

PART III
Global Shifts

CHAPTER 7

BRICS and Beyond

Mediating New Geopolitical Relationships

In the previous chapter, we considered what a global journalism would look like in the light of the changing global landscape where interdependencies and interrelationships have become much more pronounced and explicit on the terrain of the media.

A central argument in this book is that the South African media provides a perspective on global media studies that emphasizes interdependencies and interrelationships. One such interrelationship and interdependency that has increased in importance, visibility, and controversy in South Africa in recent years is its membership of the BRICS grouping of states (Brazil, Russia, India, China, and South Africa) and, within that broader geopolitical arrangement, the country's relationship to China specifically. This chapter examines how the rise of these new geopolitical relationships impacts our understanding of global media and how the South African media's location within these new networks can be illustrative of the way that shifting geopolitics necessitate new approaches to global media studies.

Background: South Africa and BRICS

The emergence of the BRICS grouping may be seen as part of larger geopolitical shifts associated with the emergence of regions outside of the old Euroamerican centers of power—what Zakaria has referred to as the "rise of the rest."[1] These shifts are reshaping global media flows—in terms of content as well as capital and human resources—to the extent that a need for more comparative media studies has become clear in order to understand how these shifts may disrupt existing theories of media systems and international communication. Despite controversies about the analytical usefulness of the BRICS category (critics have pointed to the discrepancies in the sizes of the economies of the constituent member states, their different political and economic systems, and the fact that the member states are not only allies but also economic competitors), South Africa's claim to membership acknowledges its economic leadership on the continent (even though Nigeria has now overtaken it as the African country with the biggest GDP[2]). The South African government has proclaimed the country's membership in BRICS as advantageous not only for the country's economy but also for its potential benefits for the entire continent.[3] South Africa's membership in BRICS has, however, not only given the country a strategic advantage in terms of how it positions and brands itself (e.g., by hosting the BRICS summit in Durban in 2013) but has also prompted questions about how this new set of relationships will affect its own domestic and foreign policies. Among these new geopolitical relationships, the one between South Africa and China has become especially important and controversial from the perspective of global media studies. This is because this relationship has received the most media attention in comparison with South Africa's relations with all the other BRICS countries, and because it forms part of a much bigger engagement between China and Africa, but also because the relationship raised difficult questions about the influence it might have on media norms, freedoms, and practices in South Africa and more widely on the continent.

The strengthening economic ties between South Africa and China were confirmed when an invitation was extended to South Africa by China late in 2010 to join the (then) BRIC formation of emerging economies (Brazil, Russia, India, and China). When South Africa's membership of the BRICS formation is discussed, the focus therefore often falls on the country's relationship with China.

South Africa–China Relationship

China's increased economic activity in Africa has elicited much scholarly and journalistic attention. Popular media discourses have often cast the South Africa–China relationship in stereotypical, binary terms. The debates about China's presence in Africa have assumed the now familiar contours of asking whether China is a friend or foe, imperialist or ally.[4] While the media has often facilitated these debates about China's economic engagement on the continent in general, in recent years China's activity in the African media sphere in particular has also come under scrutiny. For the past several years, China has noticeably increased its influence on the African media space. Several state-owned Chinese media houses have established offices on the continent, especially in Kenya and South Africa. These media include the news agency Xinhua, the newspaper *China Daily*, China Central Television (CCTV), and China Radio International (CRI). In South Africa, flows and contraflows of private media capital have also included investments both in and by China, such as the South African company Naspers's investment in Tencent and a Chinese consortium involved in the purchase of Independent media (more about this later).

These changes to the (South) African media landscape are ripple effects from larger geopolitical shifts, and the reaction to the Chinese media's growing presence in South Africa should be seen against these broader movements. But the interrelationships between China and South Africa on media terrain should not only be seen as occurring on the national level—they don't bypass local political contestations, and the responses to Chinese media involvement locally can also sometimes be read as proxy controversies of what is in essence criticism of the South African government. We will return to this aspect later.

Issues that emerge from these developments, to be touched on in this chapter, include:

- The coverage of the China–South African relationship in the South African media
- The views held by South African journalists of this relationship and the influence these views may have on coverage
- The flows and contraflows of media capital and human resources between China and South Africa
- The influence of this relationship on journalistic norms and practices in South Africa and the continent
- The use of media as vehicle for Chinese soft power

These are broad questions that have formed a burgeoning research area in global media studies and cannot be treated exhaustively here. The purpose of this chapter is rather to indicate the contours of these debates, provide some preliminary findings of recent research into these areas, and indicate how they illustrate some of the broader points already made in this book so far about global shifts and local contests in the media.

PART III: GLOBAL SHIFTS

China's Media Footprint in Africa

Although the increased presence of Chinese media in South Africa constitutes a noticeable inward flow, other flows and contraflows between the two countries have also taken place in recent years. Perhaps the best-known example is the South African company Naspers, which has reaped handsome benefits from its investment in the Chinese social media and gaming platform Tencent. At the end of 2015, Tencent had 853 million monthly active users on their QQ instant messaging platform and 697 million users on the app WeChat, and a 56 percent market share of Chinese online gaming.[5] Naspers owns 34 percent of Tencent, its holding now accounting for more than Naspers's total market capitalization,[6] representing a steady rise over the past few years (Naspers's stake in Tencent accounted for 80 percent of the South African company's market capitalization four years previously[7]).

The purchase in 2013 of the South African–based newspaper group Independent Media (previously owned by the Irish Independent group of Tony O'Reilly, who acquired a group of English-language newspapers in 1994 in a deal brokered by former president Mandela) by the Sekunjalo consortium, raised controversies around China's influence in the South African media landscape, as Sekunjalo's purchase was funded in part by investment from a Chinese consortium (we will return to this purchase and the discourse surrounding it below).

These shifts in ownership illustrate the extent to which South Africa, like the African region as a whole, has not been excluded from the forces of globalization and their impact on media ownership, control, and content. The Chinese influence in South Africa and on the continent more broadly should therefore be considered against the background of ongoing flows and contraflows in the global media landscape. More specifically, the growing influence of China on the media landscape can also be linked to shifting geopolitical relations, which has seen China's rise as an economic power globally, and its desire to increase its "soft power."[8] Kurlantzick has pointed out strategic efforts by China to revamp its media platforms to aim at global audiences in order to achieve this goal.[9] The use of "soft power" to describe this process has been criticized by some researchers for not adequately capturing China's media activities. A focus on "soft power" as underpinning high-level, elite interests may also obscure the informal, everyday interactions between South Africans and Chinese migrants, which may even be more influential than formal policy in shaping public views of China's involvement on the continent. These views may, for instance, be shaped by popular conceptions of Chinese goods as inferior, Chinese migrants stealing African jobs, and outrage at the illegal trade in rhino horns that is widely seen as originating in China.[10] As Anbin Shi reasoned, China's activities in Africa's media terrain may be less of an active strategy to extend the power of the nation-state than a response to existing stereotypes, which are in part sponsored by the Western media.[11] Hence, Shi sees China's media activities as a "charm defensive" rather than a "charm offensive"[12] aimed at winning hearts and minds.

Bearing this bigger picture in mind, a study of the role of the Chinese media in Africa should therefore first not be seen as a one-dimensional form of "soft power," of which Africa is on the receiving end, but as part of ongoing processes of globalized flows and contraflows in which South African media are active participants. Second, these interactions should be considered not only on the level of media and geopolitics, but as part of a wider set of engagements between the two countries, which include formal and informal, political and economic, strategic and everyday interactions. As far as Chinese investments in media on the continent are concerned, South Africa has not been a major recipient of China's media assistance in comparison with other African countries. The reason may be that its media industry is relatively robust.[13] However, perhaps because of the strength of this industry and the vibrant debates within (and meta-debates about) the South African media sphere, the involvement of China in Africa has met with criticism from local commentators, ranging from everyday concerns about fake or inferior goods (the term "Fong Kong" to denote these goods has become part of the lexicon[14]) to criticism of media freedom by media and civil society circles. The Chinese stake in the purchase of the Independent by the Sekunjalo consortium in 2014 referred to earlier prompted renewed interest in the question of how China's involvement in the African media sphere will affect freedom of expression. This human right is particularly staunchly defended in South Africa in the postapartheid, democratic era (exemplified by the vigorous opposition against the Protection of State Information Bill (POSIB) by the civil society organization Right 2 Know). This is not only because of questions about China's commitment to the freedom of the press but also because Sekunjalo is headed by Dr. Iqbal Survé, who has close ties with the African National Congress (ANC) government (raising questions about the extent to which editors and journalists in the group will be allowed the freedom to criticize the government). Survé has already fired Alide Dasnois, editor of one of the newspapers in his group, the *Cape Times*, allegedly for running a front-page story about corruption involving the awarding of a state tender for fishery vessels to a Sekunjalo subsidiary.[15] Anton Harber's comment on the Sekunjalo deal resonates with a broader fear of a "perfect storm" in which

Chinese involvement in the South African media would combine with local pressures to threaten the freedom of the press:

> We can assume that this (funding from a Chinese consortium) is tied to the Chinese authorities, and their push for a greater media presence in Africa as part of their "soft diplomacy" drive for influence on the continent. The Chinese government, let us say, is not a friend of a free, open and critical media. They are very clear about their national interests, and their firm hand on ensuring their media interests serve them. One has to wonder what will happen when their national interest does not align with ours. This is relevant when Dr Survé has been so vocal about bringing ownership back home. One can safely say now that Independent Newspapers, the country's second biggest newspaper group, is in hands that are closely tied to our ruling party, the ANC.[16]

Global media flows (China's involvement in Africa and South Africa) and local political contests (between the ANC government and its critics) have therefore coincided in their efforts to push these questions to the fore. As Alden and Wu pointed out, the South African public's perception of their own government's interests and lack of transparency is also likely to be articulated in the resistance to state- or party-level engagements between South Africa and China, as this relationship is perceived as having the potential to exacerbate the South African government's failures.[17]

South African Journalists and Chinese Soft Power

If the Chinese media are seen as a key vehicle of their soft power initiative (or in Kurlantzick's terms, "charm offensive"), the success of this initiative will depend on whether it finds the audiences it seeks. In this regard, it may compete with local media outlets that may provide contesting frames of China's involvement in Africa. At the same time, China's global media platforms—especially the wire service Xinhua—could potentially serve as a source of news for local news organizations or at least constitute a new structural relationship with local news institutions that could shape media content.[18] The question then becomes how South African media have responded to China's media push on the continent. Would South Africa's newly forged relationship with China as the leading partner in the BRICS group pave the way for an increasingly positive attitude toward China? Would China's increased economic involvement on the continent lead to more coverage, and how would this involvement be framed? Do South African journalists use Chinese media as a source, and if so, where do Chinese media rank on the "hierarchy of influences"[19] on South African news agendas? How do local developments, especially perceptions of renewed threats to freedom of the press, affect the South African media's coverage of China? The assumption is that if South African journalists draw on Chinese media sources, they could help to amplify Chinese soft power initiatives that are exercised through its media. On the other hand, if South African journalists were skeptical about China's influence in South Africa on the continent and expressed doubts on how closer involvement by China in the media sector would affect the freedom of the press and journalistic norms, they would be likely not to draw on Chinese media sources in their work, and, consequently, Chinese soft power attempts would have a much smaller chance of success. Content analyses of South African media have already found that within the BRICS alignment, the South Africa–China relationship, followed by India, received the most attention from the media.[20] These findings are in line with previous surveys of public perceptions that view China as the country's most important trading partner and an example of how to alleviate poverty and unemployment.[21] These analyses also found that coverage of the South Africa–China relationship had been cautiously optimistic for several years, perhaps mainly because coverage tended to frame China's involvement in Africa in economic and political terms as a source of development opportunities rather than in terms that can be described as the "social" cost of these engagements, such as the issue of the freedom of the press.

Previous exploratory interviews with journalists indicated that while journalists were not unequivocally positive about the South Africa–China relationship, they recognized the importance of providing coverage regarding this geopolitical alignment. Previous studies also found that journalists started using Chinese media (especially Xinhua) as sources for their own understanding of the South Africa–China relationship. Some reports showed that exposure to these media helped journalists form a nuanced understanding of China's involvement on the continent and of South Africa's place in the BRICS group. These initial findings raised the question of the possible success, albeit in an embryonic stage, of Chinese soft power in the South African media environment, and that prompted further investigation.

A further, more extensive exploration of journalists' views on the South Africa–China relationship was needed to establish in more detail the following aspects:

1. Coverage: Journalists' views on the South Africa—China relationship in general within the context of the wider BRICS grouping and their views on the media coverage of this relationship

2. Norms and practices: Journalists' views on the meaning of China's media push on the continent and involvement in the South African media landscape might mean for current norms (e.g., press freedom) and journalistic practices
3. Media as vehicle for soft power: Journalists' views on the usefulness of the Chinese media as a source in their own work and the influence of such media on their conceptions of the China–South Africa relationship

Questionnaires containing 10 questions were sent to more than 100 journalists working in print, broadcast, online, and wire service media across media houses in South Africa. After several follow-up communications, a response rate of about 20 percent was achieved. Although the total number of responses (21) was fairly small, the responses to individual questions tended to be well articulated, and substantial qualitative information was provided. Moreover, the respondent sample spanned the whole range of media platforms, which provided an overview of the entire media landscape. The intention was not to arrive at a generalizable conclusion. Instead, the aim was to provide an overview of the main themes in the responses given by the journalists in order to obtain an indication of the issues of concern, range of attitudes, and major viewpoints pertaining to the three main aspects of the research question, as listed earlier: (1) coverage; (2) norms and practices; (3) media as vehicles for soft power. The following section provides an overview of the responses in each category.

Findings

COVERAGE

The questions in this category probed journalists' views on the South Africa–China relationship in general within the context of the wider BRICS grouping and their views on the media coverage of this relationship. The questionnaire first set out to establish the importance of the South Africa–China relationship because it was likely to influence its place and prominence on the news agenda. Second, this section of the questionnaire was designed to explore journalists' views of the existing coverage of the South Africa–China story in order to obtain their self-assessments of the media's stance. In general, the journalists characterized the South Africa–China relationship as "important," "strong," and largely based on economic concerns. Several respondents remarked on the unevenness of the relationship and China's dominance of it. The journalists' views confirmed earlier content analyses that showed a "cautiously optimistic" attitude.[22] For instance:

> My general view of SA's relationship with China is positive. China is politically and economically one of the most important players and it is to SA's benefit to expand trade and relations generally.

This attitude also included criticism of the media:

> I'm fascinated by it—there's a great deal of negative and borderline xenophobic reporting about it out there, so it's interesting to try and read between the lines and see what's positive, what's negative and what's a little bit in between.

However, the journalists' responses indicated cautiousness about not naively welcoming China's growing economic presence on the continent and South Africa's relationship with that country. Several journalists remarked on the potential economic benefits:

> Although we are both part of BRICS, the two countries are vastly different in terms of political economics, culture, etc. The relationship is really just business. China sees a market here, and also used SA as its gateway to the rest of the continent. It also wants to dictate terms, as we saw with the refusal to grant the Dalai Lama a visa to attend Bishop Tutu's birthday.

The respondent quoted above touched on a highly controversial issue not only with regard to what has widely been seen as Chinese pressure on the South African government not to acknowledge the Dalai Lama (who was again unsuccessful in obtaining a visa to attend a Nobel Laureate summit in Cape Town in 2014) but also, in broader terms, how the relationship with China would play out in South African policy making. Similar concerns were expressed about South Africa's cooperation with China on global affairs, particularly during its tenure as a nonpermanent member of the UN Security Council.[23] These affairs included the countries' positions on Myanmar, Zimbabwe, and Libya. Related to the issue of China's influence on South Africa's international relations is the potential influence on South Africa's domestic policies. Another respondent remarked on the question (often mentioned in academic and journalistic accounts of China's involvement in Africa) of whether China would uphold human rights in its African engagements—specifically how it would conduct labor relations. Other concerns expressed were the implications of stronger ties with China for the historical partnerships and trade agreements that South Africa has with the United States and Europe; local casualties, such as the textile industry that was "decimated" as a result of cheap Chinese imports; and China's power to dictate the terms of economic agreements.

The potential benefits were limited to economic matters. The journalists were much more skeptical about the political implications of the increasingly close economic relationship between South Africa and China. The responses expressed both caution and concern. One journalist expressed caution:

> I think it is something that needs to be watched closely. SA should learn economic lessons from China, but not follow them on a political and ideological level. South Africa should be careful not to neglect their relationship with the west. Good relations with the east, west, and Africa are essential.

Another journalist expressed concerns about the impact that uncertainties about South Africa's relationship with China might have on the markets:

> Perhaps a greater move to a more socialist society in South Africa. Considering around 45% of the new cabinet are senior members of the SA Communist Party this may already be happening. This may lead to further uncertainty in the investment and business sector in SA.

Overall, however, the journalists acknowledged that they were not certain about the political implications of the relationship, mainly because "one is not privy to high level meetings and what goes on behind 'closed doors.'" Although several respondents expressed that it was important for South Africa to remain vigilant about the potential political pressure that China may exert, the overall stance was that of circumspection rather than negativity. The wait-and-see attitude that pervaded many of the responses was summed by one respondent:

> In general? Very congenial at the moment. The relationship can be compared to young people that like one another and are waiting for that first kiss. It can be wonderfully or horribly wrong.

Despite the pros and cons of the relationship that were weighed in most responses, there was a consensus that the China–South Africa story should remain on the news agenda. One editor of a major national newspaper remarked:

> It is very difficult for any news corporation to be agnostic about China. China has also provided a new investment area for Naspers and it is good to know that new horizons are being explored, which might make cross-subsidies possible between business entities in the company and open up new spaces for other subsidiaries in the company.

Regarding the existing coverage of the South Africa–China relationship, the journalists were critical of the media's ability to portray the complexities and nuances of the evolving story. The media was criticized for providing a "shallow representation" based on secondhand sources.

Most South African media houses do not have bureaus or correspondents in China, and they sometimes convey xenophobic attitudes. One respondent also questioned the South African media's inclination to report only China's influence on other countries and ignore its domestic development. However, several respondents pointed out that it is not the South African media's responsibility to create a better image of China. Several journalists indicated that they tended to focus on political and economic stories or big news events instead of ongoing coverage or in-depth reporting on China. This finding may indicate that when other big foreign stories break regarding the BRICS countries, such as in Ukraine/Russia, the news focus shifts away from China. The responses also confirmed Park and Alden's distinction between the "upstairs" dimensions of new geopolitical relationships (i.e., economics and politics) in contrast to the "downstairs" dimension of social and cultural implications.[24] Moreover, the South African journalists acknowledged that they focused more on the former than on the latter. However, this focus may prove to be a failure on the part of the South African media in the long run because "un-orchestrated engagements" in the "informal and subtle spaces" of South Africa–China relations could also influence the formal relationship.[25]

NORMS AND PRACTICES

Related to these concerns about China's influence on the South African culture of human rights are the recurring controversies surrounding the meaning of China's increased media presence on the continent for the way in which journalism is conceived and practiced. Journalists were asked to reflect on the freedom of the press not only in relation to how the presence of Chinese media platforms may influence attitudes toward journalists on the continent but also how Chinese investment in local media firms (e.g., the Sekunjalo deal) may affect South African media norms, such as editorial independence.

Given the voraciousness of the current debates about the freedom of the press in the country (in the responses to the POSIB and the proposed Media Appeals Tribunal), it was expected that the journalists would express strong resistance to Chinese media norms and practices as well as the fear of the Chinese threat to freedom of the press.[26] This theme was found to be less prominent in the responses, which was unexpected. Although explicit criticism and rejection of the Chinese media model were a recurring theme, this view did not translate into a strong theme of threat. The South African media was cast as strong enough to resist external pressures, and some allowances were made for positive outcomes that could result from increased exposure to Chinese media. The potential positive outcomes that emerged from the responses included the greater diversity of views that complement Western media, the creation of greater mutual understanding, and even the possibility that Chinese media may help to promote tourism in South Africa. Several respondents compared

China's expansion of its media interests on the continent with global media channels such as Russia Today, Al Jazeera, the BBC, and CNN, which were seen to play similar roles of "soft power" and public diplomacy. However, China's media were seen to be less transparent and open than these media channels. Some cautionary responses were expressed about "Chinese media culture." These responses sometimes revealed well-established tropes of China as an "expansionist" imperial power that is "tightening its grip" and that may cause "Africa to lose part of its own identity." The fact that Chinese media are state-owned and controlled was raised several times. Another strong theme was that of the uncertainty and lack of clarity about Chinese intentions. As previously mentioned, the journalists' cautious or wait-and-see attitude seemed to stem from their inability to gain a clear picture of China's intended involvement. The journalists often mentioned the great difference between South African media culture—which has constitutional guarantees of freedom of the press, transparent routines, and editorial independence—and the Chinese media culture—which is controlled by the state. Although the journalists acknowledged that the Chinese push into the continent was related to their objective of promoting soft power, the idea that Chinese media culture could "contaminate" South African media norms and practices was not a strong theme in their responses. Despite the criticism of China's media culture, the widespread belief among journalists was that the South African media were robust enough to resist pressures and had a strong history of independence that would not be easily changed by Chinese influence, and that the Chinese model was "hardly one that you would want to emulate": "SA media has a rich history and I don't think it can be easily influenced or dominated."

It was suggested that the Chinese presence could even increase the vigilance of local journalists to resist pressure on their independence. An important observation was that local pressures might have a much bigger influence on journalistic norms and practices than exposure to Chinese media culture may have:

> I think it is way too early to panic about a potential negative influence of Chinese media on South African journalism. The supposed Chinese influence on Independent Media as part of the Sekunjalo deal is overstated. Local levers of power have much more influence on news agendas than Chinese investment in a news company will ever have. Even local holders of power find it difficult to influence the news agenda, what not to say of foreign powers. Power over news is not exercised in such a direct way.

Interestingly, one respondent suggested that a reverse influence—a type of normative contraflow—might in fact be possible:

In the longer term, as contact grows, probably yes. In the very little I have seen so far, Chinese journalists tend to be quietly horrified, fascinated, intrigued, and maybe just a little bit envious at the way many South African journos go about their work, so productively freely and noisily—and, yes, sometimes irresponsibly. Maybe some of this will in time rub off on Chinese journalists, while SA journalists in turn may think a little bit more about the "nation-building positives" of people sometimes criticize[d] too harshly as "good news journalism."

In the journalists' responses, the belief in the South African media's ability to withstand political pressures, either from their own government or influences from Chinese-owned media, resonated with the belief expressed in the ability of vibrant African advocacy and civil society groups to keep questioning the cost-benefit ratio of the relationship.[27]

MEDIA AS VEHICLE FOR SOFT POWER

Regarding Reese's notion of a "hierarchy of influences" that shape media coverage,[28] the question in relation to China's use of media outlets to meet public diplomacy objectives is as follows: To what extent are Chinese media used as sources of information by South African journalists? The assumption is that if South African journalists regularly access Chinese media and trust these media enough to use them as sources for their own journalistic productions, the Chinese perspective on news events, politics, and international relations would be vastly amplified via local media platforms. A section of the questionnaire was therefore designed to explore journalists' views on both the usefulness of Chinese media as a source of their own work and the influence of such media on their conceptions of the China–South Africa relationship. A strong theme emerging from the journalists' responses was that the objective of China's extended media presence in Africa was to boost its image. The journalists' responses indicated the impression that China's media were a vehicle for the exercise of "soft power" and a "charm offensive." However, this objective was not overwhelmingly viewed in negative terms. The journalists compared Chinese media outlets in Africa with other global media platforms, such as CNN, Al-Jazeera, and the BBC, which have similar objectives but might be less explicit about their aims. However, doubt was expressed that Chinese media were effective in achieving the objective of "soft power." Not only were the journalists highly skeptical of the ability of Chinese media to resonate with South African audiences, very few of them actually used Chinese media as sources when they reported on China or the South Africa–China relationship. The chance that South African media would amplify Chinese media messages is therefore very slim. Consistent with a previous, less extensive survey in which some journalists indicated that they did consult Chinese media from time to time,[29] some respondents in the present study also indicated that they "keep an eye on Xinhua" and that they consult Chinese media to get an "inside view" on issues pertaining to China.

Nevertheless, overwhelmingly, the journalists responded that they did not use Chinese media as a source and only very rarely consumed it. Hence, a strong theme emerging from the responses in this study was the lack of trust in the credibility of Chinese media. For example:

> Personally, I am pretty skeptical about the credibility of state-owned Chinese media, and prefer to use international media sources, such as *NY Times*, *Guardian*, Bloomberg, and Reuters.

Another respondent said the following:

> I can use Xinhua for basic facts, but I am suspicious about them, I'm not convinced that they will provide all the relevant facts. The same goes for CRI. I came across them when I worked as a correspondent in West Africa, and it is clear that they do not have editorial independence. Their priorities are Chinese audiences—I have difficulty buying the argument that CRI and Xinhua are aimed at winning external hearts and minds. So overall, I am reluctant to use Chinese media as a source, and do so only very rarely.

Not only did the journalists indicate their reluctance to use Chinese media as a source of their stories because of their lack of credibility, they also doubted that Chinese media would find a large audience among South African media consumers. Consequently, the efforts of China to use their media as a vehicle to reach "hearts and minds" in South Africa would be unlikely to change xenophobic attitudes toward foreign media content. The following response was indicative:

> Chinese media are not widely used or consumed or trusted in Africa, I think. They are boring and obscure and do not seem to understand African tastes. Even the most uninformed African is also suspicious of Chinese intentions and very well aware that the sweet image China tries to portray is totally inconsistent with the reality in China.

The theme of state control over the media in China also surfaced in the responses to the question about the consumption of Chinese media. The respondents indicated that for soft power via media to be effective, the Chinese media have to gain transparency and credibility:

The communication effort will have to improve from the agents of the Chinese media themselves and these will never be really efficient [at] convincing as long as there's so much state control and censorship in China.

Conclusion

South Africa's closer relationship with China is probably the most significant geopolitical shift that has occurred in recent years insofar as it forms part of a larger reorientation of South Africa toward emerging powers as signified by the BRICS constellation of states. The increased presence of China's media on the continent is part of ongoing and much wider flows and contraflows, and the South African media has been far from a passive recipient in these processes. The South African media—especially the conglomerate Naspers—has played a dominant role on the continent itself, and has also availed itself of the processes of globalization to widen its market and increase its profitability.

Although the Chinese media presence on the continent is an important development for what it signals about China's soft power intentions, and the illustration it provides of the centrality of media content and capital in geopolitical shifts, the actual influence on local journalistic practices and news discourses is still relatively limited.

The exploratory investigation of journalists' attitudes discussed in this chapter showed that China's initiatives to disseminate soft power in South Africa through the Chinese media face major challenges. Although the South African journalists were generally positively inclined toward the country's membership of BRICS, and they expressed that this membership had piqued their interest in China as the dominant member of this group, they did not perceive that China's media had capitalized on these positive attitudes. Furthermore, the Chinese media did not contribute to the framing of these stories in the local media. Soft power initiatives could potentially be amplified by journalists if they were to use Chinese media as their sources because this would allow local stories to be framed by Chinese perspectives. However, this would not happen if journalists did not consume Chinese media or if the Chinese perspective on news events were rejected. Based on the findings, the major challenges to Chinese soft power exercised through the media are as follows:

- Access to and preference for Chinese media: A recurring theme was that journalists do not access Chinese media or see no reason to prefer Chinese media to Western sources.
- Uncertainty and mistrust: A strong theme that figured in several responses was that Chinese media are not used as a source because they

are not seen as credible. The Chinese state control of the media and bias toward official views has discredited Chinese media in the eyes of South African journalists. Although fears that the Chinese media presence in Africa would affect local freedom of the press and editorial independence were not particularly prominent themes, the South African journalists felt their integrity would be compromised if they were to rely on Chinese media sources.

- Incongruity with local news routines and agendas: Chinese media content does not seem interesting or engaging enough for it to be sought out by local journalists. The "China story" would enter local news agendas only if it satisfied news values as they are conceived in local practices and routines, and Chinese media do not yet seem able to present their content such that it is either credible or appealing to local journalists. These findings ultimately remind us that global communication is received, engaged with, and interpreted in localities. Although Chinese media may be a potentially useful vehicle to disseminate Chinese perspectives to global audiences, the messages carried by these media cannot be assumed to have a direct effect on local audiences—à la injection by hypodermic needle. In the South African context, the long struggle for democratic rights and the continued vocal resistance by local media and civil society are likely to cast serious doubts on any media content that is perceived as propagandistic in the least. Further research is needed to establish whether the same findings would hold true in other African countries, although the specificities of local audiences, histories, and power relations would likely shape the reception in various contexts. However, whatever the context, in order for Chinese media to be successful conveyors of soft power, they would have to be credible in the eyes of their audiences. As Zhu remarked in relation to CCTV's attempts to cultivate its attractiveness to global audiences: "Perceived openness and transparency are keys to successful soft power."[30] Furthermore, the local media's reception and portrayal of China's relationship with South Africa, including deals between Chinese companies and local media houses, as in the case of the Sekunjalo purchase of the Independent group, are also likely to be influenced by their stance toward the South African government. Given that the South African media's default stance toward the ANC-led government is somewhere on the spectrum between skepticism and antagonism, China's engagement in South Africa is also likely to be viewed through a lens colored by distrust and criticism.

When all these aspects are taken into account, China's attempts to use media to exert soft power in South Africa will continue to be met by considerable challenges. Nevertheless, the globalization of South African media will continue to be a major factor in years to come. What is especially important to bear in mind—as this chapter has shown in terms of how global influences were considered through the lens of local politics—is that the global and the local are intertwined and cannot be viewed as separate forces. In the next chapter, the role of new media technologies in reshaping the South African media landscape, also in relation to global influences and shifts, will be considered.

CHAPTER 8

New Pressures and Opportunities

Technology, Geopolitics, and Social Change

In the previous two chapters, we considered ways in which the South African media is located within global networks of communication, linked to new geopolitical shifts. It was argued that South African perspectives could contribute to a reconceptualization of global journalism studies, which emphasizes interrelationships and dependencies and would include viewpoints from the Global South as interventions at a theoretical level rather than merely as case studies or exemplars of theories developed elsewhere. Such a focus would be based on the understanding that the Anglo-American framework for understanding media and journalism is no longer sufficient to understand the changes and shifts occurring in media globally, especially against the background of emerging blocs like the BRICS group of nations and the growing relationship between Africa and China. The increasing interpenetrations of media content, capital, and human resources globally necessitate not only more attention to specific contexts in the Global South but also a serious theoretical engagement with the changing normative conceptions and practices of media worldwide that these shifts imply.

Another fundamental shift that has occurred in the media globally in recent years is the increased digitization of the media. The impact of digitization for traditional business models and journalistic practices, along with the "crises" that this process has set in motion, has already been discussed in Chapter 6. In this chapter, the impact of new technologies on media, changing geopolitics, and social change will be considered. Specific attention will be paid to the implications of these global trends in technology and media for social and political change in South Africa. In other words, this chapter will make the connections between global shifts in media practices and technologies, touched on in previous chapters, and local political, economic, and social contestations.

Creativity against the Odds

In discussions of digital media in Africa, the focus is often on political economic limitations that hinder access and use of these technologies. These obstacles are important to take note of, as they militate against easy transplants of celebratory Northern discourses about the emancipatory and democratizing capabilities of digital media onto Southern realities. Access and use of media technologies are often taken for granted in much of the literature emanating from the Global North in analyses of their social impact, including their use in shifting practices of journalism. While the stark difference between levels of access in different parts of the world provides solid grounds for critique of such theoretical assumptions, an analysis of digital media in Africa should go beyond merely asserting this political economic gulf. Attention to these structural limitations can direct the focus to the many creative ways in which Africans are "modernizing the indigenous and indigenizing the modern."[1] The appropriations and adaptations of media platforms by African users speak of a creativity "not only informed by cultures amenable to conviviality, interdependence, and negotiation, but also by histories of deprivation, debasement, and cosmopolitanism."[2] A recent example of this creative appropriation of technology is the development of a "please call me" service on mobile phones, which allows users who have depleted their airtime to contact another user with the request that they call them back. The impact of the exorbitant costs of mobile telephony in South Africa on especially the poor has been noted by scholars and activists.[3] The social impact of the high mobile cost structures was felt by a former employee of the South African mobile company Vodacom, Nkosana Makate. His idea for the now widely used "please call me" service offered on the Vodacom platform was born out of a "state of desperation" when he worked as a trainee accountant at Vodacom.[4] His girlfriend at the time (now his wife), was a university student, based in a town in another province (University of Fort Hare in the Eastern Cape). When one of them wanted to call the other, but did not have sufficient airtime, they would make a quick missed call (also known as "buzzing" or "beeping"). His frustration prompted him to come up with the idea of a free service that would enable users to send a free text to another user, requesting them to call back.⁵ When he shared this concept with his superiors at the mobile company, they developed the idea into software that turned out to be a very profitable service for the company, but they reneged on a verbal agreement to compensate him for his intellectual property. This led to a fifteen-year-long legal battle that ended in 2016 when Vodacom was ordered to pay Makate, now working for the South African Local Government Association, for his idea.

This example illustrates Mabweazara's view that vibrant digital cultures and practices in Africa are emerging despite infrastructural, political, and economic obstacles.⁶ The appropriation and adaptation of mobile messaging pioneered by Makate is an example of the "technological domestication" and "localized appropriations" of media technologies found in different ways across the continent.⁷ Attention to how technologies are put to use in actual contexts and impact on people's lived experience in Africa constitutes a departure from the more "techno-deterministic models of impact" often favored in economic and political discourses linked to Northern donor agencies.⁸ Optimistic predictions for what digital media might mean for social change and democratic politics in Africa have in the past frequently been based on these technologically determinist assumptions that the introduction of new technologies per se will bring about social change and deepen democratic participation. In theorizing the African digital public sphere, postulations of what ICTs might mean for African societies frequently drew on older modernization paradigms of "development": a universal, linear trajectory of progress was assumed to be facilitated through media, consisting of various stages that could be "leapfrogged" by new technologies, with an emphasis on attaining transparency, good governance, and economic growth. However, when this optimism proved to be exaggerated, questions about access, inequality, power, and quality of information returned.⁹ In contrast, approaches focusing on human capabilities and freedoms afforded by these platforms are more interested in the opportunities these technologies afford people to make their own choices and contribute to development in more areas of life than merely the economic.¹⁰

Mobile Phones

Probably the most important platform for media and communications in Africa today is the mobile phone. Mobiles have been critical in shaping everyday life on the continent, with their influence ranging from social relationships, to financial services, activism, and news media and communication.¹¹ Commentators often referred to the "explosive" spread of mobile phones on the continent as nothing short of a "revolution" that set in motion the development of new practices of communication and cultural expressions.[12] Access to the internet happens increasingly through the mobile phone rather than through fixed internet, in Africa and the Global South in general.[13] As the "please call me" example attests, mobile phones also provide ample illustrations of how technologies are appropriated in African contexts. As Chiumbu argues, mobile phones are not only "shaping social realities in African societies, but, in turn, Africans and their societies are (re)shaping the mobile phone technologies in different ways."[14] One growing form of such appropriation in Africa is that of mobilization for social activism,[15] as has been the case in many other parts of the world.[16] The use of mobile phones for this purpose has not escaped political interference, and politicians have on occasion colluded with mobile companies to suppress dissent. This was the case with the "bread riots" in the Mozambican capital Maputo in 2010, where residents took to the streets of Maputo, prompted by SMS messages that told them to "enjoy the great day of the strike" and to "protest the increase in energy, water, mini-bus taxi and bread prices." While the government at first resisted calls to stop price hikes, they later relented under pressure and reversed the bread prices. The government allegedly ordered mobile providers to suspend text-messaging services in an attempt to quell the protests—a sign that this form of protest was taken seriously.[17]

The effectiveness of mobile phones to bring about social change is highly contested. Critics dismiss new media activism as based on weak ties and therefore limited to low-risk participation. Optimistic analyses, however, stress that technologies like the mobile phone have created possibilities for communication outside mainstream media or formal channels of political communication. Ekine sees that the creative ways in which Africans have adopted and adapted the mobile phone, rather than the technology itself, is what makes mobile phones a force for social change.[18]

Assessments often hinge on the decision of whether to foreground the structural limitations of these technologies—factors like the political economy of access, or the nature of the medium that determines and limits the form and style of communication—or the agency of its users, with their creative adoptions, adaptations, and domestications of these technologies.

Mobile phones have shaped the communications landscape much more rapidly in Africa than in Europe.[19] Mobile phones are "almost always the cheapest and quickest way to communicate" in Africa,[20] because this technology does not require a network of landlines, which is often absent or inadequate on the continent.[21] Consequently, ownership of mobile phones has grown dramatically across the continent, and with 89 percent of adults owning one, mobile phones have become as common in South Africa and Nigeria as they are in the United States.[22] Africa, along with Asia-Pacific, is the region in the world with the strongest mobile growth.[23]

Figures on their own, however, do not tell the full story of access to mobiles, as handsets and subscriptions are often shared.[24] Mobile phones are used for much more than making calls—in fact sending text messages and taking pictures or videos are the most popular uses of mobile phones in Africa.[25] Africans use mobiles to text, transfer money (with the M-Pesa service in Kenya seen as a trailblazer in this regard), check market prices for agricultural products, monitor elections, and send and receive public health or emergency messages (through services such as Ushahidi or Frontline SMS). But apart from what may be considered more "serious" uses of mobiles, Africans use mobiles in everyday life to take photographs, make films, search the internet and, increasingly, for social networking.[26] The range of functionalities of mobile phones make it an "extremely versatile technology" that can be used by activists to plan campaigns long in advance or respond quickly to events.[27] Although the versatile smartphone is not yet as widely used in Africa as in the Global North,[28] older communication practices like *radio trottoir* are combined with new technologies in novel and creative ways.[29]

Against Elation

Despite the phenomenal uptake and reach of mobile telephony on the continent, the need for a "mitigated euphoria" that Nyamnjoh warned about more than a decade and a half ago is still relevant in many respects.[30] Operating a mobile phone in Africa is still much more expensive than in all other regions of the world, calculated as a percentage of gross national income (GNI).[31] Consequently, usage in many cases remains restricted to more passive usage—waiting for someone to call, or using free "beeping" or "please call me" texts to communicate, as described earlier. The nature and extent of mobile penetration and use are not uniform across African countries, nor are they equally distributed within them. As is the case with all technologies, mobile phones are not socially neutral tools but can entrench or exacerbate unequal gendered or classed power relations.[32] Even in a country such as South Africa, with one of the highest penetration rates on the continent,[33] call costs are prohibitively high, especially for the poor, who use exorbitantly priced pay-as-you-go services rather than contracts.[34] Mobile costs in South Africa are among the highest in the world, and informal settlement dwellers in a South African town typically spend 27.5 percent of their income on communications costs, using money set aside for essential items like food to buy airtime.[35] Women were more adversely affected than men by communications costs, leading to a knock-on effect on children and the infirm, for whom women are often the caregivers.[36] The high costs of mobile phone connectivity have been found to have a severely negative impact on the lives of the poor, who not only have difficulty paying for other essentials like food and electricity due to the high costs of connectivity, but also find it increasingly difficult to stay integrated in social and familial networks or take advantage of job opportunities if they cannot afford airtime.[37] These findings mitigate the euphoric notions of mobility, independence, and individuality often characterizing discourses around mobile phones in Africa. It is as a result of these difficult structural conditions that African mobile users display the remarkable creativity exemplified by the "please call me" messages or protocols to interpret different "beeps" as messages with varied meanings.[38]

In his critique of the technologically deterministic approaches that emphasizes connectivity, technology transfer, and training, Nyamnjoh has called for a socioanthropological approach to the development of ICTs that would allow Africa to "regulate, adapt and innovate ICT to its own needs and priorities for sustainable development."[39] An assessment of mobile phones in everyday life will still not tell us of their "effect" on African politics, but will help us understand how politics, popular culture, and media are entwined in intricate networks and circuits.

The view of mobiles as radically new technologies whose mere insertion into African societies would revolutionize them may also be predicated on a patronizing ideological assumption of Northern technological progress as a benevolent force for the "underdeveloped" South.[40] Much of the debate around mobile phones in Africa—whether celebratory or dismissive—seems to be based on a model of media transmission leading to direct effects. Such technologically determinist, transmission thinking bears resemblance to outdated "communication for development" approaches that tend to see technology as a modernizing force to be introduced into African settings, rather than turning the attention to the ways in which these technologies are actively contextualized and domesticated by African users.

Where the transmission model of mobile phone use is particularly concerned with issues of distribution and access, ethnographic approaches are first interested in patterns of use and deployment. In other words, the *technology-centered* model is concerned with what happens to *people* when mobile phones are used to *transmit* information *to* them; the *context-centered* model is more interested in what happens to the *technology* when it is appropriated and adapted *by* people—people that use mobile phones to *transgress* the boundaries imposed by the state, the culture, the economy, and the technology-capitalism complex itself. The domestication approach, which focuses on the adoption, adaptation, and integration of technology in everyday life as an ongoing process of negotiation,[41] is perhaps the most suitable framework within which to think of the role of mobile phones as "material objects with a particular social and economic embedding."[42]

The challenge remains, however, to link this microlevel approach to broader democratic discourses. We need to find out what the domestication of mobile phones within a specific sociocultural and politico-economic context in Africa tells us about people's engagement or disengagement with politics, how the popular relates to the political and everyday life links to democratic processes. We can expect an ethnographic approach to mobile phones to tell us more about the integration of phones in the everyday life of Africans: how they use phones to socialize, be entertained, organize their daily routines, and do their jobs. But how can we connect everyday life with the processes of democracy and the imperatives for development? Texting and tweeting might enrich our social lives, but will it lead to political and social change? Perhaps this question assumes a too rigid separation of the political and the seemingly mundane, between democratic participation and popular culture, between civic and social identities. Mobile phones are interesting in terms of their social and cultural contexts of use precisely because they tend to break down and redraw the boundaries between the private and the public.[43] While this blurring of the private/public divide may seem disconcerting for observers who prefer their politics rational and deliberative, it may pose interesting new possibilities for an understanding of the private as political and for the popular as having serious public implications. Instead of dismissing the carnival of text chats, social networking, music downloads, gossip, and so forth as having no revolutionary potential, mobile phones challenge us to pay attention to how these popular uses transgress the realm of the private into the realm of the public. Mobile phones are not external to people's lives, but an integral part of it. It therefore makes more sense not to think of mobiles as transmitting information from the outside world into people's daily environment but instead as being integrated with their daily lives, routines, and rituals. It is in this "everyday Africa" that people use mobile phones to transgress preexisting boundaries and limitations.[44]

Indeed, mobile phones in Africa are not merely technological tools that can be studied in isolation from broader social and political processes—they are *cultural* technologies that play an "indispensable role in the everyday lives of consumers" and should be investigated in terms of the cultures of consumption that they create but also how they fit within larger cultural settings.[45]

How does this transmission and transgression take place? Let us consider some of the key areas in which mobile phones are seen to make a difference in public and political life in Africa, before ending with a case study taken from South Africa.

State and Media

There has been much optimism about the potential of mobile phones for the emergence of *e-democracy* or *networked politics* in Africa. In most of Africa, the relationship between state and media has been a fragile and conflictual one. Many African states exert strong influence in or control of the airwaves, and business interests often align themselves with political power. The advent of mobile phones has been seen as providing avenues for e-democracy. Digital media have been seen as vehicles to provide information to the electorate or have been used by politicians to align themselves with popular culture or communicate with supporters. In South Africa, the opposition Democratic Alliance (DA) has been known to be especially active in this regard. Mobile phones have been used as tools for surveillance, for citizens to monitor political processes or upload reports of political violence—with the Kenyan-based platform Ushahidi having become well-known for providing this function.

These type of campaigns are, however, still hampered by unequal access to mobile social networks, and consequently subaltern counterpublics do not always gain access to a mediatized public sphere.[46] The mobilization of counterpublics via mobile phones seems to be successful for amplifying a brief political campaign or event, but it is less successful in ensuring "ongoing and higher levels of accountability."[47]

Mobile phones have proved useful to social movements such as Abahlali baseMjondolo and the Anti-eviction campaign in South Africa, for instance, to document and archive their work or mobilize for support and activism.[48]

The use of mobile phones to spread rumors during elections can either be seen as a breakdown of the rational deliberation[49] or, as Willems suggests with regards to political debate in Zimbabwe, as a way to *transgress* the limitations of the public sphere by drawing on the resources of popular culture.[50] The circulation of gossip, rumors, jokes, and "SMS Wars"[51] via mobiles can be seen as the latest incarnation of *radio trottoir*,[52] the popular and unofficial medium of discussion of political affairs in Africa. Political rumors, gossip, and jokes display the agency of mobile phone users to circumvent structural limitations (e.g., political restrictions in Zimbabwe, or economic limitations to access in South Africa) and could be read as critical comment on the political system and/or the mediatized public sphere itself. The jokes, SMS wars, and gossip-mongering should also be seen alongside the rise of satiric websites, television programs and social network sites (e.g., ZANews and *Late Night News with Loyiso Gola* in South Africa, or fake Twitter accounts making fun of politicians and TV programs like *Redykyulass* and *XYZ* in Kenya[53]). As such, the *transgression* of formal political processes and rational debate in the media that takes place on mobile networks has to be taken seriously when we try to understand the implications of mobile phones for political processes in Africa.

Digital Media and Local Politics

In countries such as South Africa (similar to other parts of the Global South, like India), social inequalities are deeply entrenched and subaltern citizens find it difficult to engage effectively with the State, especially on the level of local government.[54] This means that the Habermasian ideal of rational deliberation, as claimed by the mainstream media, is, in practice, often eschewed in favor of more informal engagement with political issues that takes the form of popular expressions. When we therefore consider the role that mobile phones may play in local politics, and how they may contribute to the practices of citizenship, we need to not restrict our focus to the "rational" aspects of *transmission* of political information such as e-government on a local level (which may include the dissemination of information about local politics, service delivery, voting, and so forth). We also need to take into account the ways in which mobile phones allow citizens to *transgress* the rules of "good citizenship" and political practices. For instance, mobile phones may allow users to opt for "strategic nonparticipation" as a political strategy (e.g., by circulating gossip or jokes in the style of *radio trottoir* instead of accessing formal political information or debates)[55] or to participate in a political culture of *clientelism* (by using mobile phone networks to gain access to powerful political stakeholders). They may choose to use their mobile phones to mobilize for street protests and activism[56] instead of behaving like good citizens and downloading government communiqués or engaging in rational debate via the exchange of texts. These informal strategies and tools might be frowned upon by donors and NGOs who want to establish a rational, liberal democracy in Africa, but they represent a real form of political engagement in postcolonial African societies marked by continued exclusions and marginalizations.[57] Indeed, the use of mobile phones to transgress the formal channels of information dissemination and consultation may substantiate the claim that "[e]veryday politics in Africa . . . is highly provisional and improvisational."[58]

Digital Entrepreneurship

We have already noted that the discourse surrounding mobile phones in Africa often avails itself of older paradigms of communication for development. The *transmission* and diffusion of technological innovation, as a knock-on effect of the introduction of mobile technology, is seen within this approach to hold the potential to modernize African societies and economies. Consequently, examples of how mobile phones succeeded in helping African entrepreneurs build businesses are often held up as an illustration of the transformative potential of mobile phones. Southwood cites the example of a plumber in Dakar who, before the advent of mobile phones, took three days to get back to desperate customers who had to leave messages at a shop where he would collect them only in the evenings after his house calls.[59] Another example Southwood cites (and which is often found in other case study literature) is that of a rural farmer who, before he could call up to get stock prices, had to take the time, effort, and expense to visit a market to find out if prices are good enough to sell his goods.

The greater ease and reach of *transmission* of information has undoubtedly benefited African economies, in the form of farmers linking to large international markets or small entrepreneurs running businesses from day to day. The personal economies of individuals in Africa are also increasingly being shaped by remittances being sent via mobile phones, which are increasingly being used as "wallets" to pay for goods and services in African cities.

But mobile phones also enable users to *transgress* the limitations and boundaries of formal economies. These limitations include the often exorbitant costs imposed by mobile phone companies themselves.[60] In the process of these transgressions, informal economies are created that crisscross formal economies, undermine them, and articulate with people's everyday lives.

From this point of view, mobile phone users in Africa are not merely the passive victims of the exploitation of big companies but are *active* consumers. As Etzo and Collender note: "A large informal economy has also emerged to support the mobile sector, with people selling airtime, charging and fixing mobiles, and renting them out."[61]

Participation in this informal economy requires a different kind of digital entrepreneurship than the kind developed by mobile companies that identify Africa as the next big market for mobile telephony.[62] It requires knowing how to unblock secondhand phones so they can use different SIM cards, knowing how to switch different prepaid SIM cards to optimally use the free minutes provided by each, how to transmit and receive money or vouchers in return for favors, how to use Bluetooth functionality to swap music between friends and develop your own social capital in the everyday circle of friends, and how to use "flashing" or "beeping" (calling and hanging up before the receiver can answer so as to avoid incurring a call cost) to develop a code of communication when you have run out of money for airtime. Airtime comes at such a high cost in South Africa that it is often offered as a prize in consumer competitions, or airtime vouchers are given as gifts or freebies. The over-the-top (OTT) internet service WhatsApp has become immensely popular as a communication platform for mobile phone users in South Africa because it transmits data at a much cheaper rate than SMS text messages sent over mobile phone data networks. In 2016, there were reportedly around 10 million WhatsApp users in South Africa, leading the mobile networks Vodacom and MTN to call for stronger regulation of OTT services.[63]

This approach to the transgressive economies of mobile phone use in Africa would ask questions other than about the affordability of contracts or prepaid calls, and assess the impact of mobile phones by the "local strategies (used) to bypass the rules of the market" as Hahn and Kibora observed in Burkina Faso, where mobile phones have become an "integral part of social life."[64]

Apart from economic capital, mobile phones also provide social capital. Southwood refers to mobile phones as being the "sports car" of its age in Africa, an aspirational status symbol within affordable reach.[65] So, if we think about mobile phones not only in terms of their economic instrumentality but also in terms of the transgressive potential they hold for African users to actively construct alternative economies, we will end up with a much more textured and varied picture than by looking at formal economic indicators alone.

The Social Is Political

If we view the use of mobile phones within the broader context of the digital platforms they give access to and consider the way in which they give expression to everyday culture to be as important as the connections they provide to more formal channels of communication, political deliberation, and activism, a serious consideration of social media becomes imperative. As a space where the personal and the political increasingly interface, especially in African contexts such as Zimbabwe where mainstream media use is largely under state control, social media platforms like Facebook can provide alternative spaces for political information, discussion, satire, and activism.[66]

In South Africa, a symbiotic relationship has developed between mainstream media and citizen bloggers, leading not only to the question of who can call themselves journalists, but also to shifting the culture of journalism from a closed, professionally oriented one to a more participatory one. This shift is also very evident in South African journalism.[67] An example of how user-generated content impacted mainstream news agendas, and eventually even made global news headlines, was when a Mozambican immigrant, Mido Macia, was handcuffed to and dragged behind a South African Police Services vehicle in Daveyton in Gauteng Province. He later died of his injuries. The incident was initially recorded on a mobile phone by a bystander and then sent to the tabloid newspaper, the *Daily Sun*, which posted it on their YouTube channel and website and reported on it in print. From there, it went viral on social media and news sites around the world—an example of how social media is not restricted to personal or private use but can connect local politics with broader global audiences and interests.

South African politics increasingly sees its agenda shaped or influenced by social media. When former senior ANC MP Vytjie Mentor decided in 2016 to go public on allegations of "state capture" by the influential Gupta family, who purportedly had direct influence on President Jacob Zuma, she did not issue a press release, but used Facebook as a medium.[68] Posts on Facebook and Twitter have also led to major controversies around racism and identity politics, ranging from racist comments made by a DA member and estate agent Penny Sparrow about Black people on South African beaches during the festive period[69] to a judge, Mabel Jansen, who claimed in a Facebook exchange that rape was "part of black culture,"[70] to the student activist Ntokozo Qwabe who used Facebook to gloat about having refused to pay a White waiter a tip until she "returns the land."[71]

Social media has been a growing influence in South African politics for a while:[72] former DA opposition party leader Helen Zille has become known for tweeting from the hip, and this has landed her in trouble for unguarded remarks. Zille's Twitter dominance, of course, reflected racial disparities (then still largely skewed to the small White minority) in internet access and use in South Africa. Not for long, though. Zille and the DA were gradually deposed by the Economic Freedom Front's (EFF) Twitter smarts (especially those of its young MP Mbuyiseni Ndlozi and its leader Julius Malema) and what passes for #BlackTwitter in South Africa.

In contrast, leaders from the ruling party—the African National Congress (ANC)—seem clueless about social media. President Jacob Zuma has 392,000 followers, but last tweeted on February 12, 2016, and before that in October 2013. In his last tweet, he thanked people who sent in comments on his State of the Nation address to the country's Parliament. And in the October 2013 tweet, he announced he was attending a church service. At the same time, Zuma has been the subject of countless memes, gifs, remixes, photoshopped pictures, and YouTube videos of his apparent innumeracy. At best, the ruling party views social media as the enemy. Recently, the ANC announced it would submit some of its members to disciplinary procedures for discussing party business on Facebook.

But perhaps the most significant example of the interface between social media, mainstream politics, and activism in recent years may be seen in the student movement of 2015.

The date October 21, 2015, will be remembered as the day mainstream media became old in South Africa. It was the day the hashtags took control. We watched as student protests morphed from #FeesMustFall to #NationalShutDown (and briefly to #ZumaMustFall) and as at least fourteen university campuses were shut down. Before we could catch our collective breath, students in Cape Town had left the University of Cape Town's (UCT) suburban campus and the nearby Cape Peninsula University of Technology (CPUT) to march on Parliament. There, they demanded to see Minister of Higher Education Blade Nzimande. The students forced open the gates of Parliament and soon—imitating #BlackLivesMatter—were marching into the grounds with their hands up. Police responded by firing tear gas and stun grenades at them. The students, defiant, began to sing the national anthem, "Nkosi Sikelel iAfrika." By nightfall, six of the main student leaders—including the offspring of a prominent liberation movement figure and the son of UCT's vice chancellor—were in custody. There were reports that the students were being charged with treason. Their lawyers were quick to react, and by nightfall, word filtered through that they would be charged with trespassing and be in court in the morning.

The protests at Parliament happened while the South African Minister of Finance, Nhlanhla Nene, went on delivering his midterm budget speech inside. Television stations were forced to choose between broadcasting democratic business as usual and democracy being remade outside. The split-screen coverage some TV stations opted for brought the point home with alarming clarity. While minister Nene was reciting figures about the "downward adjustment" of economic expectations, students were being choked, manhandled, and arrested outside. But the television coverage was of lesser importance, because the revolution was not being televised, it was being live-tweeted. Television news mattered only if it placed a camera where the protests were and left it at that.

Around the city and around the world, people were following the protests online (initially, mainstream global news channels avoided the protests) as they were unfolding. Shortly afterward, a local daily newspaper, the *Cape Argus*, announced that it would hand over the editing of its next issue to the students. This was taken by some in the industry as an indication of the media's responsiveness to the student movement. But it was perhaps more a recognition of the opposite: South Africa's mainstream media were becoming increasingly irrelevant to what was going on in the streets.

Newspapers and even mainstream online news organizations struggled to keep up with what was happening. Some online news reports consisted exclusively of cut-and-pasted Twitter updates. If they did more, they often reverted to stereotypes of protesters as irrational, violent, and disruptive. At one point, a reporter for the public SABC News, criticized for its reticence to critically report on the ruling party, told viewers "police are firing stun grenades to calm the situation."[73] After the protests, several commentators pointed out that the protesters were on the whole very disciplined and that violent clashes occurred only in response to police actions. In contrast, social media provided by-the-minute updates on situations as they developed, gave access to students' views and experiences, helped students mobilize (even providing tips on how to deal with tear gas or to ensure that one's mobile was charged) and, crucially, became a platform for alternative narratives to those of the mainstream to emerge.

The students exploited social media and the internet's full potential as a democratic sphere. Such was the power of the hashtag #FeesMustFall that it was included in a court interdict by UCT against protesting students.

We got a glimpse earlier this year of how young people interact with social media when #RhodesMustFall, #RhodesSoWhite, and #TransformWits inaugurated hashtag politics in South Africa. The hashtags articulated actual events: the hashtag #RhodesMustFall amplified on an already existing movement, mostly by Black students, at UCT against a colonial-era statue of Cecil John Rhodes. The movement was about more than the statue's removal as protesters called for curriculum reform, transformation of university faculty (a small minority of professors at South Africa's top universities are Black), and an end to outsourcing.[74]

When the #RhodesMustFall movement commenced, we could not yet foresee the internet and social media's full potential as a news source in developing countries like South Africa. Old media still by and large set the agenda for discussions around heritage, the decolonization of the university, and identity politics. This changed when the movement grew into a nationwide call for the cessation of fee increases, and protests erupted around the country. The late October protests were the death knell for old media.

That was clear when students at the University of Witwatersrand forced Vice Chancellor Adam Habib not only to meet and listen to them but also to suspend all fee increases for the next academic year. One anecdote was telling: Only a few days earlier, in a column in the country's leading business newspaper, Habib railed against students' "vanguardist" tendencies in which "theatrics replaced principled politics" and criticized them for having "the temerity to call Nelson Mandela a sellout." As Wits students upped their protests and confronted Habib, local news channels broadcast events live, their reporters and presenters talking over the images. On Twitter, the writer and broadcaster Eusebius McKaiser attempted to persuade eNCA News to play the Wits students' speeches without interruption or commentary. When he found no reward, he asked if anyone knew of a live stream. That's when the *Daily Vox*, an online news site staffed by young people (mostly recent university graduates), announced they would stream the meeting. Responded McKaiser on Twitter: "EXCELLENT! I will watch it live on Periscope. I just downloaded the app. Traditional media no longer controls us."

The *Daily Vox* reflects another key spinoff of the social media era in South Africa, with the rise of independent, online sites where students and commentators—without the mainstream's pretensions of objectivity—gave analyses and opinion of what was happening. The *Daily Vox*, *Con* (started by a group of former *Mail and Guardian* newspaper staffers), and *Daily Maverick* (the latter, while spotty, came into its own after it proved a corrective to the mainstream media narrative of the August 2012 Marikana mine massacre) stood out in this regard. The Cape Town–based online publication *GroundUp* also provided good firsthand accounts from UCT student reporter Ashleigh Furlong.

We do not want to overstate how representative the student protests were—students make up no more than 1 million of the country's nearly 50 million people and for the protests to have effects beyond campuses, they need to form alliances and capture energies in trade union, housing rights, and anti-crime movements in poor Black neighborhoods. But the protests show how out of touch conventional party politics has become. Protesters made a point of publicly turning away leaders from the DA or EFF as opportunistic. Similarly, we are not suggesting social media caused the uprising (i.e., not in the naive, ahistorical way in which some people talked about the Arab Spring, #Occupy-Nigeria, #WalktoWork in Uganda, or the protests that unseated Senegal's former president, Abdoulaye Wade), but that social media proved more adaptable and in touch with a movement that is organic in its nature.

Most of all, the student protests have proven that social media is no longer a luxury in contemporary political activism. When police and students clashed on November 11 at the University of the Western Cape—a historically Black university in Cape Town, which struggles to command the same mainstream media attention as the historically White, middle-class UCT or Stellenbosch University (where students fight over language policy)—students called for donations of vital supplies via Facebook. The order in which these were listed said it all: "We at #UWCFeesMustFall are in desperate [need] of airtime, medical and food supplies."

Conclusion

The aim of this book is to provide an overview of debates and contestations marking the South African media's role and position at the end of apartheid in that country. Although the book pays close attention to specific developments in South African politics, society, and media industry, the aim is not to consider these specifics in isolation from their articulation with global trends, regional developments, and geopolitical shifts. On the contrary—a central argument of the book is that global media studies have tended to marginalize knowledge production from the South by relegating it to the domain of "case studies," "examples," "comparative studies," or "area studies." By linking issues dominating scholarly and media discourses in South Africa in the postapartheid era with global debates and developments, the book seeks to shift the frame within which media in contexts in the South is studied. Instead of focusing on South African media as a peculiarity or special example, it is argued that it should be approached from an interrelational perspective, namely as a social, political, and cultural phenomenon that has both local specificity and global relevance. By looking at the South African media through such a "glocal" lens, the field of media studies is not merely broadened by the inclusion of another example or case study but disrupted and enriched through a dialogical process of moving in and out between the local and the global. As such, the objective is to offer a contrapuntal reading of media in the South African context that highlights its relevance for an understanding of how media operates transnationally in the current global era. In other words, the objective of the book is not only to contribute to an understanding of the South African media over the past twenty years or so but to offer a South African perspective on global media in an era of ongoing but uneven technological development, geopolitical change, political (democratic or otherwise) transitions, and social upheaval around the world. It is argued that by paying closer attention to the dynamics of the South African media in transition, scholars of global media can gain a better understanding of the media's location in social, political, and cultural transitions elsewhere as well. Ultimately, therefore, this book aims at providing an African perspective on global media.

Through its analysis of the changes that the South African media has undergone since the end of apartheid, processes of globalization and localization are considered as they play out in specific local contexts. Theoretical debates about the Africanization of media ethics, the influence of identity politics on media norms and practices, and the appropriation and adaptation of global media genres and platforms such as tabloids, mobile phones, and social media take place on the cusp of the local, regional, and global, with the recognition that each of these spatial designators contains a multitude of differences in and of itself. Using South African media as a point of departure, the book argues that the globalization and localization of media should be considered as multileveled processes that are subject to broad geopolitical shifts as well as contestations and power struggles within localities. It concludes that global media are not only appropriated and articulated in local contexts, but that local contexts often shape the way in which the global is understood and engaged with.

The book focuses on the South African media after apartheid, and its chapters span more than two decades of events and developments that followed South Africa's transition from apartheid to democracy. The research contained in this book clarifies that the media—its roles, practices, positioning, and representations—has been deeply implicated in this transition. Not merely a "mirror," "messenger," or "observer," as especially the journalistic media often claims to be, the media as institutions and infrastructures of communication has been an integral role player in political processes, policy debates, and the reimagining of democratic society. The mainstream commercial media can be counted among big business—the Naspers group has especially benefited from the new political environment by expanding its reach on the continent and globally, while the Independent group was passed back and forth between international and local capital—and as such is invested in the very economic policy decisions it reports on. In its familiar watchdog role, the South African media has performed a vital function in the postapartheid years by highlighting many instances of corruption and abuse of power on the part of the new democratic government, a role that has not endeared it to the government. Although the continued vibrancy and vigilance of the South African media, based on the constitutional guarantees of freedom of expression, can be seen as a major gain of the democratic era, the media has not always played a constructive role. The demise of the alternative media from the apartheid era has meant that the print media sector has become dominated by commercial media, which provides a very narrow perspective on society, one informed by elite audiences. The balance to this perspective that the public and community media was intended to provide has been hampered by mismanagement and political interference (in the case of the public broadcaster, the SABC) and organizational inefficiencies and funding problems (in the case of community media). Consequently, the media's ability to contribute to democratic deepening and the facilitation of citizen participation in democracy has been limited in significant ways. In many ways, therefore, the South African media's realization of the ideals of democracy remains incomplete. While the focus on the postapartheid era refers to a specific historical period, this retrospective approach should therefore not be mistaken as being based on the assumption that the arrival of formal democracy in 1994 constituted a clean break with the past. The continuities with the apartheid past are still evident in the persistent economic inequalities and current political and economic environment in a way that would undermine any simplistic bracketing of the postapartheid era as a separate epoch.

Similarly, despite the major changes that the media in the country has undergone since 1996 and which have been highlighted in this book, many of its practices remain rooted in a historical understanding of its role in society and its relationship to government; its orientation toward its audiences is influenced by market segmentation that continues to be shaped by the legacy of apartheid in terms of language, race, and class, and the reception of media content takes place within a society that remains highly unequal economically and marked by persistent social and cultural divides. Yet, at the same time, the South African media today is more robust, more vibrant, and freer than it had ever been under apartheid.

The historical transitions from apartheid to democracy and the ways the media has been a part of these changes, as well as the contestations about the media's role in this changing society, were covered in the first two sections of the book.

An analysis of the changes that the South African media underwent in the first two decades of democracy should, however, not be limited to contestations following the repositioning of the media in relation to the postapartheid state and society. Several important changes on a global level have impacted the South African media, its norms and practices, and its ability to contribute to democratic deepening and social change. Among these changes discussed in the third section of this book have been the tectonic shifts taking place globally in the economic models upon which media has historically been founded. These shifts have led to a discourse of "crisis" in journalism in particular. While the South African media has not escaped this crisis entirely, a critical reflection on this notion of crisis, and the differential ways in which South African media has responded to it, has provided us with a vantage point from which the articulation between the local and the global can be investigated.

A second global shift that has been of considerable importance for an understanding of the South African media in the period after apartheid has been the changing global geopolitical landscape. The recognition of these shifts through the formation of the BRICS grouping of emerging states, and in particular the growing relationship between China and Africa, has provided us with an additional lens through which to view the position of the South African media in the democratic era.

These changes in journalistic models and practices in response to global economic shifts, as well as the way in which local and global developments overlap, can perhaps be seen most clearly in the development and adoption of digital media technologies and social media platforms. The chapter devoted to the use of these technologies aimed to show how they can serve as an entry point into a social and cultural understanding of how media operate on the interface between the local and the global, and how these technologies relate to social and political change.

For all these reasons, the notion of South African media "after apartheid," while referring in the first instance to a specific historical juncture and a particular political moment, should serve as more than merely a temporal indicator and also signal a particular analytical approach, namely one which engages with and assesses the South African media for its contribution to a democratic society and social change. The point of departure of the book—a specific, localized vantage point on global issues and developments—indicates the complex interrelationship between the local and the global but should also be seen as a critique of approaches to global media, which often still tend to follow an "area studies" approach. It has hopefully been made clear that while contextual specificities are vitally important, especially on the level of theory-building in order to avoid totalizing pictures with universalistic claims, media in these locales can never be understood in isolation. This goes as much for media in the Global South as in the Global North. A reading of this book as yet another "case study" within a study of global media as made up of geographically bound nation-states, instead of an illustration of how local and global processes intersect, would be an incorrect one. This book illustrates how transitions and shifts always occur on several levels at once and that they continue to evolve across time and borders in ways that only a holistic approach can hope to do justice to. The monumental shifts from apartheid to democracy in South Africa, and the way in which the media have formed part of these shifts, challenge us to think about media and its various interrelationships in new and complex ways.

Most of all, it is hoped that this study of the South African media after apartheid offers a way to engage with questions of the "internationalization," "de-Westernization," or even "decolonization" of global media studies. It is only by acknowledging that global media studies is always approached from the specific of a given context, whether that context is located in the North or the South, that epistemological hierarchies in the field can start to be dismantled. As this book shows, knowledge production in the field of media studies is embedded in relations of power, and to undo these, a study of "global" media has to be rooted in the experiences of those in the South for whom "the global" has always had to be negotiated in relation to "the local."

This book takes a first step to this end.

Notes

Introduction

1. SAPA, "Media Briefed on Mandela Funeral."
2. *The Economist*, "Nelson Mandela (Obituary)."
3. For a personal reflection on the funeral and its mediation, see Wasserman, "To Come Back from Qunu."
4. Tomaselli and Shepperson, "The Absent Signifier."
5. De Waal, "Recognizing Nelson Mandela."
6. Krabill, *Starring Mandela and Cosby*, 119.
7. Ibid., 122.
8. Ibid., 124.
9. Ibid., 39.
10. Halleck, "Google (GOOG) Earnings Preview."
11. *Citizen*, "Google Doodle Marks SA Election."
12. See Wasserman and De Beer, "A Fragile Affair," for a discussion of some of these early clashes.
13. See Wasserman and Jacobs, "Media, Citizenship and Social Justice," for a fuller discussion.
14. Sparks, "South African Media in Comparative Perspective," 8.
15. Ibid.
16. Heller, "Democratic Deepening."
17. Ibid.
18. Mandela, "Address to the International Press Institute."

19. French, "Whose Freedom?"

20. See Wasserman, *Tabloid Journalism*, for a detailed discussion of the tabloid press in South Africa.

21. Fourie, "Rethinking the Role of the Media in South Africa," 27.

22. For a discussion of these principles, see Horwitz, *Communication and Democratic Reform*, 328.

23. Ibid., 330.

24. Sparks, "South African Media in Transition," 209.

25. See www.soscoalition.org.za (accessed July 14, 2017).

26. Nicolson, "Hlaudi Motsoeneng."

27. Mkonza, "Community Media and the MDDA," 115.

28. Banda, "Negotiating Distant Influences."

29. Ibid.

30. Sparks, "South African Media in Transition," 205. While the modeling of community media on a commercial media can defeat the object of community participation, some commentators (e.g., Boloka, "Diversity Goes Global," 31) see this as the only way for such media to remain sustainable, as the MDDA cannot be seen as an "infinite financier."

31. Sparks, "South African Media in Transition," 213.

32. This boycott included a ban by the British actors' union, Equity; the British Musicians' Union; celebrity signatories to the American Committee on Africa; the organization, Associated Actors and Artists of America; and the group, Artists United Against Apartheid, which protested against stars performing at Sun City in the neighboring "homeland" of Bophuthatswana. See, for instance, ANA, "Some Important Developments."

33. Switzer, "Introduction," 73; for a personal account, see Hunter-Gault, *New News out of Africa*, 9.

34. See Switzer and Adhikari, *South Africa's Resistance Press*, for a comprehensive account.

35. Lloyd, *South Africa's Media*, 6.

36. Ibid., 34.

37. Ibid., 31.

38. Louw, "Anglicising Postapartheid South Africa," 319.

39. Tomaselli, "South African Media 1994–7," 250.

40. Boloka, "Diversity Goes Global," 30.

41. Tomaselli, "South African Media 1994–7," 251.

42. See Tomaselli, "Repositioning African Media Studies," for a discussion of the complex set of deals and their ideological implications.

43. Mody, "Comparing the United Kingdom's *Guardian*," 76.

44. Tomaselli, "South African Media 1994–7," 252.

45. Strelitz, "Media Consumption and Identity Formation," 468.

46. Teer-Tomaselli, Wasserman, and De Beer, "South Africa as a Regional Media Power."

47. Tleane, *The Great Trek North*, 136–137.

48. Sparks, *Globalization, Development and the Mass Media.*
49. Wasserman, "Learning a New Language" and "South Africa and China as BRICS Partners."
50. Gagliardone, "New Media and the Developmental State in Ethiopia," 298.
51. Harber, "China's Soft Diplomacy in Africa."
52. Keita, "Africa's Free Press Problem."
53. Harber, "Update on China in African Media."
54. Harber, "Sekunjalo Consortium."
55. Hallin and Mancini, *Comparing Media Systems: Three Models.*
56. Ibid., *Comparing Media Systems beyond the Western World.*

Chapter 1. From Apartheid to a New Democracy

1. Krabill, *Starring Mandela and Cosby*, 4.
2. See Switzer and Adhikari, *South Africa's Resistance Press*, for a comprehensive historical account.
3. Daniels, *Fight for Democracy*, 24.
4. Lloyd, *South Africa's Media*, 6.
5. Tomaselli, "South African Media 1994–97," 282.
6. See Daniels, *State of the Newsroom South Africa 2013*, for an overview of the ANC's treatment of the media in the postapartheid era.
7. Peet, "Ideology, Discourse, and the Geography of Hegemony," 58.
8. Ibid., 75.
9. Tomaselli, "Political Economy," 175.
10. Jacobs, "How Good is the South African Media for Democracy?" 281.
11. For a detailed discussion of these ownership shifts and their implications, see Tomaselli, "Political Economy," on which this section draws.
12. Cowling, "Building a Nation," 325.
13. Tomaselli, "Political Economy," 170.
14. Johnnic Communications was renamed Avusa in 2007 to distinguish it from Johnnic Holdings, and in 2012, it was acquired by Mvelaphanda Holdings and renamed Times Media Group (TMG). TMG then bought the remaining 50 percent stake in the business titles *Business Day* and *Financial Mail* from Pearson, marking a flow back of media capital from a company based abroad to one based locally. Similarly, the Sekunjalo consortium, which bought back the Independent group of newspapers from the Irish-based company, is also an example of media capital flowing back to a locally owned company (if the stake of the Chinese consortium is set aside).
15. Tomaselli, "Political Economy," 170–171.
16. See Wasserman, "Learning a New Language," for a more detailed discussion of the repositioning of the Afrikaans media.
17. Lloyd, *South Africa's Media*, 17.
18. Anton Harber, quoted in Wright, "The Perils of Foreign Owners."

19. Harber, "Journalism in the Age of the Market."
20. This was also found in a skills audit commissioned by the South African National Editors' Forum some years later; see De Beer and Steyn, "Sanef's 2002 South African National Journalism Skills Audit."
21. Harber, "Journalism in the Age of the Market," and Jacobs, "Public Sphere, Power and Democratic Politics," 149.
22. Duncan, "Another Journalism Is Possible"; French, "Whose Freedom?"; Jacobs, "Public Sphere, Power and Democratic Politics."
23. Jacobs, "Public Sphere, Power and Democratic Politics," 146.
24. We will return to this issue in a separate section later.
25. Lloyd, *South Africa's Media*, 11.
26. Ibid., 12.
27. See, for example, Bond, *Elite Transition*, and Marais, *South Africa: Limits to Change*.
28. Horwitz, *Communication and Democratic Reform*, 42–43.
29. See Wasserman, "Learning a New Language," for a case study of how the Afrikaans media repositioned itself after apartheid.
30. Turner, *Ordinary People and the Media*, 20.
31. Ibid.
32. Ibid.
33. Sparks, "South African Media in Transition."
34. Tomaselli, "Political Economy," 175.
35. Ibid., 176.
36. Lloyd, *South Africa's Media*, 10.
37. Horwitz, *Communication and Democratic Reform*, 36.
38. Horwitz, *Communication and Democratic Reform*.
39. Ibid., 56.
40. Ibid., 63.
41. Lloyd, *South Africa's Media*, 10.
42. Wasserman, *Tabloid Journalism*.
43. Lloyd, *South Africa's Media*, 17.
44. Ibid.
45. Ibid., 6.
46. Ibid., 13.
47. Ibid., 14.
48. Nicolson, "Hlaudi Motsoeneng," and Davis, "SABC Interim Board."
49. Sparks, "South African Media in Transition," 205.
50. Benjamin, "Knock-and-Drop Case."
51. Ibid.
52. Lloyd, *South Africa's Media*, 15.
53. Cited in ibid., 19.
54. As mentioned in the introduction, Independent was sold in 2014 to the Sekunjalo consortium in a deal that raised concerns about the influence of Chinese investors and

the owner's (Iqbal Survé's) close ties to the ANC. This will be returned to later in this book.

55. Bassey, "The Rise and Fall of *ThisDay*," 68.
56. Lloyd, *South Africa's Media*, 16.
57. Ibid.
58. Malala, "The Truth."
59. Lloyd, *South Africa's Media*, 32. Only small media who do not pose a competitive threat to the major media houses are allowed to contribute to the MDDA.
60. Sparks, "South African Media in Transition."
61. Froneman, "Redes vir die gebrek."
62. Giffard, De Beer, and Steyn, "New Media for the New South Africa."
63. De Vos, "A Lot of Hot Air."
64. Barratt, *Part of the Story*, 22.
65. Ibid.
66. Nerone, *Last Rights*.
67. Christians and Nordenstreng, "Social Responsibility Worldwide."
68. Retief, *Media Ethics*.
69. Barratt, *Part of the Story*, 5.
70. Ibid., 7.
71. Ibid., 16, 29.
72. Ibid., 34–35.
73. Parsons, *The Social System*.
74. Personal communication, March 18, 2014.
75. Christians and Nordenstreng, "Social Responsibility Worldwide."
76. Ibid.
77. Ibid.
78. Harber, "Journalism in the Age of the Market," and Haffajee, "A Review of the Media."
79. Duncan, "Another Journalism Is Possible," 7.
80. Duncan, "Another Journalism Is Possible."
81. Christians and Nordenstreng, "Social Responsibility Worldwide," 16.
82. See Mandela, "Address to the International Press Institute."
83. Duncan, "Another Journalism Is Possible," 5.
84. Jacobs, "Public Sphere, Power and Democratic Politics," 132.
85. See Krabill, "Symbiosis," 591–596.
86. Johnson and Jacobs, "Democratisation and the Rhetoric of Rights," 91.
87. Ibid., 95.
88. Ibid., 98.
89. Barratt, *Part of the Story*, 4.
90. Krabill, "Symbiosis," 573.
91. Ibid.
92. Ibid.

93. Barratt, *Part of the Story*, 17.

94. Krabill, "Symbiosis," 576, 578.

95. Ibid., 579.

96. Lloyd, *South Africa's Media*, 9.

97. Ibid., 19.

98. Sparks, "South African Media in Transition," 195.

99. Blankson, "Media Independence and Pluralism," 19.

100. Sparks, "South African Media in Transition," 195.

101. Voltmer, "The Mass Media," 1.

102. Olorunnisola, Tomaselli, and Teer-Tomaselli, "Political Economy, Representation, and Transformation," 1.

103. Heller, "Democratic Deepening."

104. Sparks, "South African Media in Transition," 195.

105. Sparks, "South African Media in Transition," and Splichal, "Media Privatization and Democratization."

106. Sparks, "South African Media in Transition," 195.

107. Carothers cited in ibid.

108. Sparks, "South African Media in Transition," 196.

109. Ibid.

110. Ibid.

111. Ibid., 197.

112. Ibid., 199.

113. Ibid., 203–204.

114. Ibid., 208.

115. Ibid., 212.

116. Ibid., 213.

117. Ibid., 214.

118. As formulated by Heller, "Democratic Deepening."

119. Murphy, "Media and Democracy," 2.

120. Voltmer, "The Mass Media," 3.

121. Sparks, "South African Media in Transition."

122. Voltmer, "The Mass Media," 4.

123. Ibid.

124. Gurevitch and Blumler, "State of the Art," 178, 338.

125. Voltmer, "The Mass Media," 5; Wasserman and De Beer, "A Fragile Affair."

126. Christians and Nordenstreng, "Social Responsibility Worldwide."

127. Blankson, "Media Independence and Pluralism," 24.

128. Teer-Tomaselli and Tomaselli, "Transformation," 123.

129. Couldry, "Media Meta-Capital," 671.

130. Turner, *Ordinary People and the Media*, 20.

131. Couldry, "Media Meta-Capital," 671.

132. Macdonald, *Exploring Media Discourse*.

133. Jacobs, "How Good is the South African Media?" 281.
134. Mbeki, "I Am an African."
135. Adebayo, "Appraising Mandela and Mbeki."
136. Ross and Derman, *Mapping the Margins*, 2.
137. For how this was being done by the SABC, see Teer-Tomaselli, "Nation Building."
138. Servaes and Lie, "Media, Globalisation and Culture," 9.
139. Alexander, "New Meanings of Pan-Africanism."
140. Suttner, "Op-Ed."
141. See Krabill, "Symbiosis"; Steenveld, "Transforming the Media"; Steenveld and Strelitz, "The 1995 Rugby World Cup"; Teer-Tomaselli, "Nation Building."
142. Mangcu, "The State of Race Relations," 108.
143. Ibid., 110.
144. See Dawson, "Documenting Democratization"; Wasserman and Jacobs, Introduction.
145. Satgar, "Thabo Mbeki," 168.
146. Mbeki, "Address."
147. Ibid.
148. Malala, "The Truth."

Chapter 2. "This Time for Africa"?

1. Wasserman, *Tabloid Journalism*.
2. Curran and Park, *De-Westernizing Media Studies*.
3. Thussu, *International Communication*, 1.
4. Löffelholz and Weaver, *Global Journalism Research*.
5. Obijiofor and Hanusch, *Journalism across Cultures*.
6. For example: Ward, *Global Journalism Ethics*; Ward and Wasserman, *Media Ethics beyond Borders*.
7. Hallin and Mancini, *Comparing Media Systems beyond the Western World*.
8. Nordenstreng and Thussu, *Mapping the BRICS Media*.
9. For instance, Tomaselli, "Ideological Contestation."
10. Shome, "Post-Colonial Reflections."
11. Shome, "When Postcolonial Studies Meets Media Studies."
12. Ibid, 247.
13. Ibid.
14. Ibid.
15. Shome, "Post-Colonial Reflections." Also see Wasserman, "Introduction: Taking It to the Streets."
16. Comaroff and Comaroff, "Theory from the South," 113.
17. Ibid.
18. Ibid., 114.
19. Shiva, *Staying Alive*, 118.

20. Some random examples: Wasserman, *Tabloid Journalism*; Hasty, *The Press and Political Culture in Ghana*; Hachten, *Muffled Drums*.
21. Mamdani, "The Importance of Research."
22. Green, "Taylor & Francis Presentation."
23. See, for instance, Ndangam, "Gombo."
24. Mamdani, "The Importance of Research."
25. Chakrabarty, *Provincializing Europe*, 5.
26. Zakaria, *The Post-American World*.
27. Chakrabarty, *Provincializing Europe*, 16.
28. Bunce, Franks, and Paterson, "Introduction: A New Africa's Media Image?" 3.
29. Jacobs, "Media Perspectives."
30. Willems and Mano, *Everyday Media Culture in Africa*.
31. Nordenstreng, "Media Studies."
32. I owe this metaphor to Bruce Girard.
33. Wainaina, "How to Write about Africa."
34. Comaroff and Comaroff, "Theory from the South," 121.
35. Ibid., 122.
36. Spivak, *The Post-Colonial Critic*.

Chapter 3. A Changing Media Culture

1. Deuze, "What Is Journalism?" 446.
2. Cf. Thussu, *Media on the Move*.
3. Horwitz, *Communication and Democratic Reform*, 42–43.
4. French, "Whose Freedom?"
5. Zelizer, "Why Memory's Work," 80.
6. Ibid., 81.
7. Kitch, "Placing Journalism inside Memory," 313.
8. Conboy, "The Paradoxes," 6.
9. Zelizer, "Why Memory's Work," 81.
10. Deuze, "What Is Journalism?" 446.
11. Ibid., 447.
12. The findings from those interviews were first published in Wasserman, "The Presence of the Past."
13. Tomaselli, "South African Media 1994–7."
14. Ibid., 287.
15. Wasserman, "Freedom's Just Another Word?"
16. The quote "A critical, independent and investigative press is the lifeblood of any democracy" has been a favorite rhetorical gesture in recent debates about the proposed Media Appeals Tribunal, although it is seldom mentioned that the same speech (Mandela, "Address to the International Press Institute") also contained a blistering attack on the White, male domination of the South African press.

17. Harber, "Nat Nakasa."
18. Ibid.
19. Ibid.
20. Ibid.
21. Wasserman, "The Presence of the Past."
22. Cf. Zelizer, "Why Memory's Work," 81.
23. See Wasserman, "The Presence of the Past," for more detailed information about this study and its outcomes.
24. Berkowitz and TerKeurst, "Community as Interpretive Community," 125.
25. E.g., Fourie, "Rethinking the Role of the Media," and "'n Terugkeer na die onderdrukking."
26. *Mail and Guardian*, 2010, "Media May Be under Dire Threat."
27. Ibid., "Media Tribunal."
28. Ibid., "News Agencies."
29. *Biznews*, "Activists Stepping Up."
30. Cf. Deuze, "What Is Journalism?" 447.
31. Sparks, "South African Media in Transition," and "South African Media in Comparative Perspective."
32. *Mail and Guardian*, "Zuma."

Chapter 4. Is This Freedom?

1. Cf. Murphy, "Media and Democracy," 2, for similar processes in other new democracies.
2. Sparks, "South African Media in Transition," and Splichal, "Media Privatization and Democratization."
3. Bond, *Elite Transition*.
4. Friedman, "Whose Freedom?"
5. Caldwell, "Between Proceduralism and Substantialism," 61.
6. Ibid.
7. Ibid., 60–61.
8. Sen, *The Idea of Justice*; see Rao, "Global Media Ethics," for an application of these concepts to the Indian media.
9. Rao, "Global Media Ethics."
10. Heller, "Democratic Deepening."
11. Caldwell, "Between Proceduralism and Substantialism," 65–66.
12. Boyd-Barrett, "Media Imperialism."
13. Herman and McChesney, *The Global Media*.
14. Louw, "Soft Power."
15. Obijiofor and Hanusch, *Journalism across Cultures*, 2.
16. Hanitzsch, "Deconstructing Journalism Culture," 33.
17. Eide, Kunelius, and Phillips, "Contrapuntal Readings," 15.

18. De Liefde, *Lekgotla*.
19. Tomaselli, "Our Culture."
20. Rønning and Kasoma, *Media Ethics*; Wasserman and De Beer, "Covering HIV/AIDS."
21. Macdonald, *Exploring Media Discourse*, 11.
22. See, for instance, Black and Barney, "Search"; Christians et al., "Toward a Global Media Ethics"; Cooper et al., *Communication Ethics*; Wasserman, "The Search."
23. Christians et al., "Toward a Global Media Ethics," 138.
24. Christians and Nordenstreng, "Social Responsibility Worldwide," 4.
25. Ibid., 6.
26. See Johannesen, "Diversity, Freedom, and Responsibility."
27. Rao and Wasserman, "Global Journalism Ethics"; Wasserman and Rao, "The Glocalization."
28. Christians and Nordenstreng, "Social Responsibility Worldwide."
29. See Hlongwane, "The ANC's Best Friend."
30. Wines, "Media Turn Up the Heat."
31. *Ubuntu*, derived from the isiZulu saying *umuntu ngumuntu ngabantu*, "a person is a person through other persons." Applied to media ethics, this philosophy could be characterized as an African form of a communitarian media ethic (see Christians, "Ubuntu").
32. AllAfrica, "South Africa."
33. Leshilo, "Enemies of the People?"
34. See Wasserman, "Freedom's Just Another Word?" for findings of an empirical study of how "responsibility" and "freedom" were interpreted differently by various stakeholders in the political communication process.
35. For a related critique of discourses of "internationalization" in the field of cultural studies, see Shome, "Post-Colonial Reflections."
36. Christians, "Communication Ethics," 178.
37. Bickford, *The Dissonance of Democracy*; Dreher, "Listening across Difference"; Wasserman, "Journalism."
38. UNESCO, "Declaration of Windhoek."
39. E.g., Lodamo and Skjerdal, "Freebies"; Ndangam, "Gombo."
40. Rao and Wasserman, "Global Journalism Ethics"; Wasserman, "Globalised Values."
41. See Kasoma, *Journalism Ethics*; "The Foundations" and *The Press*.
42. E.g., Banda, "Kasoma's Afriethics"; Nyamnjoh, *Africa's Media*, 91.
43. Cf. critique by Tomaselli, "Our Culture."
44. Christians, "Ubuntu"; Fourie, "Ubuntuism."
45. Ibid.
46. Keita, "Africa's Free Press Problem"; Allison, "Tencent."
47. Xiaoge, "Development Journalism," 357.
48. Christians et al., *Normative Theories*, 200.
49. Ibid., 198.
50. Ogan, "Development Journalism," 10.

51. Christians et al., *Normative Theories*, 198–199.
52. Shah, "Modernization."
53. De Beer et al., "Binary Opposites."
54. www.worldsofjournalism.org (accessed July 1, 2017).
55. De Beer et al., "Binary Opposites."
56. This is in line with the traditional liberal model of the role of the media, or what Christians et al., *Normative Theories*, describes as the "monitorial" role.
57. This is a stance that is more in line with the conventional developmental model of the role of the media, or "collaborative" in Christians et al., *Normative Theories*.
58. Musa and Domatob, "Who Is a Development Journalist?" 315.
59. Ibid., 317.
60. Ibid., 320.
61. Kasoma, *Journalism Ethics*, 3.
62. See Banda, "Kasoma's Afriethics," for a recent summary and reassessment.
63. Kasoma, *Journalism Ethics*, 4.
64. Ibid., 8.
65. Ibid., 19.
66. Ibid., 28.
67. Tomaselli, "Our Culture." 430.
68. Ibid.
69. Banda, "Kasoma's Afriethics," 236; Tomaselli, "Repositioning African Media Studies," 13.
70. Fourie, "Ubuntuism."
71. Ibid.; Tomaselli, "Repositioning African Media Studies."
72. Banda, "Kasoma's Afriethics."
73. Berger, "Problematizing 'Media Development.'"
74. Ibid., 552.
75. Mfumbusa, "Newsroom Ethics," 143.
76. White, "The Moral Foundations."

Chapter 5. Global Genres and Local Context

1. Wasserman, "Attack."
2. Bloom, "*Daily Sun*."
3. Wasserman, "Attack."
4. Manson, "ABC Analysis."
5. Wasserman, "Attack," 787.
6. Cowling, "Building a Nation."
7. Zelizer, *The Changing Faces of Journalism*.
8. Steenveld and Strelitz, "Trash or Popular Journalism?" 532.
9. See Wasserman and Mbatha, "Tabloid TV."
10. Sparks and Tulloch, *Tabloid Tales*.

11. See Wasserman, "Tackles and Sidesteps," 66, for discussion.
12. Berger, "Remarks."
13. Friedman, "Whose Freedom?"
14. Manson, "No Responsibility Please."
15. Berger, "Current Challenges," 19.
16. Conboy, *The Press*, 35.
17. See Wasserman, *Tabloid Journalism*, for results of an audience study among tabloid readers.
18. IOL, "Video Shows Man Dragged."
19. De Beer and Steyn, "Sanef's 2002."
20. Daniels, *State of the Newsroom*.
21. Ibid., 3, 43.
22. Dayan and Katz, *Media Events*.
23. See Evans, *Broadcasting*, 10.
24. Although, as Couldry and Hepp, Introduction, 9, point out, the feasibility of such a function is limited in fragmented settings where a shared set of values may be absent, such as in the South African context where the legitimacy of the event was viewed differently depending on various social and political positions.
25. See Couldry and Hepp, Introduction, 11–12, for an overview of this concept, which draws on the work of Douglas Kellner and Guy Debord.
26. Ibid., 14.
27. Ibid., 15–17.
28. Zelizer, *The Changing Faces of Journalism*.
29. See ibid. for a discussion of this term.
30. See Botma, "Going Back"; Jacobs, *Tensions*; and Sparks, "South African Media," for an overview of some of the positions in these debates and conflicts.
31. Christians et al., *Normative Theories*.
32. See footage captured in *City Press*, "Watch—Marikana," and discussed in Wasserman, "Journalism."
33. Marinovich, "The Murder Fields of Marikana."
34. De Waal, "Marikana."
35. Wasserman, *Tabloid Journalism*, 105.
36. Christians et al., *Normative Theories*.
37. Wasserman, "Freedom's Just Another Word?"
38. De Waal, "Marikana."
39. Duncan, "Marikana."
40. Hook, "For the Love of Mandela."
41. Malila et al., "Making Meaning of Citizenship."
42. Dahlgren, *Media and Political Engagement*, 84.
43. Bakhtin, *Rabelais*, 7–9.
44. See, for instance, Bird, "News We Can Use," 35; Fiske, *Understanding Popular Culture*, 84; Langer, *Tabloid Television*, 160.
45. See Dewa and Prinsloo, "I Am a Man!" for a South African example.

46. Zelizer, *The Changing Faces of Journalism*, 5.
47. Ibid., 7–8.
48. Nicolson, "Mamphela Ramphele's Agang."
49. Hardt and Negri, *Empire*.
50. Ibid., 321–322.
51. SAPA, "Gender Commission."
52. Steinberg, "How SA Fell out of Love."
53. Dahlgren, *Media and Political Engagement*, 46.
54. One reporter even wrote frivolously about how journalists keep themselves busy while there was no news about the former president's condition. See Kings, "Seven Things to Do."
55. SABC, "Vuyo Mvoko Speaks to Makaziwe Mandela."
56. Smith, "Desmond Tutu."
57. Schechter, "Nelson Mandela's Final Battle."
58. Ibid.
59. Zakariah, *The Post-American World*.

Chapter 6. Rethinking Global and Local

1. Zelizer, *The Changing Faces of Journalism*.
2. See, for instance, the special issues by the leading scholarly journal, *Journalism Studies*, on "The Future of Journalism," based on papers presented at a series of international conferences held at the University of Cardiff on the same theme: Franklin, "The Future of Journalism," and "The Future of Journalism 2011."
3. Zelizer, "Terms of Choice," 890.
4. Ibid., 889.
5. Ibid.
6. Ibid., 891, 894, 896.
7. Ibid., 895.
8. Ibid., 900.
9. Berger, "A Paradigm in Process"; Wasserman, "Tackles and Sidesteps."
10. Daniels, *State of the Newsroom South Africa 2013* and *State of the Newsroom South Africa 2014*.
11. Harber and Krüger, Preface.
12. Daniels, *State of the Newsroom South Africa 2014*, vii.
13. Waisbord, "Remaking 'Area Studies,'" 35.
14. Berglez, *Global Journalism*, 26.
15. Robertson, *Global News*; Silverstone, *Media and Morality*.
16. Berglez, *Global Journalism*, 5.
17. Ibid., 13.
18. Rao and Wasserman, *Media Ethics and Justice*; Robertson, *Mediated Cosmopolitanism*; Ward, *Global Journalism Ethics* and *Global Media Ethics*.
19. De Beer, "News."

20. Reese, "Understanding the Global Journalist," 178.
21. Moorthy and Jamal, *Indian Ocean Studies*, 11.
22. Wicks, "The Panama Papers."
23. See Ghemawat, "Why the World Isn't Flat," and Marshall, "Sorry, Thomas Friedman," for critiques on Thomas Friedman's 2005 book, *The World Is Flat*.
24. Thussu, "Why Internationalize," 19.
25. De Beer, *Global Journalism*; Wahl-Jorgensen and Hanitzsch, *Handbook*; Weaver, *The Global Journalist*.
26. E.g., in Wahl-Jorgensen and Hanitzsch, *Handbook*.
27. Cf. the one sub-Saharan country versus seven European countries in the first round of the "Worlds of Journalism" project, www.worldsofjournalism.org (accessed July 3, 2017). (This project has subsequently been broadened to include other African countries, and, in the interest of disclosure, it should be mentioned that the author of this book has been involved in the revision of this project.) Or, cf. the one (North) African country included in Weaver, *The Global Journalist*.
28. Shiva, *Staying Alive*, 118.
29. Timmons, "Newspapers on Upswing."
30. Wasserman, *Tabloid Journalism*.
31. Nordenstreng, "Media Studies," 255.
32. Löffelholz and Weaver, *Global Journalism Research*.
33. Thussu, *Internationalizing Media Studies*.
34. http://wjec.ru.ac.za/ (accessed July 3, 2017).
35. Weaver and Löffelholz, "Questioning National, Cultural and Disciplinary Boundaries," 3.
36. Wasserman, "African Journalism Studies," 1.
37. Waisbord, "Remaking 'Area Studies,'" 30.
38. Ibid., 31.
39. UNESCO, *Many Voices, One World*.
40. Thussu, *Media on the Move*; Berger, "How the Internet Impacts."
41. E.g., Parameswaran, "Local Culture," 312.
42. Former editor of the *Guardian*, Alan Rusbridger's notion of "mutualised" journalism in his "Hugh Cudlipp Lecture" is apposite in this regard.
43. Sparks, "What's Wrong with Globalization?" 155.
44. Berger, "How the Internet Impacts."
45. Jay Rosen, "The People," even refers to "the people formerly known as the audience."
46. Mabweazara, "Mainstreaming," 1.
47. Berger, "How the Internet Impacts."
48. Mabweazara, "Mainstreaming," 4.
49. Rao, "The 'Local' in Global Media Ethics," 784.
50. Wasserman, *Tabloid Journalism*.
51. Thussu, *News as Entertainment*.
52. Nordenstreng and Thussu, *Mapping the BRICS Media*.

53. Thussu, "Why Internationalize," 18.
54. Tomaselli, "Repositioning African Media Studies," 17.
55. Curran and Park, *De-Westernizing Media Studies*.
56. Shome, "Post-Colonial Reflections."
57. Thussu, "Why Internationalize," 14.
58. Ibid., 15.
59. Wasserman, "Learning a New Language."
60. Tomaseli, "South African Media 1994–7."
61. Berger, "How the Internet Impacts," 364.
62. Rusbridger, "The Hugh Cudlipp Lecture."
63. Ibid.
64. Berger, "How the Internet Impacts," 365.
65. Ibid., 366.
66. Robertson, *Mediated Cosmopolitanism*, 20.
67. Thussu, *News as Entertainment*.
68. Sainath, "Where India Shining."
69. See Sparks, "What's Wrong with Globalization?"
70. Ward and Wasserman, *Media Ethics beyond Borders*.
71. Chouliaraki, *The Spectatorship*; Moeller, *Compassion Fatigue*; Silverstone, *Media and Morality*.
72. See Banda's reappraisal of "Kasoma's Afriethics" in this regard.
73. Tomaselli, "Our Culture"; Fourie, "Ubuntuism."
74. Chouliaraki, *The Spectatorship*; Robertson, *Mediated Cosmopolitanism*; Silverstone, *Media and Morality*.
75. Robertson, *Mediated Cosmopolitanism*, 11.
76. Nordenstreng, "Media Studies," 261.
77. Berger, "How the Internet Impacts," 356.
78. Ibid., 357.
79. Rusbridger, "The Hugh Cudlipp Lecture."
80. De Bruijn et al., *The New Talking Drums*.
81. Wasserman and Kabeya-Mwepu, "Creating Connections."
82. Wasserman, "Is a New World Wide Web Possible?"

Chapter 7. BRICS and Beyond

1. Zakaria, *The Post-American World*, 2.
2. See *The Economist*, "Africa's New Number One."
3. Nkoane-Mashabane, "South Africa's Role in BRICS."
4. Alden, *China in Africa*; Sautman and Yan, "Fu Manchu in Africa"; Waldron, *China in Africa*.
5. Cook, "Digital Business."
6. Ibid.

7. Steyn, "Naspers Rides"; see also Peacock, "Tencent's Worth."
8. Nye, *Soft Power*.
9. Kurlantzick, *Charm Offensive*.
10. Alden and Wu, *South Africa and China*, 25, 27.
11. Shi, "Strategies and Objectives."
12. Kurlantzick, *Charm Offensive*.
13. See Wu, *The Rise of China's State-led*, for an itinerary of Chinese media assistance projects on the continent.
14. Alden and Wu, *South Africa and China*, 25.
15. Vecchiato, "Firing."
16. Harber, "Sekunjalo Consortium."
17. Alden and Wu, *South Africa and China*, 26.
18. See Reese, "Understanding the Global Journalist," 182, on how such sources and relationships form part of a "hierarchy of influences."
19. Ibid.
20. Wasserman, "China in South Africa" and "South Africa and China as BRICS Partners."
21. Alden and Wu, *South Africa and China*, 26.
22. Wasserman, "China in South Africa" and "South Africa and China as BRICS Partners."
23. Alden and Wu, *South Africa and China*, 12.
24. Park and Alden, "Upstairs and Downstairs."
25. Alden and Wu, *South Africa and China*, 25.
26. E.g., Harber, "Sekunjalo Consortium."
27. Alden and Wu, *South Africa and China*, 25. See examples of this resistance elsewhere on the continent, such as in Ghana, as highlighted by French, *China's Second Continent*.
28. Reese, "Understanding the Global Journalist."
29. Wasserman, "South Africa and China as BRICS Partners."
30. Zhu, *Two Billion Eyes*, 7.

Chapter 8. New Pressures and Opportunities

1. Nyamnjoh, *Africa's Media*, 4.
2. Ibid.
3. E.g., Duncan, "Mobile Network Society?"; R2K, "Demand the Right."
4. Mapumolo, "Please Call Me Inventor."
5. Ibid.
6. Mabweazara, "Mainstreaming," 1.
7. Ibid.
8. Chib, "Research on the Impact," 6.
9. Chiumbu, "Exploring Mobile Phone Practices," 193; Mudhai, Tettey, and Banda, *African Media*, 1.

10. Chib, "Research on the Impact," 5–6.
11. Mabweazara, "Mainstreaming," 2.
12. Chiumbu, "Exploring Mobile Phone Practices," 193.
13. Donner, *After Access*, 19.
14. Chiumbu, "Exploring Mobile Phone Practices," 194.
15. Ibid.; Ekine, *SMS Uprising*.
16. See Van de Donk et al., *Cyberprotest*.
17. Jacobs and Duarte, "Protest in Mozambique."
18. Ekine, *SMS Uprising*, xi.
19. Hahn and Kibora, "The Domestication of the Mobile Phone," 88.
20. Etzo and Collender, "The Mobile Phone 'Revolution,'" 659.
21. Ekine, *SMS Uprising*, x.
22. Pew Research Center, "Cell Phones in Africa."
23. ITU, "Statistics."
24. Etzo and Collender, "The Mobile Phone 'Revolution,'" 660.
25. Pew Research Center, "Cell Phones in Africa."
26. Berger, "1001 Uses for a Cellphone"; Essoungou, "Africa's Social Media Revolution"; Etzo and Collender, "The Mobile Phone 'Revolution.'"
27. Ekine, *SMS Uprising*, xi.
28. Pew Research Center, "Cell Phones in Africa."
29. Mabweazara, "'New' Technologies," 14.
30. Nyamnjoh, "Africa and the Information Superhighway."
31. ITU, "Measuring the Information Society," 103.
32. Etzo and Collender, "The Mobile Phone 'Revolution,'" 660, 666.
33. Smith, "Africa Calling."
34. Duncan, "Mobile Network Society?"
35. Ibid.
36. Ibid.
37. Ibid.
38. Ibid.; Etzo and Collender, "The Mobile Phone 'Revolution,'" 666.
39. Nyamnjoh, "Africa and the Information Superhighway," 31.
40. Mabweazara, "'New' Technologies," 13–14.
41. Ling, *The Mobile Connection*, 26.
42. Hahn and Kibora, "The Domestication of the Mobile Phone," 103.
43. Goggin, *Cell Phone Culture*, 4.
44. De Bruijn et al., *The New Talking Drums*.
45. Goggin, *Cell Phone Culture*, 2–3.
46. Walton and Donner, "Read-Write-Erase."
47. Ibid.
48. See www.abahlali.org (accessed June 30, 2017) and Chiumbu, "Exploring Mobile Phone Practices."
49. Walton and Donner, "Read-Write-Erase."

50. Willems, "At the Crossroads," 56.
51. Walton and Donner, "Read-Write-Erase."
52. Ellis, "Tuning In," 321.
53. See Ogola, "If You Rattle a Snake."
54. Heller, "Democratic Deepening," 132.
55. Cf. Robins, Cornwall, and Von Lieres, "Rethinking 'Citizenship,'" 1072.
56. Ekine, *SMS Uprising*.
57. Robins, Cornwall, and Von Lieres, "Rethinking 'Citizenship,'" 1070.
58. Ibid., 1080.
59. Southwood, *Less Walk, More Talk*, xiv.
60. Cf. the political economy critique of Duncan, "Mobile Network Society?" mentioned earlier.
61. Etzo and Collender, "The Mobile Phone 'Revolution,'" 659.
62. As described in Southwood, *Less Walk, More Talk*.
63. Van Zyl, "WhatsApp."
64. Hahn and Kibora, "The Domestication of the Mobile Phone," 94–96.
65. Southwood, *Less Walk, More Talk*, xvi.
66. Mare, "Facebook, Youth and Political Action."
67. Jones and Pitcher, "Traditions, Conventions and Ethics," 105.
68. Tandwa, "Vytjie Mentor."
69. Thomas, "Estate Agent."
70. ANA, "Judiciary Body."
71. *GroundUp*, "Rhodes Must Fall Leader."
72. This section until the end of the chapter draws on Jacobs and Wasserman, "The Day Mainstream Media Became Old."
73. In general, South African media also use Twitter but then mainly to aggregate and amplify their news products.
74. Services like cleaning, catering, and campus security had been handed over to private companies, which meant the loss of benefits like tuition discount for the children of campus service staff.

References

Adebayo, Adekeye. "Appraising Mandela and Mbeki." *Sunday Independent*, February 27, 2012. Accessed May 26, 2016. http://www.iol.co.za/sundayindependent/appraising-mandela-and-mbeki-1.1243712.

Alden, Chris. *China in Africa*. London: Zed Books, 2007.

Alden, Chris, and Yu-Shan Wu. *South Africa and China: The Making of a Partnership*. Global Powers in Africa Programme. SAIIA Occasional Paper, no. 199. Johannesburg: South African Institute of International Affairs, 2014.

Alexander, Neville. "New Meanings of Pan-Africanism in the Era of Globalisation." Fourth Annual Frantz Fanon Distinguished Lecture, DePaul University. Chicago: October 8, 2003. Accessed May 26, 2016. http://ccs.ukzn.ac.za/files/Panafri1.pdf.

AllAfrica. "South Africa: SABC in Media War." 2007. Accessed May 25, 2015. http://allafrica.com/stories/200709140594.html.

Allison, Simon. "Tencent, WeChat and Chinese Censorship: Does Naspers Have a Free Speech Problem?" *Daily Maverick*, November 20, 2014. Accessed May 25, 2015. http://www.dailymaverick.co.za/article/2014-11-20-tencent-wechat-and-chinese-censorship-does-naspers-have-a-free-speech-problem/.

ANA (African News Agency). "Judiciary Body to Investigate Complaint about Judge's Racist Remarks." *Mail and Guardian*, May 10, 2016. Accessed May 25, 2016. http://mg.co.za/article/2016-05-10-judiciary-body-to-investigate-complaint-about-judges-racist-remarks/.

———. "Some Important Developments in the Movement of a Cultural Boycott against South Africa." November 25, 1983. Accessed May 26, 2016. http://www.anc.org.za/show.php?id=6869&t=Boycotts.

Bakhtin, Mikhail. *Rabelais and His World*, translated by Hélêne Iswolsky. Bloomington: Indiana University Press, 1984.

Banda, Fackson. "Kasoma's Afriethics: A Reappraisal." *International Communication Gazette* 71, no. 4 (2009): 227–242.

———. "Negotiating Distant Influences: Globalization and Broadcasting Policy Reforms in Zambia and South Africa." *Canadian Journal of Communication* 31, no. 2 (2006). Accessed May 25, 2016. http://cjc-online.ca/index.php/journal/article/view/1785/1907.

Barratt, Elizabeth. *Part of the Story: 10 Years of the South African National Editors' Forum*. Rosebank: SANEF, 2006.

Bassey, Eno A. "The Rise and Fall of *ThisDay* Newspaper: The Significance of Advertising to Its Demise." MA diss., University of the Witwatersrand, 2006. Accessed May 26, 2016. http://wiredspace.wits.ac.za/handle/10539/1549.

Benjamin, Chantelle. "Knock-and-Drop Case Is Big News." *Mail and Guardian*, May 23, 2014. Accessed June 30, 2016. http://mg.co.za/article/2014-05-23-knock-and-drop-case-is-big-news.

Berger, Guy. "1001 Uses for a Cellphone." *Mail and Guardian*, October 18, 2008. Accessed May 25, 2016. http://www.mg.co.za/article/2008-10-16-1-uses-for-a-cellphone.

———. "Current Challenges." In *Changing the Fourth Estate: Essays on South African Journalism*, edited by Adrian Hadland, 19–26. Cape Town: HSRC Press, 2005.

———. "How the Internet Impacts on International News." *International Communication Gazette* 71, no. 5 (2009): 355–371.

———. "A Paradigm in Process: What the Scapegoating of Vusi Mona Signalled about South African Journalism." *Communicatio* 34, no. 1 (2008): 1–20.

———. "Problematizing 'Media Development' as a Bandwagon Gets Rolling." *International Communication Gazette* 72, no. 7 (2010): 547–565.

———. "Remarks at Mondi Shanduka Newspaper Journalism Awards." April 20, 2005. Accessed May 26, 2016. guyberger.ru.ac.za/fulltext/mondi05.doc.

Berglez, Peter. *Global Journalism: Theory and Practice*. New York: Peter Lang, 2013.

Berkowitz, Dan, and James V. TerKeurst. "Community as Interpretive Community: Rethinking the Journalist-Source Relationship." *Journal of Communication* 49, no. 3 (1999): 125–136.

Bickford, Susan. *The Dissonance of Democracy: Listening, Conflict and Citizenship*. Ithaca: Cornell University Press, 1996.

Bird, Elizabeth S. "News We Can Use: An Audience Perspective on the Tabloidization of News in the United States." *The Public* 5, no. 3 (1998): 33–49.

Biznews. "Activists Stepping Up to Defend Cape Times Editor Alide Dasnois after Her Firing by New CEO Iqbal Survé." *Biznews*, December 20, 2013. Accessed May 25, 2016. http://www.biznews.com/interviews/2013/12/20/mark-weinberg-right-2-know-campaign/.

Black, Jay, and Ralph Barney, eds. "Search for a Global Media Ethic." Special issue, *Journal of Mass Media Ethics* 17, no. 4 (2002).

Blankson, Isaac A. "Media Independence and Pluralism in Africa: Opportunities and Challenges of Democratization and Liberalization." In *Negotiating Democracy: Media*

Transformation in Emerging Democracies, edited by Isaac Blankson and Patrick Murphy, 15–34. Albany: SUNY Press, 2007.

Bloom, Kevin. "Daily Sun Outshines All." *Mail and Guardian*, March 3, 2003. Accessed May 25, 2016. http://mg.co.za/article/2004-03-03-daily-sun-outshines-all.

Boloka, Mashilo. "Diversity Goes Global." *Rhodes Journalism Review* 24 (2004): 30–31.

Bond, Patrick. *Elite Transition: From Apartheid to Neoliberalism in South Africa*. Pietermaritzburg: University of Natal Press, 2000.

Botma, Gabriel J. "Going Back to the Crossroads: Visions of a Democratic Media Future at the Dawn of the New South Africa." *Ecquid Novi: African Journalism Studies* 32, no. 2 (2011): 75–89.

Boyd-Barrett, Oliver. "Media Imperialism Reformulated." In *International Communication: A Reader*, edited by Daya Thussu, 139–153. Abingdon: Routledge, 2010.

Bunce, Mel, Suzanne Franks, and Chris Paterson. "Introduction: A New *Africa's Media Image*?" In *Africa's Media Image in the 21st Century: From the 'Heart of Darkness' to 'Africa Rising'*, edited by Mel Bunce, Suzanne Franks, and Chris Paterson, 1–14. Abingdon: Routledge, 2017.

Caldwell, Marc. "Between Proceduralism and Substantialism in Communication Ethics." In *Communication and Media Ethics in South Africa*, edited by Natalie Hyde-Clarke, 58–75. Cape Town: Juta, 2011.

Chakrabarty, Dipesh. *Provincializing Europe*. Princeton: Princeton University Press, 2007.

Chib, Arul. "Research on the Impact of the Information Society in the Global South: An Introduction to SIRCA." In *Impact of Information Society Research in the Global South*, edited by Arul Chib, Julian May, and Roxana Barrantes, 1–17. Singapore: Springer Open, 2015.

Chiumbu, Sarah. "Exploring Mobile Phone Practices in Social Movements in South Africa: The Western Cape Anti-Eviction Campaign." *African Identities* 10, no. 2 (2012): 193–206.

Chouliaraki, Lilie. *The Spectatorship of Suffering*. London: Sage, 2006.

Christians, Clifford. "Communication Ethics in Postnarrative Terms." In *Key Concepts in Critical Cultural Studies*, edited by Linda Steiner and Clifford Christians, 173–186. Urbana: University of Illinois Press, 2010.

Christians, Clifford G. "Ubuntu and Communitarianism in Media Ethics." *Ecquid Novi: African Journalism Studies* 25, no. 2 (2004): 235–256.

Christians, Clifford G., and Kaarle Nordenstreng. "Social Responsibility Worldwide." *Journal of Mass Media Ethics* 19, no. 1 (2004): 3–28.

Christians, Clifford G., Shakuntala Rao, Stephen J. Ward, and Herman Wasserman. "Toward a Global Media Ethics: Exploring New Theoretical Perspectives." *Ecquid Novi: African Journalism Studies* 29, no. 2 (2008): 135–172.

Christians, Clifford G., Theodore L Glasser, Denis Mcquail, Kaarle Nordenstreng, and Robert A White. *Normative Theories of the Media: Journalism in Democratic Societies*. Urbana: University of Illinois Press, 2009.

Citizen. "Google Doodle Marks SA Election." *Citizen*, May 7, 2014. Accessed May 25, 2016. http://citizen.co.za/171873/google-doodle-marks-sa-election/.

City Press. "Watch—Marikana: Who Shot First?" *City Press*, August 21, 2012. Accessed May 25, 2016. http://www.news24.com/Archives/City-Press/Watch-Marikana-Who-shot-first-20150429.

Comaroff, Jean, and John Comaroff. "Theory from the South: Or, How Euro-America Is Evolving Toward Africa." *Anthropological Forum* 22, no. 2 (2012): 113–131.

Conboy, Martin. "The Paradoxes of Journalism History." *Australian Journalism Review* 32, no. 1 (2010): 5–13.

———. *The Press and Popular Culture*. London: Sage, 2002.

Cook, David. "Digital Business in China." *Corospondent* (April 2016): 40–44.

Cooper, Thomas W., Clifford G. Christians, Frances F. Plude, and Robert A. White, eds. *Communication Ethics and Global Change*. White Plains: Longman, 1989.

Couldry, Nick. "Media Meta-Capital: Extending the Range of Bourdieu's Field Theory." *Theory and Society* 32 (2003): 653–677.

Couldry, Nick, and Andreas Hepp. "Introduction: Media Events in Globalized Media Cultures." In *Media Events in a Global Age*, edited by Nick Couldry and Andreas Hepp, 1–20. Abingdon: Routledge, 2010.

Cowling, Lesley. "Building a Nation: The *Sowetan* and the Creation of a Black Public." *Journal of Southern African Studies* 40, no. 2 (2014): 325–341.

Curran, James, and Miyung-Jin Park. *De-Westernizing Media Studies*. London: Routledge, 2000.

Dahlgren, Peter. *Media and Political Engagement: Citizens, Communication and Democracy*. Cambridge: Cambridge University Press, 2009.

Daniels, Glenda. *Fight for Democracy: The ANC and the Media in South Africa*. Johannesburg: Wits University Press, 2012.

———, ed. *State of the Newsroom South Africa 2013: Disruptions and Transitions*. Johannesburg: Wits Journalism, 2013. Accessed May 26, 2016. http://www.journalism.co.za/wp-content/uploads/2014/03/State_of_the_newroom_20131.pdf.

———, ed. *State of the Newsroom South Africa 2014: Disruptions Accelerated*. Johannesburg: Wits Journalism, 2014. Accessed May 26, 2016. http://www.journalism.co.za/wp-content/uploads/2014/10/State-of-the-newsroom-2014.pdf.

Davis, Gaye. "SABC Interim Board Must End Climate of Fear—Parly Committee." *Eyewitness News*, January 24, 2017. Accessed February 20, 2017. http://ewn.co.za/2017/01/24/sabc-new-board-tasked-with-ensuring-free-fair-working-environment.

Dawson, Ashley. "Documenting Democratization: New Media Practices in Post-Apartheid South Africa." In *Media in Transition*, edited by David Thorburn, 225–244. Boston: MIT Press, 2003.

Dayan, Daniel, and Elihu Katz. *Media Events: The Live Broadcasting of History*. Cambridge: Harvard University Press, 1992.

De Beer, Arnold S., ed. *Global Journalism: Topical Issues and Media Systems*. 5th ed. Boston: Pearson, 2008.

———. "News from and in the 'Dark Continent.'" *Journalism Studies* 11, no. 4 (2010): 596–609.

De Beer, Arnold S., and Elanie Steyn. "Sanef's 2002 South African National Journalism Skills Audit." *Ecquid Novi: African Journalism Studies* 23, no. 1 (2002): 11–86.

De Beer, Arnold S., Vanessa Malila, Sean Beckett, and Herman Wasserman. "Binary Opposites: Can South African Journalists Be Both Watchdogs and Developmental Journalists?" *Journal of African Media Studies* 8, no. 1 (2016): 35–53.

De Bruijn, Mirjam, Francis Nyamnjoh, and Inge Brinkman, eds. *The New Talking Drums of Everyday Africa*. Leiden: Africa Studiecentrum, 2009.

De Liefde, Willem. *Lekgotla: The Art of Leadership through Dialogue*. Houghton: Jacana, 2003.

Deuze, Mark. "What Is Journalism? Professional Identity and Ideology of Journalists Reconsidered." *Journalism: Theory, Practice, Criticism* 6, no. 4 (2005): 442–464.

De Vos, Pierre. "A Lot of Hot Air about Section 205." *Constitutionally Speaking*, January 22, 2010. Accessed May 25, 2016. http://constitutionallyspeaking.co.za/a-lot-of-hot-air-about-section-205/.

Dewa, Nhlanhla, and Jeanne Prinsloo. "'I Am a Man!' The *Daily Sun* Campaign and Gender Violence." *Ecquid Novi: African Journalism Studies* 33, no. 2 (2010): 20–35.

De Waal, Alex. "Recognizing Nelson Mandela." *African Arguments*, December 10, 2013. Accessed May 25, 2016. http://africanarguments.org/2013/12/10/recognizing-nelson-mandela-by-alex-de-waal/.

De Waal, Mandy. "Marikana: What Really Happened? We May Never Know." *Daily Maverick*, August 23, 2012. Accessed May 25, 2016. http://dailymaverick.co.za/article/2012-08-23-marikana-what-really-happened-we-may-never-know.

Donner, Jonathan. *After Access*. Boston: MIT Press, 2015.

Dreher, Tanja. "Listening across Difference: Media and Multiculturalism beyond the Politics of Voice." *Continuum* 23, no. 4 (2009): 445–458.

Duncan, Jane. "Another Journalism Is Possible: Critical Challenges for the Media in South Africa." Memorial Lecture, Harold Wolpe Lecture Series. University of KwaZulu-Natal, October 30, 2003. Accessed May 26, 2016. http://ccs.ukzn.ac.za/files/wolpe2.pdf.

———. "Marikana and the Problem of Pack Journalism." *SABC News Online*, October 7, 2012. Accessed May 25, 2016. http://www.sabc.co.za/news/a/00f7e0804cfe58899b00bf76c8dbd3db/Marikana-and-the-problem-of-pack-journalism-20121007.

———. "Mobile Network Society? Affordability and Mobile Phone Usage in Grahamstown East." *Communicatio* 39, no. 1 (2013): 35–52.

The Economist. "Africa's New Number One." *The Economist*, July 7, 2014. Accessed May 25, 2016. http://www.economist.com/news/leaders/21600685-nigerias-suddenly-supersized-economy-indeed-wonder-so-are-its-still-huge.

———. "Nelson Mandela (Obituary)." *The Economist*, December 14, 2013. Accessed May 25, 2016. http://www.economist.com/news/obituary/21591539-nelson-mandela-man-who-freed-south-africa-apartheid-died-december-5th-aged.

Eide, Elisabeth, Risto Kunelius, and Angela Phillips. "Contrapuntal Readings: Transnational Media Research and the Cartoon Controversy as a Global News Event." In *Transnational Media Events: The Mohammed Cartoons and the Imagined Clash of*

Civilizations, edited by Elisabeth Eide, Risto Kunelius, and Angela Phillips, 11–27. Göteborg: Nordicom, 2008.

Ekine, Sokari, ed. *SMS Uprising: Mobile Activism in Africa*. Oxford: Fahamu, 2010.

Ellis, Stephen. "Tuning In to Pavement Radio." *African Affairs* 88, no. 352 (1989): 321–330.

Essoungou, André-Michel. "Africa's Social Media Revolution." *Bizcommunity*, December 13, 2010. Accessed May 25, 2016. http://www.bizcommunity.com/Article/410/16/55280.html.

Etzo, Sebastiana, and Guy Collender. "The Mobile Phone 'Revolution' in Africa: Rhetoric or Reality?" *African Affairs* 109, no. 437 (2010): 659–668.

Evans, Martha. *Broadcasting the End of Apartheid: Television and the Birth of the New South Africa*. London: IB Taurus, 2014.

Fiske, John. *Understanding Popular Culture*. Boston: Unwin Hyman, 1989.

Fourie, Pieter. "'n Terugkeer na die onderdrukking van vryheid van spraak? Ooreenkomste tussen die apartheidsregering(s) en die ANC se optrede teen die media" [A Return to the Repression of Freedom of Speech? Similarities between the Apartheid Government(s) and the ANC's Actions against the Media]. *Tydskrif vir Geesteswetenskappe* 49, no. 1 (2009): 62–84.

———. "Rethinking the Role of the Media in South Africa." *Communicare* 21, no. 1 (2002): 17–40.

———. "Ubuntuism as a Framework for South African Media Practice and Performance: Can It Work?" *Communicatio* 34, no. 1 (2008): 53–79.

Franklin, Bob, ed. "The Future of Journalism." Special issue, *Journalism Studies* 11, no. 4 (2010).

———, ed. "The Future of Journalism 2011: Developments and Debates." Special issue, *Journalism Studies* 13, no. 5–6 (2012).

French, Howard. *China's Second Continent: How a Million Migrants Are Building a New Empire in Africa*. New York: Knopf, 2014.

Friedman, S. "Whose Freedom? South Africa's Press, Middle-Class Bias and the Threat of Control." *Ecquid Novi: African Journalism Studies* 32, no. 2 (2011): 106–121.

Friedman, Thomas L. *The World Is Flat: A Brief History of the Twenty-First Century*. New York: Farrar, Straus and Giroux, 2005.

Froneman, Johannes D. "Redes vir die gebrek aan 'n ingeligte, lewendige debat oor media-etiek" [Reasons for the Lack of Intelligent, Lively Debate about Media Ethics]. *Ecquid Novi: African Journalism Studies* 15, no. 1 (1994): 123–128.

Gagliardone, Iginio. "New Media and the Developmental State in Ethiopia." *African Affairs* 113, no. 451 (2014): 279–299.

Ghemawat, Pankaj. "Why the World Isn't Flat." *Foreign Policy*, October 14, 2009. Accessed July 11, 2016. http://foreignpolicy.com/2009/10/14/why-the-world-isnt-flat/.

Giffard, Anthony C., Arnold S. De Beer, and Elanie Steyn. "New Media for the New South Africa." In *Press Freedom and Communication in Africa*, edited by Festus Eribo and William Jong-Ebot, 75–99. Trenton: Africa World Press, 1997.

Goggin, Gerard. *Cell Phone Culture*. London: Routledge, 2006.

Green, David. "Taylor & Francis Presentation (Based on figures from the International Association of Scientific, Technical and Medical Publishers)" at an Editor's Indaba, Cape Town, October 7, 2016.

GroundUp. "Rhodes Must Fall Leader Tells Waiter: 'We Will Give Tip When You Return the Land.'" *GroundUp*, April 29, 2016. Accessed May 25, 2016. http://www.groundup.org.za/article/rhodes-must-fall-leader-waiter-we-will-give-tip-when-return-land/.

Gurevitch, Michael, and Jay G. Blumler. "State of the Art of Comparative Political Communication Research: Poised for Maturity?" In *Comparing Political Communication*, edited by Frank Esser and Barbara Pfetsch, 325–343. Cambridge: Cambridge University Press, 2004.

Hachten, William A. *Muffled Drums: The News Media in Africa*. Ames: Iowa State University Press, 1971.

Haffajee, Ferial. "A Review of the Media in the First Decade of Democracy." Public lecture at the South African National Editors' Forum Media Seminar Series, Cape Town, July 2, 2004.

Hahn, Hans Peter, and Ludovic Kibora. "The Domestication of the Mobile Phone: Oral Society and New ICT in Burkina Faso." *Journal of Modern African Studies* 46, no. 1 (2008): 87–109.

Halleck, Thomas. "Google (GOOG) Earnings Preview Q3 2013: World's Biggest Search Engine to Book 14% Jump in Profit." *International Business Times*, October 16, 2013. Accessed May 25, 2016. http://www.ibtimes.com/google-goog-earnings-preview-q3-2013-worlds-biggest-search-engine-book-14-jump-profit-1427634.

Hallin, Daniel C., and Paolo Mancini, eds. *Comparing Media Systems beyond the Western World*. Cambridge: Cambridge University Press, 2012.

———. *Comparing Media Systems: Three Models of Media and Politics*. Cambridge: Cambridge University Press, 2004.

Hanitzsch, Thomas. "Deconstructing Journalism Culture: Toward a Universal Theory." In *Cultural Meanings of News: A Reader*, edited by Daniel Berkowitz, 33–47. London: Sage, 2011.

Harber, Anton. "China's Soft Diplomacy in Africa." *Ecquid Novi: African Journalism Studies* 34, no. 3 (2013): 149–151.

———. "Journalism in the Age of the Market." Harold Wolpe Memorial Lecture, University of KwaZulu-Natal, September 2002. Accessed May 26, 2016. http://ccs.ukzn.ac.za/default.asp?3,28,10,452.

———. "Nat Nakasa." *African Journalism Studies* 36, no. 1 (2015): 141–143.

———. "Sekunjalo Consortium Details Announced: Some Preliminary Thoughts on a Chinese Puzzle." *Harbinger*, June 20, 2013. Accessed May 26, 2016. http://www.theharbinger.co.za/wordpress/2013/06/20/sekunjalo-consortium-details-announced-some-preliminary-thoughts-on-a-chinese-puzzle/.

———. "Update on China in African Media." *Harbinger*, July 8, 2013. Accessed May 26, 2016. http://www.theharbinger.co.za/wordpress/2013/07/08/update-on-china-in-african-media/.

Harber, Anton, and Franz Krüger. Preface. In *State of the Newsroom South Africa 2014: Disruptions Accelerated*, edited by Glenda Daniels, vi. Johannesburg: Wits Journalism, 2014. Accessed May 26, 2016. http://www.journalism.co.za/wp-content/uploads/2014/10/State-of-the-newsroom-2014.pdf.

Hardt, Michael, and Antonio Negri. *Empire*. Cambridge: Harvard University Press, 2000.

Hasty, Jennifer. *The Press and Political Culture in Ghana*. Bloomington: Indiana University Press, 2005.

Heller, Patrick. "Democratic Deepening in India and South Africa." *Journal of Asian and African Studies* 44 (2009): 123–149.

Herman, Edward, and Robert McChesney. *The Global Media: The New Missionaries of Corporate Capitalism*. London: Continuum, 1997.

Hlongwane, Sipho. "The ANC's Best Friend: Brett Murray and the Spear." *Daily Maverick*, May 22, 2012. Accessed May 26, 2016. http://dailymaverick.co.za/article/2012-05-22-the-ancs-best-friend-brett-murray-the-spear.

Hook, Derek. "For the Love of Mandela." *Mail and Guardian Thought Leader*, July 4, 2013. Accessed May 26, 2016. http://www.thoughtleader.co.za/readerblog/2013/07/04/for-the-love-of-mandela/.

Horwitz, Robert B. *Communication and Democratic Reform in South Africa*. Cambridge: Cambridge University Press, 2001.

Hunter-Gault, Charlayne. *New News out of Africa: Uncovering Africa's Renaissance*. Oxford: Oxford University Press, 2006.

IOL. "Video Shows Man Dragged behind Police Van." *IOL News*, February 28, 2013. Accessed May 26, 2016. http://www.iol.co.za/news/crime-courts/video-shows-man-dragged-behind-police-van-1.1478398#.VdTvYvmqqko.

ITU (International Telecommuncation Union). "Measuring the Information Society Report," 2015. Accessed May 26, 2016. http://www.itu.int/en/ITU-D/Statistics/Documents/publications/misr2015/MISR2015-w5.pdf.

———. "Statistics," 2014. Accessed May 26, 2016. http://www.itu.int/en/ITU-D/Statistics/Pages/stat/default.aspx.

Jacobs, Sean. "How Good Is the South African Media for Democracy?" *African and Asian Studies* 14 (2002): 279–302.

———. "Media Perspectives: New Media and African Engagement with the Global Public Sphere." In *Africa's Media Image in the 21st Century: From the 'Heart of Darkness' to 'Africa Rising'*, edited by Mel Bunce, Suzanne Franks, and Chris Paterson, 190–192. Abingdon: Routledge, 2017.

———. "Public Sphere, Power and Democratic Politics: Media and Policy Debates in Post-Apartheid South Africa." PhD thesis, Birkbeck College, London, 2003.

———. *Tensions of a Free Press: South Africa after Apartheid*. Research Paper R-22, Joan Shorenstein Center, Harvard University, 1999. Accessed May 26, 2016. http://shorensteincenter.org/wp-content/uploads/2012/03/r22_jacobs.pdf.

Jacobs, Sean, and Diana Duarte. "Protest in Mozambique: The Power of SMS." *Afronline*, September 16, 2010. Accessed May 26, 2016. http://www.afronline.org/?p=8680.

Jacobs, Sean, and Herman Wasserman. "The Day Mainstream Media Became Old in South Africa." *Washington Post*, November 25, 2015. Accessed July 11, 2016. https://www.washingtonpost.com/news/monkey-cage/wp/2015/11/25/the-day-mainstream-media-became-old-in-south-africa/.

Johannesen, Richard L. "Diversity, Freedom, and Responsibility in Tension." In *Communication Ethics in an Age of Diversity*, edited by Josina M. Makau and Ronald C. Arnett, 157–186. Urbana: University of Illinois Press.

Johnson, Krista, and Sean Jacobs. "Democratisation and the Rhetoric of Rights: Contradictions and Debate in Post-Apartheid South Africa." In *Rights and Politics of Recognition in Africa*, edited by Francis Nyamnjoh and Harry Englund, 84–102. London: Zed Books, 2004.

Jones, Nicola. "When the Public Interest Is Not What Interests the Public: An Investigation of Privacy as Media Ethic in Contemporary South Africa." In *Communication and Media Ethics in South Africa*, edited by Natalie Hyde-Clarke, 162–175. Cape Town: Juta, 2011.

Jones, Nicola, and Sandra Pitcher. "Traditions, Conventions and Ethics: Online Dilemmas in South African Journalism." In *The Citizen in Communication—Re-visiting Traditional, New and Community Media Practices in South Africa*, edited by Nathalie Hyde-Clarke, 97–112. Claremont: Juta, 2010.

Kasoma, Francis P. "The Foundations of African Ethics (Afriethics) and the Professional Practice of Journalism: The Case for Society-Centred Media Morality." *Africa Media Review* 10, no. 3 (1996): 93–116.

———, ed. *Journalism Ethics in Africa*. Nairobi: ACCE, 1994.

———. *The Press and Multiparty Politics in Africa*. Tampere: University of Tampere, 2000.

Keita, Mohamed. "Africa's Free Press Problem." *New York Times*, April 15, 2012. Accessed May 26, 2016. http://www.nytimes.com/2012/04/16/opinion/africas-free-press-problem.html?_r2&ref.

Kings, Sipho. "Seven Things to Do When There's No News on Mandela." *Mail and Guardian*, June 13, 2013. Accessed May 26, 2016. http://mg.co.za/article/2013-06-13-8-things-to-do-when-theres-no-more-news-on-mandela.

Kitch, Carolyn. "Placing Journalism inside Memory—and Memory Studies." *Memory Studies* 1, no. 3 (2008): 311–320.

Krabill, Ron. *Starring Mandela and Cosby: Media and the End(s) of Apartheid*. Chicago: University of Chicago Press, 2010.

———. "Symbiosis: Mass Media and the Truth and Reconciliation Commission of South Africa." *Media, Culture and Society* 23, no. 5 (2001): 585–603.

Kurlantzick, Joshua. *Charm Offensive: How China's Soft Power Is Transforming the World*. New Haven: Yale University Press, 2007.

Langer, John. *Tabloid Television: Popular Journalism and the "Other News."* New York: Routledge, 1998.

Leshilo, Thabo. "Enemies of the People?" *Mail and Guardian*, September 7, 2007. Accessed May 26, 2016. http://mg.co.za/article/2007-09-07-enemies-of-the-people.

Ling, Rich. *The Mobile Connection: The Cell Phone's Impact on Society.* San Francisco: Morgan Kaufmann, 2004.

Lloyd, Libby. *South Africa's Media 20 Years after Apartheid.* A Report to the Center for International Media Assistance. Washington, D.C.: Center for International Media Assistance, 2013. Accessed May 26, 2016. http://cima.ned.org/publications/south-africas-media-20-years-after-apartheid.

Lodamo, Berhanu, and Terje Skjerdal. "Freebies and Brown Envelopes in Ethiopian Journalism." *Ecquid Novi: African Journalism Studies* 30, no. 2 (2009): 134–154.

Löffelholz, Martin, and David Weaver, eds. *Global Journalism Research: Theories, Methods, Findings, Future.* Oxford: Blackwell, 2008.

Louw, P. Eric. "Anglicising Postapartheid South Africa." *Journal of Multilingual and Multicultural Development* 25, no. 4 (2004): 318–332.

———. "Soft Power, Being Attractive to Others, and Nation Branding in an Epoch Where the Pax Americana Sets the Pace." *Ecquid Novi: African Journalism Studies* 34, no. 3 (2013): 141–148.

Mabweazara, Hayes M. "Mainstreaming African Digital Cultures, Practices and Emerging Forms of Citizen Engagement." *African Journalism Studies* 36, no. 4 (2015): 1–11.

———. "'New' Technologies and Journalism Practice in Africa: Towards a Critical Sociological Approach." In *The Citizen in Communication: Re-visiting Traditional, New and Community Media Practices in South Africa*, edited by Natalie Hyde-Clarke, 11–30. Claremont: Juta, 2010.

Macdonald, Myra. *Exploring Media Discourse.* London: Arnold, 2003.

Mail and Guardian. "Media May Be under Dire Threat Once More." *Mail and Guardian*, July 26, 2010. Accessed May 26, 2016. http://www.mg.co.za/article/2010-07-26-media-may-be-under-dire-threat-once-more.

———. "Media Tribunal Would Be a 'Very Dangerous Move.'" *Mail and Guardian*, July 30, 2010. Accessed May 26, 2016. http://www.mg.co.za/article/2010-07-30-media-tribunal-would-be-a-very-dangerous-move.

———. "News Agencies Sound Warning over Media Tribunal." *Mail and Guardian*, September 8, 2010. Accessed May 26, 2016. http://www.mg.co.za/article/2010-09-08-news-agencies-sound-warning-over-media-tribunal.

———. "Zuma: Media Tribunal to 'Complement' Self-Regulation." *Mail and Guardian*, September 9, 2010. Accessed May 26, 2016. http://www.mg.co.za/article/2010-09-09-zuma-media-tribunal-to-complement-selfregulation.

Malala, Justice. "The Truth behind the 'White Monopoly Capital' Propaganda Assault." *Rand Daily Mail*, January 23, 2017. Accessed February 20, 2017. https://www.businesslive.co.za/rdm/politics/2017-01-23-justice-malala-the-truth-behind-the-white-monopoly-capital-propaganda-assault/.

Malila, Vanessa, Marietjie Oelofsen, Anthea Garman, and Herman Wasserman. "Making Meaning of Citizenship: How 'Born Frees' Use Media in South Africa's Democratic Evolution." *Communicatio* 39, no. 4 (2013): 415–431.

Mamdani, Mahmood. "The Importance of Research in a University." *Pambazuka News*. April 21, 2011. Accessed October 12, 2016. http://www.pambazuka.org/resources/importance-research-university.

Mandela, Nelson. "Address to the International Press Institute." Cape Town, February 14, 1994. Accessed May 26, 2016. http://www.anc.org.za/show.php?id=3651.

Mangcu, Xolela. "The State of Race Relations in Post-Apartheid South Africa." In *State of the Nation: South Africa 2003–2004*, edited by John Daniel, Adam Habib, and Roger Southall, 105–117. Cape Town: HSRC Press, 2003.

Manson, Herman. "ABC Analysis Q4 2014: The Biggest Circulating Newspapers in South Africa." *Marklives.com*, February 19, 2015. Accessed May 26, 2016. http://www.marklives.com/2015/02/abc-analysis-q4–2014-biggest-circulating-newspapers-south-africa/.

———. "No Responsibility Please, We're Journalists." *Media Toolbox* 7(13), April 11, 2005. Accessed July 4, 2005. http://www.mediatoolbox.co.za/pebble.asp?relid=3325.

Mapumolo, Zinhle. "Please Call Me Inventor: It Wasn't Only About Money." *City Press*, May 1, 2016. Accessed May 26, 2016. http://city-press.news24.com/News/please-call-me-inventor-it-wasnt-only-about-money-20160501.

Marais, Hein. *South Africa: Limits to Change: The Political Economy of Transition*. Cape Town: Palgrave Macmillan, 2001.

Mare, Admire. "Facebook, Youth and Political Action: A Comparative Study of Zimbabwe and South Africa." PhD diss., Rhodes University, 2016.

Marinovich, Greg. "The Murder Fields of Marikana: The Cold Murder Fields of Marikana." *Daily Maverick*, September 8, 2012. Accessed May 26, 2016. www.dailymaverick.co.za/article/2012–08–30-the-murder-fields-of-marikana-the-cold-murder-fields-of-marikana.

Marshall, Stephen. "Sorry, Thomas Friedman, the World Is Round." *Alternet*, June 4, 2007. Accessed July 11, 2016. http://www.alternet.org/story/55418/sorry,_thomas_friedman,_the_world_is_round.

Mbeki, Thabo. "Address at the South African National Editors' Forum on the Media, African Union, Nepad and Democracy." Johannesburg, April 12, 2003. Accessed May 26, 2016. http://www.dfa.gov.za/docs/speeches/2003/mbek0412.htm.

———. "I Am an African—Thabo Mbeki's Speech at the Adoption of the Republic of South Africa Constitution Bill." Cape Town, May 8, 1996. Accessed May 26, 2016. http://www.anc.org.za/show.php?id=4322.

Mfumbusa, Bernadin F. "Newsroom Ethics in Africa: Quest for a Normative Framework." *African Communication Research* 1, no. 2 (2008): 139–158.

Mkonza, Khanyi. "Community Media and the MDDA." *Ecquid Novi: African Journalism Studies* 25, no. 1 (2004): 115–151.

Mody, Bella. "Comparing the United Kingdom's *Guardian* Newspaper with Its Co-Owned South African *Mail and Guardian Online*: Towards Productive Global North-South Collaborations in the Digital World Information Order." *Ecquid Novi: African Journalism Studies* 35, no. 1 (2014): 74–91.

Moeller, Susan D. *Compassion Fatigue*. London: Routledge, 1999.
Moorthy, Shanti, and Ashraf Jamal, eds. *Indian Ocean Studies: Cultural, Social and Political Perspectives*. London: Routledge, 2010.
Mudhai, Fred O., Wisdom Tettey, and Fackson Banda, eds. *African Media and the Digital Public Sphere*. New York: Palgrave Macmillan, 2009.
Murphy, Patrick D. "Media and Democracy in the Age of Globalization." In *Negotiating Democracy: Media Transformation in Emerging Democracies*, edited by Isaac Blankson and Patrick Murphy, 1–11. Albany: SUNY Press, 2007.
Musa, Bala A., and Jerry Domatob. "Who Is a Development Journalist? Perspectives on Media Ethics and Professionalism in Post-Colonial Societies." *Journal of Mass Media Ethics* 22, no. 4 (2007): 315–331.
Ndangam, Lilian. "'Gombo': Bribery and the Corruption of Journalism Ethics in Cameroon." *Ecquid Novi: African Journalism Studies* 27, no. 2 (2006): 179–199.
Nerone, John C., ed. *Last Rights: Revisiting Four Theories of the Press*. Urbana: University of Illinois Press, 1995.
Nicolson, Greg. "Hlaudi Motsoeneng: Another Court Defeat, but Still Fighting." *Daily Maverick*, May 23, 2016. Accessed May 26, 2016. http://www.dailymaverick.co.za/article/2016-05-23-hlaudi-motsoeneng-another-court-defeat-but-still-fighting/#.VobXyuSV3IV.
———. "Mamphela Ramphele's Agang, One Week Later." *Daily Maverick*, February 28, 2013. Accessed May 26, 2016. http://www.dailymaverick.co.za/article/2013-02-28-mamphela-rampheles-agang-one-week-later/#.UeaiJ2o7Wys.
Nkoane-Mashabane, Maite. "South Africa's Role in BRICS, and Its Benefits to Job Creation and the Infrastructure Drive in South Africa." Speech presented at the New Age Business Briefing, Johannesburg, July 7, 2014. Accessed May 26, 2016. http://www.brics.utoronto.ca/docs/120911-nkoana-mashabane.html.
Nordenstreng, Kaarle. "Media Studies as an Academic Discipline." In *Internationalizing Media Studies*, edited by Daya Thussu, 254–266. London: Routledge. 2009.
Nordenstreng, Kaarle, and Daya Thussu, eds. *Mapping the BRICS Media*. London: Routledge, 2015.
Nyamnjoh, Francis B. "Africa and the Information Superhighway: The Need for Mitigated Euphoria." *Ecquid Novi: African Journalism Studies* 20, no. 1 (1999): 31–49.
———. *Africa's Media: Democracy and the Politics of Belonging*. London: Zed Books, 2005.
Nye, Joseph S. *Soft Power: The Means to Success in World Politics*. New York: Public Affairs, 2004.
Obijiofor, Levi, and Folker Hanusch. *Journalism across Cultures: An Introduction*. London: Palgrave Macmillan, 2011.
Ogan, Christine. "Development Journalism/Communication: The Status of the Concept." *International Communication Gazette* 29, no. 1 and 2 (1982): 3–13.
Ogola, George. "'If You Rattle a Snake, Be Prepared to Be Bitten': Popular Culture, Politics and the Kenyan News Media." In *Popular Media, Democracy and Development in Africa*, edited by Herman Wasserman, 123–136. London: Routledge, 2010.

Olorunnisola, Anthony A., Keyan G. Tomaselli, and Ruth E. Teer-Tomaselli. "Political Economy, Representation, and Transformation in South Africa." In *Political Economy of Media Transformation in South Africa*, edited by Anthony Olorunnisola and Keyan G. Tomaselli, 1–13. Cresskill: Hampton Press, 2011.

Parameswaran, Radhika. "Local Culture in Global Media: Excavating Colonial and Material Discourses in National Geographic." *Communication Theory* 12 (2002): 287–315.

Park, Yoon J., and Christopher Alden,. "Upstairs and Downstairs Dimensions of China and the Chinese in South Africa." In *State of the Nation 2012–2013*, edited by Udesh Pillay, Gerard Hagg, and Francis Nyamnjoh, 643–662. Cape Town: HSRC Press, 2013.

Parsons, Talcott. *The Social System*. New York: Free Press, 1951.

Peacock, Brendan. "Tencent's Worth Turns into Naspers' Fortune." *Business Day*, July 10, 2014. Accessed May 26, 2016. http://www.bdlive.co.za/business/media/2014/02/09/tencent-s-worth-turns-into-naspers-s-fortune.

Peet, Richard. "Ideology, Discourse, and the Geography of Hegemony: From Socialist to Neoliberal Development in Postapartheid South Africa." *Antipode: A Radical Journal of Geography* 34, no. 1 (2002): 54–84.

Pew Research Center. "Cell Phones in Africa: Communication Lifeline." April 15, 2015. Accessed May 26, 2016. http://www.pewglobal.org/2015/04/15/cell-phones-in-africa-communication-lifeline/.

R2K (Right to Know Campaign). "Demand the Right to Communicate: Vula 'ma Connexion." April 15, 2013. Accessed May 26, 2016. http://www.r2k.org.za/2013/04/15/right2communicate/.

Rao, Shakuntala. "Global Media Ethics, Justice and Indian Journalism." In *Global Media Ethics: Problems and Perspectives*, edited by Stephen Ward, 235–252. New York: Wiley-Blackwell, 2013.

———. "The 'Local' in Global Media Ethics." *Journalism Studies* 12, no. 6 (2010): 780–790.

Rao, Shakuntala, and Herman Wasserman. "Global Journalism Ethics Revisited: A Postcolonial Critique." *Global Media and Communication* 3, no. 1 (2007): 29–50.

———, eds. *Media Ethics and Justice in the Age of Globalization*. New York: Palgrave Macmillan, 2015.

Reese, Stephen. "Understanding the Global Journalist: A Hierarchy-of-Influences Approach." *Journalism Studies* 2, no. 2 (2001): 173–187.

Retief, Johan. *Media Ethics: An Introduction to Responsible Journalism*. Cape Town: Oxford University Press, 2002.

Robertson, Alexa. *Global News: Reporting Conflicts and Cosmopolitanism*. New York: Peter Lang, 2015.

———. *Mediated Cosmopolitanism*. Cambridge: Polity, 2010.

Robins, Steven, Andrea Cornwall, and Bettina von Lieres. "Rethinking 'Citizenship' in the Postcolony." *Third World Quarterly* 29, no. 6 (2008): 1069–1086.

Rønning, Helge, and Francis Kasoma. *Media Ethics*. South Africa: Juta, 2002.

Rosen, Jay. "The People Formerly Known as the Audience." *Huffington Post*, June 30, 2006. Accessed July 10, 2016. http://www.huffingtonpost.com/jay-rosen/the-people-formerly-known_1_b_24113.html.

Ross, Karen, and Deniz Derman. *Mapping the Margins: Identity Politics and Media.* Cresskill: Hampton Press, 2003.

Rusbridger, Alan. "The Hugh Cudlipp Lecture: Does Journalism Exist?" *Guardian,* January 25, 2010. Accessed on May 26, 2016. http://www.guardian.co.uk/media/2010/jan/25/cudlipp-lecture-alan-rusbridger.

SABC. "Vuyo Mvoko Speaks to Makaziwe Mandela," YouTube video, 15:40, posted by "SABC Digital News," June 26, 2013. Accessed May 26, 2016. http://www.youtube.com/watch?v=DnFuQYkMaXQ.

Sainath, Palagummi. "Where India Shining Meets Great Depression." *The Hindu,* April 1, 2006. Accessed May 26, 2016. http://www.thehindu.com/todays-paper/tp-opinion/where-india-shining-meets-great- depression/article3140861.ece.

SAPA. "Gender Commission: Media Focus on Pistorius Overlooks Women Abuse." *Mail and Guardian,* February 19, 2013. Accessed May 26, 2016. http://mg.co.za/article/2013-02-19-gender-commission-media-focus-on-pistorius-ignores-gender-violence.

———. "Media Briefed on Mandela Funeral." *IOL News,* December 13, 2013. Accessed May 26, 2016. http://www.iol.co.za/news/south-africa/eastern-cape/media-briefed-on-mandela-funeral-1.1622325#.UwXcyYUU1A5.

Satgar, Vishwas. "Thabo Mbeki and the South African Communist Party." In *Thabo Mbeki's World,* edited by Sean Jacobs and Richard Calland, 163–177. Scottsville: University of Natal Press, 2002.

Sautman, Barry, and Hairong Yan. "Fu Manchu in Africa: The Distorted Portrayal of China's Presence in the Continent." *South African Labour Bulletin* 31 (2007): 34–38.

Schechter, Danny. "Nelson Mandela's Final Battle: Dying with Dignity." *AlJazeera,* July 19, 2013. Accessed May 26. 2016. http://www.aljazeera.com/indepth/opinion/2013/07/201371711254473893.html.

Sen, Amartya. *The Idea of Justice.* Cambridge: Belknap Press, 2009.

Servaes, Jan, and Rico Lie. "Media, Globalisation and Culture: Issues and Trends." *Communicatio* 29, no. 1 and 2 (2003): 7–23.

Shah, Hemant. "Modernization, Marginalization, and Emancipation: Toward a Normative Model of Journalism and National Development." *Communication Theory* 6, no. 2 (1996): 143–166.

Shi, Anbin. "Strategies and Objectives to Attract New Audiences Abroad." Paper presented at the FoMe Symposium, "Promoting Alternative Views in a Multipolar World: BRICS and Their Role in Developing Media Markets," Berlin, October 10, 2013.

Shiva, Vandana. *Staying Alive: Women, Ecology, and Development.* London: Zed Books, 1989.

Shome, Raka. "Post-Colonial Reflections on the 'Internationalization' of Cultural Studies." *Cultural Studies* 23, no. 5 and 6 (2009): 694–719.

———. "When Postcolonial Studies Meets Media Studies." *Critical Studies in Media Communication* 33, no. 3 (2016): 245–263.

Silverstone, Roger. *Media and Morality: On the Rise of the Mediapolis.* Cambridge: Polity, 2007.

Smith, David. "Africa Calling: Mobile Phone Usage Sees Record Rise after Huge Investment." *The Guardian*, October 22, 2009. Accessed July 12, 2016. https://www.theguardian.com/technology/2009/oct/22/africa-mobile-phones-usage-rise.

———. "Desmond Tutu: Nelson Mandela Family Feud 'Is like Spitting in Mandela's Face.'" *Guardian*, July 5, 2013. Accessed May 26, 2016. http://www.guardian.co.uk/world/2013/jul/05/desmond-tutu-nelson-mandela-family-feud-mandiba.

Southwood, Roger. *Less Walk, More Talk: How Celtel and the Mobile Phone Changed Africa*. Chichester: Wiley, 2008.

Sparks, Colin. *Globalization, Development and the Mass Media*. London: Sage, 2007.

———. "South African Media in Comparative Perspective." *Ecquid Novi: African Journalism Studies* 32, no. 2 (2011): 5–19.

———. "South African Media in Transition." *Journal of African Media Studies* 1, no. 2 (2009): 195–220.

———. "What's Wrong with Globalization?" *Global Media and Communication* 3, no. 2 (2007): 133–155.

Sparks, Colin, and John Tulloch, eds. *Tabloid Tales: Global Debates over Media Standards*. Lanham, Md.: Rowman and Littlefield, 2000.

Spivak, Gayatri Chakravorty. *The Post-Colonial Critic: Interviews, Strategies, Dialogues*, edited by Sarah Harasym. New York: Routledge, 1990.

Splichal, Slavko. "Media Privatization and Democratization in Central-Eastern Europe." *International Communication Gazette* 49, no. 1 and 2 (1992): 3–22.

Steenveld, Lynette. "Transforming the Media: A Cultural Approach." *Critical Arts* 18, no. 1 (2004): 92–115.

Steenveld, Lynette, and Larry N. Strelitz. "The 1995 Rugby World Cup and the Politics of Nation Building in South Africa." *Media, Culture and Society* 20, no. 4 (1998): 609–629.

———. "Trash or Popular Journalism? The Case of South Africa's *Daily Sun*." *Journalism* 11, no. 5 (2010): 531–547.

Steinberg, Jonny. "How SA Fell out of Love with Oscar Pistorius." *Mail and Guardian*, May 27, 2013. Accessed May 26, 2016. http://mg.co.za/article/2013-05-27-how-oscar-pistorius-fell-off-track-with-sa.

Steyn, Lisa. "Naspers Rides Big Chinese Wave." *Mail and Guardian*, March 21, 2012. Accessed May 26, 2016. http://mg.co.za/article/2012-08-31-naspers-rides-big-chinese-wave.

Strelitz, Larry N. "Media Consumption and Identity Formation: The Case of the 'Homeland' Viewers." *Media, Culture and Society* 24 (2002): 459–480.

Suttner, Raymond. "Op-Ed: Who Is an African?" *Daily Maverick*, June 4, 2014. Accessed May 26, 2016. http://www.dailymaverick.co.za/article/2014-06-04-op-ed-who-is-an-african.

Switzer, Les. "Introduction: South Africa's Resistance Press under Apartheid." In *South Africa's Resistance Press: Alternative Voices in the Last Generation under Apartheid*, edited by Les Switzer and Mohamed Adhikari, 1–75. Athens: Ohio University Press, 2000.

Switzer, Les, and Mohamed Adhikari, eds. *South Africa's Resistance Press: Alternative Voices in the Last Generation under Apartheid*. Athens: Ohio University Press, 2000.

Tandwa, Lizeka. "Vytjie Mentor to 'Tell More' to Media Tomorrow—Facebook Page Disappears." *Biznews*, March 17, 2016. Accessed May 26, 2016. http://www.biznews.com/briefs/2016/03/17/vytjie-mentor-to-tell-more-tomorrow-facebook-page-disappears/.

Teer-Tomaselli, Ruth. "Nation Building, Social Identity and Television in a Changing Media Landscape." In *Culture in the New South Africa*, edited by Robert Kriger and Abebe Zegeye, 117–138. Cape Town: Kwela Books, 2001.

Teer-Tomaselli, Ruth, and Keyan G. Tomaselli. "Transformation, Nation-Building and the South African Media, 1993–1999." In *Media, Democracy and Renewal in Southern Africa*, edited by Keyan Tomaselli and Hopeton Dunn, 123–150. Colorado Springs: International Academic Publishers, 2001.

Teer-Tomaselli, Ruth, Herman Wasserman, and Arnold De Beer. "South Africa as a Regional Media Power." In *Media on the Move: Global Flow and Contra-flow*, edited by Daya Thussu, 153–164. London: Routledge, 2007.

Thomas, Stuart. "Estate Agent Calls Black People 'Monkeys' in Racist Facebook Post." *Memeburn*, January 3, 2016. Accessed May 26, 2016. http://memeburn.com/2016/01/estate-agent-calls-black-people-monkeys-in-racist-facebook-post/.

Thussu, Daya K., ed. *International Communication: A Reader*. London: Routledge, 2010.

———, ed. *Internationalizing Media Studies*. London: Routledge, 2009.

———, ed. *Media on the Move: Global Flow and Contra-Flow*. London: Routledge, 2007.

———. *News as Entertainment: The Rise of Global Infotainment*. London: Sage, 2007.

———. "Why Internationalize Media Studies and How?" In *Internationalizing Media Studies*, edited by Daya K. Thussu, 13–31. London: Routledge, 2009.

Timmons, Heather. "Newspapers on Upswing in Developing Markets." *New York Times*, May 20, 2008. Accessed May 26, 2016. http://www.nytimes.com/2008/05/20/business/worldbusiness/20newspapers.html?_r=1&ref=media.

Tleane, Console. *The Great Trek North: The Expansion of South African Media and ICT Companies into the SADC Region*. Braamfontein: Freedom of Expression Institute, 2006.

Tomaselli, Keyan G. "Ideological Contestation and Disciplinary Associations: An Autoethnographic Analysis." *Communicatio* 42, no. 2 (2016): 276–292.

———. "'Our Culture' vs. 'Foreign Culture': An Essay on Ontological and Professional Issues in African Journalism." *Gazette* 65, no. 6 (2003): 427–441.

———. "Political Economy of the Transformation and Globalization of South African Media 1994–1997." In *Political Economy of Media Transformation in South Africa*, edited by Anthony Olorunnisola and Keyan G. Tomaselli, 167–180. Cresskill: Hampton Press, 2011.

———. "Repositioning African Media Studies: Thoughts and Provocations." *Journal of African Media Studies* 1, no. 1 (2009): 9–21.

———. "South African Media 1994–7: Globalizing via Political Economy." In *De-Westernizing Media Studies*, edited by James Curran and Myung-Jin Park, 279–292. London: Routledge, 2000.

Tomaselli, Keyan G., and Arnold Shepperson. "The Absent Signifier: The Morphing of Nelson Mandela." In *Cultural Icons*, edited by Keyan Tomaselli and David Scott, 25–42. Walnut Creek: Left Coast Press, 2009.

Turner, Graeme. *Ordinary People and the Media: The Demotic Turn*. London: Sage, 2010.
UNESCO. "Declaration of Windhoek." May 3, 1991. Accessed May 5, 2015. http://www.unesco.org/webworld/fed/temp/communication_democracy/windhoek.htm.
———. *Many Voices, One World: Towards a More Just and More Efficient World Information and Communication Order*. Report by the International Commission for the Study of Communication Problems. Paris: UNESCO, 1981. Accessed May 26, 2016. http://unesdoc.unesco.org/images/0004/000400/040066eb.pdf.
Van de Donk, Wim, Brian D. Loade, Paul G. Nixon, and Dieter Rucht, eds. *Cyberprotest: New Media, Citizens and Social Movements*. London: Routledge, 2004.
Van Zyl, Gareth. "WhatsApp Faces Possible Regulation in SA." *Fin24*, January 13, 2016. Accessed May 26, 2016. http://www.fin24.com/Tech/News/whatsapp-faces-possible-regulation-in-south-africa-20160113.
Vecchiatto, Paul. "Firing of Cape Times' Editor Raises Eyebrows." *Business Day*, December 9, 2013. Accessed May 26, 2016. http://www.bdlive.co.za/national/media/2013/12/09/firing-of-cape-times-editor-raises-eyebrows.
Verbaan, Aly. "Changing the Face of Africa." *Cape Times*, February 11, 2015.
Voltmer, Katrin. "The Mass Media and the Dynamics of Political Communication in Processes of Democratization." In *Mass Media and Political Communication in New Democracies*, edited by Katrin Voltmer, 1–20. London: Routledge, 2001.
Wahl-Jorgenson, Karin, and Thomas Hanitzsch, eds. *The Handbook of Journalism Studies*. New York: Routledge, 2008.
Wainaina, Binyavanga. "How to Write about Africa." *Granta*, January 19, 2006. Accessed February 20, 2017. https://granta.com/how-to-write-about-africa/.
Waisbord, Silvio. "Remaking 'Area Studies' in Journalism Studies." *African Journalism Studies* 36, no. 1 (2015): 30–36.
Waldron, Arthur, ed. *China in Africa*. Washington, D.C.: Jamestown Foundation, 2009.
Walton, Marion, and Jonathan Donner. "Read-Write-Erase: Mobile-Mediated Publics in South Africa's 2009 Elections." In *Mobile Communication: Dimensions of Social Policy*, edited by James E. Katz, 117–132. New Brunswick: Transaction Publishers, 2011.
Ward, Stephen J. A. *Global Journalism Ethics*. Montreal: McGill-Queen's University Press, 2010.
———, ed. *Global Media Ethics: Problems and Perspectives*. Malden: Wiley-Blackwell, 2013.
Ward, Stephen, and Herman Wasserman. *Media Ethics beyond Borders*. New York: Routledge, 2010.
Wasserman, Herman. "African Journalism Studies in a Globalised World." *African Journalism Studies* 36, no. 1 (2015): 1–10.
———. "Attack of the Killer Newspapers! The 'Tabloid Revolution' in South Africa and the Future of Newspapers." *Journalism Studies* 9, no. 5 (2008): 786–797.
———. "China in South Africa: The Media's Response to a Developing Relationship." *Chinese Journal of Communication* 5 (2012): 336–354.
———. "Freedom's Just Another Word? Perspectives on Media Freedom and Responsibility in South Africa and Namibia." *International Communication Gazette* 72, no. 7 (2010): 567–588.

———. "Globalised Values and Postcolonial Responses: South African Perspectives on Normative Media Ethics." *The International Communication Gazette* 68, no. 1 (2006): 71–91.

———. "Introduction: Taking It to the Streets." In *Popular Media, Democracy and Development in Africa*, edited by Herman Wasserman, 1–16. London: Routledge, 2011.

———. "Is a New World Wide Web Possible? An Explorative Comparison of the Use of ICTs by Two South African Social Movements." *African Studies Review* 50, no. 1 (2007): 109–131.

———. "Journalism in a New Democracy: The Ethics of Listening." *Communicatio* 39, no. 1 (2013): 67–84.

———. "Learning a New Language: Culture, Ideology and Economics in Afrikaans Media after Apartheid." *International Journal of Cultural Studies* 12, no. 1 (2009): 59–78.

———. "The Presence of the Past: The Uses of History in the Discourses of Contemporary South African Journalism." *Journalism Practice* 5, no. 5 (2011): 584–598.

———. "The Search for Global Journalism Ethics." In *Philosophical Approaches to Journalism Ethics*, edited by Christopher Meyers, 69–84. Oxford: Oxford University Press. 2010.

———. "South Africa and China as BRICS Partners: Media Perspectives on Geopolitical Shifts." *Journal of Asian and African Studies* 50, 1 (2015): 109–123. doi: 0.1177/0021909613514191.

———. *Tabloid Journalism in South Africa: True Story!* Bloomington: Indiana University Press, 2010.

———. "Tackles and Sidesteps: Normative Maintenance and Paradigm Repair in Mainstream Media Reactions to Tabloid Journalism." *Communicare* 25, no. 1 (2006): 59–80.

———. "To Come Back from Qunu." *Africa Is a Country*, December 17, 2013. Accessed May 26, 2016. http://africasacountry.com/to-come-back-from-qunu/.

Wasserman, Herman, and Arnold S. De Beer. "Covering HIV/Aids: Towards a Heuristic Comparison between Communitarian and Utilitarian Ethics." *Communicatio* 30, no. 2 (2004): 84–97.

———. "A Fragile Affair: An Overview of the Relationship between the Media and State in Post-Apartheid South Africa." *Journal of Mass Media Ethics* 20, no. 2 and 3 (2005): 192–208.

Wasserman, Herman, and Loisa Mbatha. "Tabloid TV in Zambia: A Reception Study of Lusaka Viewers of Muvi TV News." *Journal of African Media Studies* 4, no. 3 (2012): 275–391.

Wasserman, Herman, and Patrice Kabeya-Mwepu. "Creating Connections: Exploring the Intermediary Use of ICTs by Congolese Refugees at Tertiary Educational Institutions in Cape Town." *Southern African Journal of Information and Communication* 6 (2005): 94–103.

Wasserman, Herman, and Sean Jacobs. Introduction. In *Shifting Selves: Postapartheid Essays on Mass Media, Culture and Identity*, edited by Herman Wasserman and Sean Jacobs, 15–28. Cape Town: Kwela, 2003.

———. "Media, Citizenship and Social Justice in South Africa." In *State of the Nation 2012–2013*, edited by Udesh Pillay, Gerard Hagg, and Francis Nyamnjoh, 333–354. Cape Town: HSRC Press, 2013.

Wasserman, Herman, and Shakuntala Rao. "The Glocalization of Journalism Ethics." *Journalism: Theory, Practice Criticism* 9, no. 2 (2008): 163–181.

Weaver, David, ed. *The Global Journalist: News People around the World*. Cresskill: Hampton Press, 1998.

Weaver, David, and Martin Löffelholtz. "Questioning National, Cultural and Disciplinary Boundaries: A Call for Global Journalism Research." In *Global Journalism Research: Theories, Methods, Findings, Future*, edited by Martin Löffelholz and David Weaver, 3–12. Oxford: Blackwell, 2008.

White, Robert A. "The Moral Foundations of Media Ethics in Africa." *Ecquid Novi: African Journalism Studies* 31, no. 1 (2010): 42–67.

Wicks, Jeff. "The Panama Papers and the Zuma Link." *News24*, April 4, 2016. Accessed May 26, 2016. http://www.news24.com/SouthAfrica/News/the-panama-papers-and-the-zuma-link-20160404.

Willems, Wendy. "At the Crossroads of the Formal and Popular: Convergence Culture and New Publics in Zimbabwe." In *Popular Media, Democracy and Development in Africa*, edited by Herman Wasserman, 46–62. London: Routledge, 2010.

Willems, Wendy, and Winston Mano, eds. *Everyday Media Culture in Africa: Audiences and Users*. London: Routledge, 2017.

Wines, Michael. "Media Turn Up the Heat on South Africa's Health Minister." *New York Times*, August 20, 2007. Accessed May 26, 2016. http://www.nytimes.com/2007/08/20/world/africa/20iht-saf.4.7188583.html?_r=0.

Wright, Joanna. "The Perils of Foreign Owners." *The Media Online*, February 26, 2014. Accessed May 26, 2016. http://themediaonline.co.za/2014/02/the-perils-of-foreign-owners/.

Wu, Yu-Shan. *The Rise of China's State-Led Media Dynasty in Africa*. SAIIA Occasional Paper, no. 117. Johannesburg: South African Institute of International Affairs, 2012.

Xiaoge, Xu. "Development Journalism." In *The Handbook of Journalism Studies*, edited by Karen Wahl-Jorgensen and Thomas Hanitzsch, 357–370. New York: Routledge, 2009.

Zakaria, Fareed. *The Post-American World: Release 2.0*. New York: Norton, 2011.

Zelizer, Barbie. *The Changing Faces of Journalism: Tabloidization, Technology and Truthiness*. Abingdon: Routledge, 2009.

———. "Terms of Choice: Uncertainty, Journalism and Crisis." *Journal of Communication* 65 (2015): 888–908.

———. "Why Memory's Work on Journalism Does Not Reflect Journalism's Work on Memory." *Memory Studies* 1, no. 1 (2008): 79–87.

Zhu, Ying. *Two Billion Eyes: The Story of China Central Television*. New York: New Press, 2012.

Index

African culture, 88, 89
African ethical norms, 90
African ethics, 130
Africa News Network, 27
Africanization, 27, 44–45, 84, 85; of media ethics, 168
African journalism, 91
African journalists, 92, 93; communal orientation, 93
African media ethics, 89, 90, 93, 97; "Afriethics," 93
African media practice, 94
African media studies, 50
African National Congress, 3, 5–6, 30, 35, 39; government, 95, 140; and social media, 163
African values, 85, 88, 94
Afrikaans media, 21, 22, 24, 34, 104
ANC. *See* African National Congress
ANN7. *See* Africa News Network
apartheid, 2–3, 8, 67–68, 71–74; to democracy, 17–46
Argus, 21
audience studies, 126–128; anthropological approaches, 127; ethnographic methods, 127

BCCSA. *See* Broadcasting Complaints Commission of South Africa
BEE. *See* Black Economic Empowerment
BEF. *See* Black Editors' Forum
Bill of Rights, 3
Black: capital, 19, 20–21, 28; editors, 22; empowerment consortium (*see* National Empowerment Consortium); journalists, 19, 30, 34; ownership, 5, 6, 22, 25
Black Economic Empowerment, 20, 39
Black Editors' Forum, 30. *See also* South African National Editors' Forum
boycott, 7
BRICS, 8, 10, 13, 49, 53, 91, 111, 135–151; economic ties, 136; and new geopolitical relationships, 135–151
broadcasting, 109
Broadcasting Complaints Commission of South Africa, 29–30, 83
Brown, Karima, 21
Business Day, 20
Business Times, 20

Cape Argus, 20
Cape Times, 21, 66

Caxton, 26
changing media culture, 58–75
Charlie Hebdo, 85
China, 9, 10–11, 13, 38, 48, 91, 116, 126, 138–139; and Africa, 136–137; flow of media capital, 137, 138; and issue of freedom of the press, 141; news agency Xinhua, 137, 140, 148
China Central Television, 137
China Daily, 111, 137
China Radio International, 137
China's: media footprint in Africa, 138–140, 146, 147; use of media outlets, 147
Chinese media, 111, 139, 140–141, 146, 149; and credibility, 149–150; and editorial independence, 150; and freedom of expression, 139; incongruity with local news routines, 150; messages, 147–148; norms, 145; and South Africa, 91, 137, 138, 139, 141; stance towards the South African government, 150; state controlled, 146, 149
Chinese soft power, 140–142, 149, 150–151; major challenges, 149–150, 151
Citizen, 72
citizen bloggers, 162
citizenship, 79, 80; practice, 83; status, 83
City Press, 21, 22
civil society, 81
climate change, 116, 117
CoE. *See* Conference of Editors
colonialism, 7
commercialization, 23, 36, 47, 63, 71, 107; and tabloidization, 107–110
commercial media, 4–5, 36, 84
Commission for Gender Equality, 109; gender-based violence in South Africa, 109
communication, 123; for development, 160–161; studies, 125
community media, 6, 8, 22, 25–26, 28, 36, 39; print, 115
community radio stations, 5, 111
The Con, 48, 166
Conference of Editors, 30. *See also* South African National Editors' Forum
controversies and tabloidization, 97–111
Criminal Procedure Act, 29
critical: global journalism, 121–124; regionalism, 123; regional studies, 124
criticism of government, 94

creativity, 153–154

Daily Maverick, 48, 104, 111, 166
Daily News, 20
Daily Sun, 25
Daily Vox, 165, 166
Dasnois, Alide, 66, 139
decolonization of media studies, 49–51, 57, 87
democracy, 79
Democratic Alliance, 159
democratic institutions, 82; and processes, 82–83
Democratic Republic of the Congo, 118
democratization, 81
deracialization, 62
developing world, 122, 131
development: and democracy, 129
development journalism, 91, 128, 129; framework, 91–92
Die Antwoord (music group), 10
digital: entrepreneurship, 160–162; media and local politics, 159, 160; media technologies, 122–123; revolution, 123
digitization of the media, 152
discourses, 42–45; of identity, 43, 45; media meta-discourse, 43; official discourse, 44; public discourse, 44–45
diversification, 18, 24–28
dominant norms and standards, 100

economic: justice, 81; policies, 81
e-democracy. *See* mobile phones
editorial: composition, 18, 19–24; freedom, 80; staff representativity, 80
electronic media, 109
elite: continuity, 37–42, 46, 71; interests, 31; markets, 22, 36; perspectives, 28; renewal, 28
English-language media, 104
entertainment media, 7
equitable global communication systems, 86–87
establishment journalism, 128
ethical: frameworks, 90–91; institutions, 83; standards, 80
ethics, 79, 83
ethnographic audience studies, 127
e.tv, 9

Index

Facebook, 163; posts, 163
#FeesMustFall movement, 125, 164, 165; curriculum reform, 125; decolonization of the curriculum, 125
Financial Mail, 20, 105
Fourth Estate, 3, 23
freedom and independence, 80
freedom of expression, 29, 30, 33, 60, 69, 82, 83, 87, 95, 139; Bill of Rights, 3; Media Appeals Tribunal, 95; new democracy, 40; Protection of State Information Bill, 95, 139; threats, 28
freedom of the press, 140, 145
Fugard, Athol, 10
future of journalism, 25, 99, 112, 114, 125, 126; global and South African perspectives, 112–132

GEAR. *See* Growth, Employment and Redistribution
Genderlinks, 99
gender representation, 22, 72
geopolitical change, 168, 170
geopolitics, 80, 135
global: audiences, 130, 138; communication, 122; coverage, 111; crisis in journalism, 79; economic downturn, 117; genres and local context, 97–111; interconnectedness, 115; journalism, 113, 115–121, 122, 124, 127, 132; journalism studies, 112, 124, 129, 152; media, 23, 135, 168, 170; media ethics, 84, 86–89, 90, 96, 97, 116, 118; media flows, 140; media inequalities, 123; media studies, 47–57, 124, 135, 167, 171; media styles, 111; news environment, 117; political economy, 116; research, 120–121; shifts, 133–171; social changes, 122
globalization, 7, 17, 47–49, 50, 63, 81, 122, 129; after apartheid, 10, 168; journalism ethics, 129–130; of media, 84, 98, 103, 110–111, 118, 151; of the media industry, 128; reaction against, 44
Global North, 7, 25, 49, 84, 95, 112, 116, 119, 130, 170; in academia, 46, 51–53
Global South, 88, 116–117, 119, 127, 132, 152, 170
"glocalization," 98, 123
Gold-Net News, 26
Goudveld Forum, 26

government interests, 140
GroundUp, 48
Growth, Employment and Redistribution, 22
Guardian, 127, 128
Gupta family, 27, 45, 163. *See also* state capture

Haffajee, Ferial, 21
Harber, Anton, 139–140
hashtag politics, 165
hashtags, 54
higher education, 49, 50
history of media, 50
Huffington Post, 21
human: dignity, 81, 87; rights, 80

IAMCR. *See* International Association for Media and Communication Research
ICA. *See* International Communication Association
Icasa. *See* Independent Communications Authority
identities, 10, 42–46, 59–75
identity politics, 85
Independent Communications Authority, 5
Independent Media, 138
Independent Newspapers, 9, 11, 20, 66, 115, 126, 168; links to ruling party, 140
indigenization of ethics, 92–94
indigenous African values, 92
individual rights, 81
infotainment, 123, 128
International: journalism, 119, 124, media, 8, 17
International Association for Media and Communication Research, 49
International Communication Association, 49
Internationalization, 171; of media studies, 49–51, 87
Internet, 8, 25, 48, 123

JCI. *See* Johannesburg Consolidated Investments
Johannesburg Consolidated Investments, 20, 23
Johnnic. *See* Johannesburg Consolidated Investments

213

Index

journalism, 97, 123; as continuity, 71; in crisis, 113–115, 170; as cure, 68–71; democracy and development, 128–129; education, 124; as global journalism, 125; in an interconnected world, 121; practices, 102, 131; research, 120; as resistance, 67–68; studies, 84, 119, 132; Western norms, 91

journalistic standards, 99, 146

journalists: ability to withstand political pressures, 147; black, 19–20; and China, 142–143; coverage of BRICS grouping, 142; foreign, 8; and geopolitical alignment with China, 141; identities, 59–75; past to present, 62–67; political, 65; reluctance to use Chinese media sources, 148; remain vigilant, 80; on South Africa and China, 143–144; started using Chinese media, 141; use of Chinese media, 142, 148; views on China's media push in Africa, 142

justice, 82, 83

Kasoma, Francis, 93; "Afriethics," 93. *See also* African media ethics

liberalization, 38

limits of press freedom, 91

local: contestations and debates, 112; contexts, 120, 123, 168; and global interface, 170; media, 7, 10, 21, 48, 63; politics, 160; tabloids, 99

localization, 168

Machel, be Graça, 2

Mail & Guardian, 8, 9, 21, 32, 33

mainstream media, 98, 160, 164; and the government, 107; inclination towards middle-class audiences, 105

mainstream news reporting, 97

Makate, Nkosana, 153–154; compensation by Vodacom, 154

Malala, Justice, 21

Mandela, Nelson, 1–3, 17, 106–107, 110

Maputo bread riots, 155

Marikana massacre, 105–106, 110; media analysis of sources, 106

marketization, 4, 38, 41

market segmentation, 169; shaped by apartheid legacy, 169

mass market of newspaper readers, 99

MAT. *See* Media Appeals Tribunal

Mbeki, Thabo, 2–3, 31, 43–45

McKaiser, Eusebius, 165–166

MDDA. *See* Media Development and Diversity Agency

media: business models, 102; contexts in the South, 167; cultures, 84; and political power relationship, 32–35; as a political role player, 104–107; relationship to government, 169; society and state, 114; in South Africa's transition to democracy, 168; as vehicle for soft power, 147–149

Media Appeals Tribunal, 4, 35, 104, 145

media assistance, 94

media ban. *See* ban

media coverage, 142–145

media development, 94, 95

Media Development and Diversity Agency, 6, 25, 36, 39, 115

media ethical procedures, 82, 83

media ethics, 49, 86, 88–89; in Africa, 89–91; African culture and universal values, 79–96; local versus global, 89; in a new democracy, 81–84; in postapartheid South Africa, 82

media freedom, 33, 41, 80, 81, 86, 136

media imperialism, 84

Media Monitoring Project, 99

media ownership, 80, 138; and representativity, 80

media practices and technology, 152–153

media practitioners, 12

media professionalism, 94

media research, 142–151

media responsibility, 83; and democratic values, 79; towards South African citizens, 79

media spectacle, 109

media's role to promote development, 91

media standards, 100, 113; debates, 100

media studies, 120; about Africa, 51–53; from Africa, 53–55; with Africa, 55–57

media systems, 13, 86

Media24, 26

214

Index

Media Workers Association of South Africa, 30
M-Net, 20
mobile messaging, 154
mobile phones, 25, 48, 154–156, 160, 168; costs, 156–158; as cultural technologies, 158; and e-democracy, 159; mobilization for social activism, 155; ownership growth, 155–156; payment 'wallets,' 161; penetration, 156; please call me, 153–154, 155, 157; politics and media networks, 157; social and cultural contexts, 158; and social movements, 159; transformative potential, 161; transmission of information, 161; use in Africa, 156, 157, 158; users, 161
morality, 89
Motsoeneng, Hlaudi, 6, 25–26
MultiChoice, 9, 90
Muthambi, Faith, 6, 26
MWASA. *See* Media Workers Association of South Africa

NAB. *See* National Association of Broadcasters
Nakasa, Nat, 63–64
Naspers, 10, 20–21, 26, 34, 90, 126, 138, 168; and gaming platform Tencent, 138; global expansion, 117
National Association of Broadcasters, 30
National Empowerment Consortium, 20
National Party, 2, 7, 20, 39
Ncube, Trevor, 10
NEC. *See* National Empowerment Consortium
Neoliberalism, 7, 9, 13, 22
new: geopolitical relationships, 135–151; media platforms, 110–111; media technologies, 84, 130–131; pressures and opportunities, 152–166; technologies, 114
New Age, 27
news, 126; and its audiences 126; from a domestic perspective, 116
news media, 104
newspapers, 9, 20–22, 164; *Argus*, 21; *Business Day*, 20, 106; *Business Times*, 20; *Cape Argus*, 20, 164; *Cape Times*, 21, 66; *Citizen*, 72; *City Press*, 21, 22, 87; *Daily News*, 20; *Daily Sun*, 25, 98, 105, 163; *Daily Voice*, 98; *Die Son*, 101; *Financial Mail*, 20; *Gold-Net News*, 26; *Goudveld Forum*, 26; *Huffington Post*, 21; *Independent Newspapers*, 11; *Kaapse Son*, 98; *Mail & Guardian*, 8, 9, 21, 32, 33; *New Age*, 27; *Pretoria News*, 20, 21; *Sowetan*, 20, 98; *Star*, 20, 21; *Sunday Times*, 20, 21, 33, 87; *Sunday Tribune*, 21; *ThisDay*, 21, 26; *Weekly Mail*, 9
news stories, 102; death of President Mandela, 102, 103; Marikana massacre, 102, 103; Oscar Pistorius trial, 102, 103
News24, 48
normative frameworks, 18, 28–32, 41, 52, 58, 79, 80, 84, 86, 89, 96
norms and practices, 145–147
NP. *See* National Party

online audiences, 114
online media, 48, 54, 117; *Con, The*, 48; *Daily Maverick*, 48; *GroundUp*, 48; *News24*, 48. *See also* internet
opposition political parties, 105
O'Reilly, Tony, 9, 20
ownership, 18, 19–24

Panama Papers leaks, 118
political: economy of journalism, 126; power struggles, 86; processes, 159–160; system, 81; transition, 168
postapartheid: era, 80; ethical framework, 94; identities, 85; society, 102–104; South Africa, 80
postcolonialism, 50
postcolonial society, 81
press codes, 80, 95
press freedom, 89, 104
Pretoria News, 20, 21
print media, 169; dominated by commercial media, 169; political role, 105
private media, 19–21
procedural ethics, 82, 83
professional ideologies, 58–75
professionalism and social responsibility, 94–96
professionalization, 32, 63
professional norms, 86

professional values, 92
Pro-Journ, 31
Protection of State Information Bill, 3–4, 29, 35, 104
public and community media, 169
public broadcaster. *See* South African Broadcasting Corporation
public sphere, 24–28; diversification, 18, 24–28

radio, 24, 25; community, 5, 26
Rantao, Jovial, 21
RDP. *See* Reconstruction and Development Programme
Reconstruction and Development Programme, 22
regulatory: bodies, 80; frameworks, 18, 28–32
#RhodesMustFall, 165
Right to Know Campaign, 66, 95

SABC. *See* South African Broadcasting Corporation
SAHRC. *See* South African Human Rights Commission
Sainath, Palagummi, 128–129
sanctions, 17
SANEF. *See* South African National Editors' Forum
SASJ. *See* South African Society of Journalists
scholarship, 49–57
Secrecy Bill. *See* Protection of State Information Bill
Sefara, Makhudu, 21
Sekunjalo consortium, 115, 138; funded by a Chinese consortium, 138
Sen, Amartya, 82; and a just society, 82
sensationalism, 107
service delivery, 19
shifts, theorizing, 35–37
social justice, 81
social media, 25, 27, 54, 80, 125, 162, 168; platforms, 162–166, 168; and political activism, 166; racism and identity politics, 163; and South African politics, 163
social responsibility, 87; theory, 86
social upheaval, 168

South Africa: and BRICS, 135–136; and China, 136–137, 149–151
South African Broadcasting Corporation, 5–6, 24–26, 34, 39, 72, 88, 169; news, 164–165
South African Human Rights Commission, 33–35
South African journalism, 113, 120, 162
South African journalists: and Chinese soft power, 140–142
South African media, 79, 86, 93, 104, 117,167, 168, 170, 171; contribution to democratic society, 170; global relevance, 167; highlighted corruption, 168; independence, 86; market, 80; and social change, 170; and society, 97–111; support for political parties, 105; in transition, 168
South African National Editors' Forum, 27, 29, 30–32, 34, 45, 88, 99, 101
South African perspective(s): on the future of journalism, 112–113; on global media, 168
South African politics, 167
South African reorientation towards emerging powers, 149
South African Society of Journalists, 30. *See also* South African Union of Journalists
South African student protests, 125
South African tabloids, 101; journalists, 99; and politics, 101; and the trust of communities, 101
South African Union of Journalists, 30
Sowetan, 20
Standard Bank Sikuvile awards, 108
Star, 20, 21
state and media, 159–160
Stellenbosch University, 166
substantive ethics, 82
Sunday Times, 20, 21, 33
Sunday Tribune, 21
Survé, Iqbal, 66, 139. *See also* Sekunjalo consortium

tabloid: format, 112; genres, 96, 112; journalism, 79, 97, 107; media, 108; newspapers, 80, 97, 98–99, 123; revolution, 98
tabloidization, 108, 109; controversies, 96, 97, 101; of print media, 103

Index

tabloids, 5, 12, 25, 36, 98, 99–102, 108, 168; in South Africa, 113
teaching global journalism, 124–131
technological: advances, 103–104; development, 168
technology, geopolitics and social change, 152–166
television, 8, 17, 25, 89, 104, 130; stations, 164
terrorism, 118
tertiary education, 124, 125
ThisDay, 21, 26
Time Magazine, 2
Time Warner, 9
Times Media Limited, 20
TML. *See* Times Media Limited
transitions from apartheid to a new democracy in South Africa, 17–46, 81, 169
transitology, 37–42, 81
transnational news, 118
TRC. *See* Truth and Reconciliation Commission
Truth and Reconciliation Commission, 31, 33–35
Tsedu, Mathatha, 21, 27
Tsotsi (film), 10

ubuntu, 88, 93
UNESCO, 87
Universal Declaration of Human Rights, 89
universalism, 90
universal values: and African culture, 84–86
University of Cape Town, 166
University of the Western Cape, 166
University of the Witwatersrand, 165; student protests, 165

values of media freedom, 88
Vodacom, 162

web-based publications, 111
Weekly Mail, 9
Western ethics, 130
WhatsApp, 161–162
Wikileaks, 118
Williams, Moegsien, 21
Windhoek Declaration on Promoting an Independent and Pluralistic African Press, 89

Zambia: tabloid television, 99
Zille, Helen, 163
Zimbabwe, 159
Zuma, Jacob, 27, 45, 66, 71, 105, 106–107, 118, 163
Zuma, Khulubuse, 118
#ZumaMustFall, 164

HERMAN WASSERMAN is a professor of media studies and director of the Centre for Film and Media Studies at the University of Cape Town. He is the author of *Tabloid Journalism in South Africa: True Story!*. He is editor of *Taking It to the Streets: Popular Media, Democracy and Development in Africa* and coeditor of *Media Ethics Beyond Borders*.

THE GEOPOLITICS OF INFORMATION

Digital Depression: Information Technology and Economic Crisis   *Dan Schiller*
Signal Traffic: Critical Studies of Media Infrastructures   *Edited by Lisa Parks
    and Nicole Starosielski*
Media in New Turkey: The Origins of an Authoritarian Neoliberal State   *Bilge Yesil*
Goodbye iSlave: A Manifesto for Digital Abolition   *Jack Linchuan Qiu*
Networking China: The Digital Transformation of the Chinese Economy   *Yu Hong*
The Media Commons: Globalization and Environmental Discourses   *Patrick D. Murphy*
Media, Geopolitics, and Power: A View from the Global South   *Herman Wasserman*

The University of Illinois Press
is a founding member of the
Association of American University Presses.

University of Illinois Press
1325 South Oak Street
Champaign, IL 61820-6903
www.press.uillinois.edu